Labour Forces

LABOUR
FORCES

From Ernest Bevin
to Gordon Brown

Edited by
Kevin Jefferys

I.B. Tauris *Publishers*
LONDON • NEW YORK

Published in 2002 by I.B.Tauris & Co Ltd
6 Salem Road, London W2 4BU
175 Fifth Avenue, New York NY 10010
www.ibtauris.com

In the United States of America and in Canada distributed by
Palgrave Macmillan, a division of St Martin's Press
175 Fifth Avenue, New York NY 10010

ISBN 1 86064 743 X

A full CIP record for this book is available from the British Library
A full CIP record for this book is available from the Library of Congress

Library of Congress catalog card: available

Project management by Steve Tribe, Andover
Printed and bound in Great Britain by MPG Books Ltd, Bodmin

Contents

Acknowledgements

I am grateful to all the contributors for their helpful comments at various stages of the project. I would also like to express my thanks to Lester Crook at I.B. Tauris for his support and to Steve Tribe for his careful and constructive editing of the text.

For supplying photographs of the various figures in the book, I would like to thank Philip Dunn and the National Museum of Labour History. The photograph of Roy Jenkins is reproduced courtesy of Hulton Getty Images.

Kevin Jefferys
June 2002

Notes on contributors

TIM BALE teaches political science at Victoria University of Wellington in New Zealand, but maintains a keen interest in the politics and political history of the British Labour Party. He wrote the chapter on Harold Wilson in the collection *Leading Labour: From Keir Hardie to Tony Blair*, and contributed to Brian Brivati and Richard Heffernan's edited collection celebrating Labour's centenary. He is the author of *Sacred Cows and Commons Sense* (1999), which examines the symbolic role played by welfare policy in Labour's political culture in the post-war period.

LEWIS BASTON is Senior Research Fellow at the Centre for the Understanding of Society and Politics (CUSP) at Kingston University. He is author of *Sleaze* (2000) and the forthcoming *Reggie: A Life of Reginald Maudling*, co-author of *Politico's Guide to the General Election* (2000, with Simon Henig) and *The Future Labour Offered You: Labour's election campaigns since 1945* (with Brian Brivati). He was associate author of *Major: A Political Life* (1997) and historical consultant on BBC1's *The Major Years* (1999).

BRAIN BRIVATI is Professor of Contemporary History at Kingston University. His single-volume abridgement of Alan Bullock's biography of Ernest Bevin is published by Politico's. His publications include *Hugh Gaitskell* (1996), *New Labour in Power: Precedent and Prospects* (edited with Tim Bale, 1997), *Lord Goodman* (1999), *The Labour Party: A Centenary History* (edited with Richard Heffernan, 2000), *Guiding Light: The collected speeches of John Smith* (2000) and *The Future Labour Offered You: Labour's election campaigns since 1945* (with Lewis Baston, Politico's, 2001).

STEPHEN HOWE is Tutor in Politics at Ruskin College, Oxford. He is author of *Anticolonialism in British Politics* (1993), *Afrocentrism* (1998) and *Ireland and Empire* (2000), editor of *Lines of Dissent* (1998), and a former *New Statesman* journalist. He is currently working on some pictures of rabbits for his nephew George (aged 2), and on the odd bit of writing.

KEVIN JEFFERYS is Reader in Contemporary History at the University of Plymouth. His publications include *The Labour Party since 1945* (1993), the biography *Anthony Crosland* (1999) and, as editor, *Leading Labour: From Keir Hardie to Tony Blair* (1999).

DAVID LIPSEY is a Labour peer. He was political adviser to Anthony Crosland from 1972 to 1977 and to James Callaghan from 1977 to 1979. A former economics editor at the *Sunday Times*, editor of *New Society* and political editor of the *Economist*, he is also a past chair of the Fabian Society. His book *The Secret Treasury* was published in 2000.

KENNETH O. MORGAN was Fellow and Tutor, The Queen's College, Oxford, 1966–89, Vice-Chancellor of the University of Wales, Aberystwyth, 1989–95, and Visiting Professor at the University of the Witwatersrand, South Africa, 1997–2000. His books include *Keir Hardie: Radical and Socialist* (1975), *Labour in Power 1945–1951* (1984), *Labour People* (1987), *Callaghan: A Life* (1997) and *The People's Peace: Britain since 1945* (new edn., 2001). He became a life peer in March 2000.

EDWARD PEARCE read PPE at Oxford, worked for the *Daily Telegraph*, the *Guardian* and the *Scotsman* and has published ten books, including a study of the Irish Home Rule crisis, *Lines of Most Resistance* (1999). His biography *Denis Healey: A Life in our Times* was published in the spring of 2002.

ROBERT PEARCE teaches history at St Martin's College, Lancaster. He has published on colonialism and decolonisation in Africa, on twentieth-century British political history and on the historicity of George Orwell's writings. He is editor of *History Review* and general editor of Routledge Historical Biographies.

RAYMOND PLANT is a Labour member of the House of Lords. From 1994 to 2000 he was Master of St Catherine's College, Oxford. At the time of writing the chapter on Crosland he was Professor of European Political Thought at Southampton University. From January 2002 he becomes Professor of Legal Philosophy at King's College, London University. He is the author of eight books on political theory.

KEITH ROBBINS is Vice-Chancellor of the University of Wales, Lampeter. He was formerly Professor of Modern History at Glasgow University, President of the Historical Association and Editor of *History*. His numerous publications include *Politicians, Diplomacy and War in Modern British History* (1994), *Great Britain: Identities, Institutions and the Idea of Britishness* (1997) and *The World since 1945: A Concise History* (1998).

GREG ROSEN is the editor of the *Dictionary of Labour Biography* (Politico's, 2001). He has written for *Tribune*, the *Fabian Review*, *Renewal* and contributed 'John P. Mackintosh: His Achievements and Legacy,' to *The Political Quarterly* (Vol. 70, No. 2, April–June 1999). A member of the Fabian Society Executive Committee, he has been the President of London Young Fabians since 1997 under the auspices of which the Herbert Morrison Memorial Lecture was recently re-founded. Formerly Policy and Research Officer at Britain in Europe he currently works in the General Secretary's Office at the Amalgamated Engineering and Electrical Union.

ERIC SHAW is Senior Lecturer in Politics at the University of Stirling. Prior to entering academic life he worked as a researcher for the Labour Party during the period of the Callaghan government.

List of abbreviations

BMA	British Medical Association
BR	British Rail
BUPA	British United Provident Association
CAP	Common Agricultural Policy
CLP	Constituency Labour Party
CND	Campaign for Nuclear Disarmament
DEA	Department of Economic Affairs
DEP	Department of Employment and Productivity
EDC	European Defence Community
EEC	European Economic Community
GDP	Gross Domestic Product
GEC	General Electrical Company
GLC	Greater London Council
ILP	Independent Labour Party
IMF	International Monetary Fund
LCC	London County Council
LPTB	London Passenger Transport Board
MEP	Member of the European Parliament
MIRAS	Mortgage interest relief at source
NALT	National Association of Labour Teachers
NATO	North Atlantic Treaty Organisation
NEC	National Executive Committee
NEDC	National Economic Development Council
NHS	National Health Service
ODM	Ministry of Overseas Development
PEP	Political and Economic Planning
PLP	Parliamentary Labour Party
PPS	Parliamentary Private Secretary
PSBR	Public Sector Borrowing Requirement
SDP	Social Democratic Party
SERPS	State Earnings Related Pension Scheme
TGWU	Transport & General Workers' Union
UDC	Urban District Council

INTRODUCTION

Kevin Jefferys

This book aims to provide a series of fresh and accessible biographical studies of leading figures in the history of Labour politics since the Second World War. It follows on directly from the collection of essays entitled *Leading Labour: From Keir Hardie to Tony Blair*, one of several works published in 2000 to coincide with the hundredth anniversary of the foundation of the Labour Party.[1] Whereas the earlier book assessed the successes and failings of each party leader, this volume starts with a question. Which individuals, outside the ranks of the leadership, have had most impact on Labour's recent history? Countless numbers of local activists, trade unionists, party officials and MPs have, of course, long provided the backbone of left-wing politics. But in a political movement formed to embody collective action there has always been – ironically – a strong attachment to the 'cult of personality'.[2] What follows is partly a history of would-be Labour leaders. Many of the figures assessed here coveted the leadership and some almost reached it. Others, however, were less concerned about reaching the 'top of the greasy pole', yet still had a major influence on Labour's development. This work is therefore best regarded as a collection of expert and up-to-date surveys of the key figures – leadership contenders and otherwise – in Labour history from 1945 onwards. The contributors set out to demonstrate how their chosen subjects played critical roles in British political life, leaving their mark on the fortunes of the party and often on the broader history of the nation.

There were two main issues to be addressed in preparing the book. The first, and most obvious, was that of selection: who should be included? All of those assessed here, from Ernest Bevin to Gordon Brown, have a strong claim to be included in the Labour pantheon. This is not to underrate the achievements of others whose name might appear in any list of the party's great and good. Readers will have their own preferences, and in a longer work it would have been possible to include profiles of more senior ministers such as Richard Crossman, of maverick figures like Manny Shinwell, and of more prominent Labour women such as Ellen Wilkinson, Jennie Lee and Margaret Beckett. But, as ministers are fond of reminding us, tough choices sometimes have to be made. With the exception of Gordon Brown, whose influence in government since 1997 has been manifest, it was decided to exclude contemporary figures such as John Prescott and Robin Cook, concentrating instead on those whose role can reasonably be appraised from a historical perspective.

After selecting those for inclusion, a second question had to be addressed: in what order should those chosen appear in the book? To present the biographical studies in alphabetical order, starting with Tony Benn and ending with Herbert Morrison, would have been arbitrary and would require readers to jump back and forth in terms of themes and issues that have arisen in Labour politics across several decades. Another possibility would be – in deference to New Labour's obsession with the 'people's game' – to set out the selection in the format of a football team. After all, the party's 'First XI' – those assessed in *Leading Labour* – selected itself, as there have been 11 'Leaders' since that term was adopted – in place of 'Chairman' – in 1922.

In a similar vein, the 'Second XI' might have been presented here in the 3-5-2 formation favoured by many football managers. The midfield, for example, could be made up of five figures who have served as Labour Chancellors. On the right side there would be Roy Jenkins, Chancellor in the late 1960s. Adding bite alongside him in the David Batty role would be the pugnacious Denis Healey, prone to telling opponents – as he did the IMF – to 'sod off'. Central midfield would have to be occupied by Gordon Brown, the real powerhouse of the team. On the left of midfield that would leave two Chancellors who helped to secure full employment while Britain recovered from the ravages of the Second World War. Hugh Dalton, arguably Labour's most committed egalitarian at the Treasury, would be playing beside Stafford Cripps, who was no stranger to the early bath. His working day began with a cold dip at four o'clock in the morning and it was his relentless energy that helped to ensure the welfare state survived the economic difficulties of the late 1940s.

But the presentation of the figures in this volume as a 'Second XI' is fraught with difficulty. For one thing there are more than 11 individuals under scrutiny, each highly influential in his or her own way. None of them would be happy failing to make it onto the team-sheet and being relegated to the substitutes' bench. Most, for another thing, would resist the idea that they should be seen as part of a second XI, believing their contribution to the Labour cause has been equal, if not greater, than several of those who made it to the party leadership. The 'Second XI' certainly has strength in depth, though as a hypothetical team there are question marks over its discipline and collective spirit. Two of its members, Cripps and Bevan, were known for getting sent off (both were temporarily expelled from the Labour party) and another, Roy Jenkins, went off to join a different club: more, of course, a 'gang of four' than a team of 11. Of the rest, Gordon Brown clearly hopes he will yet move up to join the ranks of the 'first team'.

The order in which the individuals in this book appear was therefore ultimately determined along more conventional lines. It was decided to divide the volume chronologically to correspond with broad phases in the party's history, with each figure being allocated to the period in which his or her influence was primarily (though not exclusively) felt. The section on the immediate post-war years begins with assessments of Attlee's two most senior colleagues: his closest ally, Ernie Bevin, and his archrival, Herbert Morrison. This is followed by reviews of successive incumbents at the Treasury, Dalton and Cripps. Part I is completed with a study of Nye Bevan, who more so than Attlee's other ministers continued to play a pivotal role through to the end of the 1950s. The second section starts with overviews of the careers of three Oxford contemporaries who vied for high office during the era of Wilson and Callaghan in the 1960s and 1970s: Jenkins, Crosland and Healey. Part II also contains chapters on the mercurial George Brown and on arguably the most important woman politician in Labour history, Barbara Castle. The final section of the book reflects the party's fluctuating fortunes since 1979. Tony Benn and Roy Hattersley were prominent figures during the dark days of the 1980s, while Gordon Brown has been closely associated with the electoral revival of the 1990s and the present day. It is the immense contribution and legacy of these personalities – the driving forces of the modern Labour party – that the following chapters seek to illuminate.

Notes

1. Kevin Jefferys (ed.), *Leading Labour: From Keir Hardie to Tony Blair* (London, 1999); Brian Brivati and Richard Heffernan (eds), *The Labour Party: A Centenary History* (Basingstoke and London, 2000); Duncan Tanner, Pat Thane and Nick Tiratsoo (eds), *Labour's First Century* (Cambridge, 2000); Duncan Tanner, Chris Williams and Deian Hopkin (eds), *The Labour Party in Wales* 1900–2000 (Cardiff, 2000).
2. Kenneth O. Morgan, *Labour People – Leaders and Lieutenants: Hardie to Kinnock* (Oxford, 1987), p 1.

Part I
The
Attlee Years

1

Ernest Bevin

Robert Pearce

Ernest Bevin, b.1881–d.1951. General Secretary Transport and General Workers' Union 1922–40; Labour MP for Central Wandsworth 1940–50, and for East Woolwich 1950–51. Minister of Labour and National Service 1940–45; Foreign Secretary 1945–51; Lord Privy Seal March–April 1951.

Bevin is surely ripe for revisionism. Partly this is due to the excesses of his major biographers, who have revelled in his 'larger-than-life' personality, partly to the passage of events which, at the start of the twenty-first century, now makes him seem a veritable beached whale of proletarian militancy. The personification of Old Labour, no one seems less at home in the brave slick world of New Labour than Ernie Bevin.

To his first biographer, Trevor Evans, Bevin was 'not so much a man as a phenomenon' who mirrored 'the soul of millions of the English people'.[1] Francis Williams subtitled his 1952 biography 'Portrait of a Great Englishman'. In the first volume of his massive biographical trilogy, Alan Bullock called Bevin 'the outstanding trade-union leader yet produced by this, or perhaps any other, country'.[2] In volume two he meted out major praise. Not only did Bevin ensure that Britain achieved a high degree of mobilisation for war – higher than that of the Nazis – but he saw to it that increased efficiency brought about important and much-needed gains for British workers. Bevin's 'concern for ordinary men and women' ran 'like a scarlet thread through everything he touched'.[3] In the final volume, covering 1945–51, he resolutely defended his record as Foreign Secretary and praised him as one of 'that small group of men who can be said to have had a decisive impact on the history of their own times'. The key to Bevin's achievements, according to Bullock, is that he 'sought not to raise himself but the class from which he came'.[4] Yet to revisionists, such a cosy biographical consensus is ripe for shaking. The work begun in Peter Weiler's 1993 biography seems likely to intensify.

Bevin's image now counts against him. There was no media-friendly elegance about the man. He did not hold a pen between his fingers (which looked 'like a bunch of bananas')[5] – he would hold one with his whole fist. His table manners also left much to be desired. He would rarely keep quiet during meals, and his habit of talking while eating meant that he would often spit his food about. It was not a pleasant experience for those sitting in the vicinity. 'Several times I had to pick bits off my hand and sleeve,' reported one of his victims.[6] At a dinner in 1943 in honour of the Viceroy of India, Lord Linlithgow, at which the War Cabinet and the Chiefs of Staff were present, he twice brought out his false teeth, fingered them and put them back again.[7] During a meeting with foreign statesmen, a few years later, he was observed cleaning his fingernails with a pen from the tray placed in front of him.[8]

Excessive eating rendered him an unedifying figure. Despite being short, he weighed 18 stones from his middle years and consequently waddled rather than walked. He smoked heavily and also consumed vast and unhealthy quantities of alcohol. According to one of his secretaries, Bevin as Foreign Secretary after 1945 used alcohol as a car uses petrol, and it was rumoured that he once consumed one and a quarter bottles of whiskey in an hour and a half. His doctor urged him to drink either whiskey or champagne, but at official luncheons or dinners he could rarely resist both. He regularly supped not wisely but too well. According to a Foreign Office official, the hours he spent at his official papers each morning 'tended to vary inversely with the number of glasses of brandy he had consumed' the night before. Nor was he averse to 'tossing back vodka'.[9] He also had a penchant for Nuits St-Georges, which he pronounced 'Newts'.[10] Inevitably his performance was sometimes affected. At one cabinet meeting, having indulged himself in a particularly good dinner with a representative from Afghanistan, he was guilty of a 'drunken monologue'. At 12.30 a.m. he lurched towards the door enquiring, 'Where do we sleep tonight – in 'ere?'[11]

Towards the end of his life Bevin was told by Sir Alec McCall, his doctor, that there was no sound part of his body except his feet. He was suffering from angina pectoris, arteriosclerosis, sinusitis, an enlarged liver and damaged kidneys. His first heart attack occurred during the Second World War, and thereafter angina was a constant anxiety. A private detective was usually on hand with a box of pills (his 'pellets') if the condition became alarming.

In addition, he was much given to egotism. Hence he reacted self-righteously to any criticism, which he all too often regarded as a 'stab in the back'. He also boasted about his achievements. He even boasted that he had won the general strike of 1926. The words 'my, me, mine' fell effortlessly from his lips. 'It was Ernest Bevin's way,' Michael Foot has noted, 'to imagine that the universe was kept moving not solely by his major excursions in policy but hardly less by the hints and half-hints of wisdom dropped casually in his ceaseless monologue.'[12] He spoke endlessly about *my* policy, *my* proposals, *my* demands, *my* union, *my* people. Alone I did it.

In 1940 J.B. Priestley famously described Bevin as 'a powerful, thick-set, determined figure of a man, a fine lump of that England which we all love'.[13] He was indeed a 'lump'. But can we agree with Priestley's gloss, which must have been partly dictated by the requirements of wartime propaganda? Can we continue to see Bevin's stature in a symbolically positive way: was he a huge block of a man who, in his very person, defied first the interwar British capitalists, then the Nazis and finally the Soviets? Where stands Bevin today in our history?

Trade Unionist

Bevin's career was so long that it defies any mere summary. Yet for a long time it seemed he would have no career at all. He was born in March 1881 at Winsford in Somerset into real poverty. He was the youngest of seven children. His mother worked sporadically as the village midwife; no one knew who his father was, though he was almost certainly a farm labourer. When he was eight his mother died, and he went to live with a half-sister and her husband in Crediton. He left school at the age of 11, having reached the Fourth Standard, with the ability to read and write, and then had a variety of unskilled jobs, on a farm, in a bake house and as a conductor on a tram. He showed no particular aptitude and seemed unlikely to make a mark. His likely permanent job was that of drayman in Bristol. For 11 years, until the age of 29, he was content to drive a horse and cart delivering mineral water.

Everyone needs to be blessed with disadvantages, but Bevin's seemed strangely debilitating. He learned something at school, but probably more reading the *Bristol Mercury* aloud to one of his employers. Most important of all, he lacked ambition. The life of a drayman seemed suited to his solitary and inward temperament; and his 11–hour stint six days a week enabled him to earn sufficient to allow him to marry in 1908. At this time he was a teetotaller and had no taste for the luxuries of life. He seemed content with his lot.

There were signs of change from the year of his marriage. He joined

the Bristol Socialist Society and took on unpaid, spare-time work with
the Bristol Right-to-Work Committee. But the real turning point came
in 1910, when there was a strike at the Avonmouth and Bristol docks,
which involved the carters. Bevin now joined the Dockers' Union and
organised a carters' branch. The following year he became a paid official.
Union work was the making of Bevin. His career as an active trade
unionist lasted from 1910 to 1940, three times as long as his career as a
politician, and it left its stamp on that subsequent career. Finally he had
found a cause that unleashed his latent ability and ambition.

His rise was rapid. Hard work, dedication, strength of character and not
a little ruthlessness paid off. All these qualities were needed. He learned to
shout down opponents and to fight strikebreakers and rival unions. Rumour
has it that he once walked over to a big Irish navvy who was interrupting his
speech and without a word flung him into the dock, before resuming the
speech. With good reason was the sobriquet 'Napoleon' applied to him.[14]
He also learned the importance of organisation and efficient administration.
By 1914 he was one of the union's three national organisers. In 1916 he was
elected to the Executive Council of the Transport Workers' Federation and
in May 1920 he became Assistant General Secretary of the Dockers' Union.
Lloyd George said of him in 1919 that he was 'a powerful fellow, a born
leader … Mark my words, you will hear more of Bevin!'[15] Soon the PM was
hearing too much of him. Bevin organised resistance to British support for
the Poles in their war against the Bolsheviks and showed himself far from
over-awed in an interview with Lloyd George. Later he showed that he could
be over-awed by no one. He also helped organise a General Council for the
Trade Union Congress; and in 1922 he amalgamated 22 separate unions
into the Transport and General Workers' Union (TGWU), which could soon
boast a membership larger than that of any other trade union in the world.
Bevin became its first General Secretary, a post he held until 1940.

Bevin was now a nationally-known figure and the *bête noire* of portions
of the press. To them he seemed an unreasonable figure, bombastic and
belligerent, bent on class war, wreckage and revolution. Certainly he
seemed impatient of all opposition, insisting that the employers would
beat us 'until we are too strong for them to beat us any longer'.[16] According
to the *Athenaeum* in 1922, no other trade union leader 'has assumed an
attitude so truculent and irresponsible as Mr Bevin'. Another paper called
him 'the manipulator of more industrial disputes than any man of his
generation'.[17] This is an interpretation which Bevin's involvement in the
general strike may seem to justify. Yet such a view is simplistic.

Bevin was certainly not, on principle, against strikes, especially if he
judged they could be won. But he knew that strikes were only one weapon
in the workers' armoury. There were other weapons, including the

mobilisation and manipulation of public opinion. On several occasions he publicised the plight of his men with real imagination. The first was on a Sunday morning in 1909 when, in the Right-to-Work campaign, he marched a column of unemployed and ill-fed, hungry men into Bristol Cathedral during a service. At its end, they silently marched out – 'a mute challenge to the conscience of every worshipper'.[18] The second occasion was a few years later, when a drayman had been sentenced to jail for taking apples from a waste bin at the Bristol docks. Bevin organised a procession of marchers through the city. Two apples were impaled on their protest banner, and the campaign did not stop until a re-trial was accepted. But his greatest *coup de théâtre* came with the famous Shaw Enquiry of 1920. Here Bevin became the 'Dockers' KC'.

Instead of striking to obtain the dockers' claim of a national minimum wage of 16 shillings (80p) a day, Bevin took the opportunity to press his claims before an independent tribunal. The owners' case was marshalled by Sir Lynden Macassey, KC, one of the most experienced counsels in Britain in industrial cases. Yet he proved no match for Bevin, backed up by his redoubtable assistant Miss May Forcey. Bevin's opening speech lasted 11 hours. In it he showed a complete mastery of the evidence to prove that dockers' wages had failed to keep up with inflation and that the employers could afford to pay more. Allied to hard evidence he used sarcasm, wit and righteous indignation. 'I am no orator, as Brutus is ...' he might have begun. It was a bravura performance. Then he cross-examined witnesses. When experts pontificated about the diet dockers could live on, Bevin brought in actual plates of food to show how much food – or, rather, how little – particular calorific values actually meant. He also produced a menu from the Savoy Hotel, a contrast that was not lost on the tribunal. He pointedly asked the Chairman of the Cunard Shipping Company whether he thought he mattered more to the community 'than the docker who handles your ship ... Do you think it right to ask a man to live and maintain himself on what you would not dream of asking your own family to live upon?'[19] The dockers were awarded their claim of 16 shillings a day for a 44-hour week.

It is often said that Bevin was a poor speaker – and he often was, especially later as a member of the House of Commons. He would read out a prepared statement relentlessly and poorly – and 'the listener found no relief in grace of language or charm of delivery'.[20] Sometimes he was so ungrammatical as to be incoherent.[21] But occasionally he could speak with tremendous force and conviction: according to three very different observers, his words could amount to a 'tidal wave' of a speech, they could be 'shattering' and there was 'a touch of imagination, almost of poetry' about his simplicity and honesty.[22]

Bevin was not the sort of man to wear his heart on his sleeve, but in his address to the Shaw Inquiry he came closer than ever to giving his credo. He did not want a violent revolution, but he did demand an equitable distribution of wealth and a fair deal for the working class:

> I say that if the Captains of Industry cannot organize their concerns so as to give labour a living wage then they should resign from their captaincy. If you refuse our claim then I suggest you must adopt an alternative. You must go to the Prime Minister. You must go to the Minister of Education and tell him to close down our schools and teach us nothing. We must get back then to the purely fodder basis. For it is no use to give us knowledge if we are not to be given the possibility of using it, to give a sense of the beautiful without allowing us ever to have a chance to obtain the enjoyment of it. Education creates aspirations and a love of the beautiful. Are we to be denied the wherewithal to secure these things? It is a false policy. Better to let us live in the dark if our claims are not be met.[23]

Later he insisted that 'no tongue exists, no voice is capable, no pen can write, no artist can paint, the real human tragedy that is behind it all'.[24] Here was the wrath which transformed Bevin from drayman to trade union leader and more. His basic message was a simple one. It was not just a call for 16 shillings a day: it was a plea for greater equality and for manual workers to be treated with respect as full citizens. During the Second World War he described his quest very simply: 'Treat people like people'. Inevitably it was a long crusade, one with setbacks and defeats as well as victories.

A major setback came back in 1926, with the defeat of the General Strike. Bevin did more than anyone else to improvise some organisation for the TUC during the strike, and it remained solid to the last. Partly as a result of this he emerged from the strike, at least according to the *Sunday Express*, as the only trade union leader 'whose reputation was enhanced' by the stoppage.[25] But it had not been a strike of his choosing: he believed that the Samuel Report had provided a basis for a just settlement, and he long blamed Churchill for the failure of the last-minute negotiations. He also played a key role in the hard decision of 12 May: the strike would not be won and had to be called off, despite the miners' insistence on staying out. It was virtually unconditional surrender, though he never admitted as much. Publicly he insisted that the strike had taught the governing classes a lesson, and he refused to say 'never again'. This was sensible damage-limitation. It would have been foolish to say anything else. Yet he was unwise to blame the miners for letting the TUC down, and as late as September 1940 he was still boasting that 'We' won the strike.[26] There was an element of egotism in everything Bevin touched.

After the strike came the task of rebuilding. Bevin, a self-proclaimed 'revolutionary conservative' not a syndicalist,[27] was a leading figure in the constructive Mond-Turner talks of 1928 and, along with Walter Citrine and others, helped to bring about the revival of trade unionism during the 1930s. Membership of the TGWU fell after the general strike to 286,000, but by 1940 its ranks had swollen to 650,000 members. Bevin was a leading figure in battling against communist influence in the TGWU, and he was also a key figure on the Macmillan Committee, set up by the second Labour Government in 1930. Here he was an apt pupil of Maynard Keynes. Indeed in some ways he out-keynesed Keynes: he called for Britain to abandon the gold standard before Keynes accepted the wisdom of the idea. His resistance to cuts in benefits in the summer of 1931 was therefore a reasoned position. The result was a split in MacDonald's cabinet and the resignation of the government. MacDonald and Bevin had long disliked each other, certainly since the first Labour government of 1924, when Bevin led two strikes and MacDonald declared a state of emergency. Now the rift was complete. Part of the price to be paid was the formation of a National Government and the depletion of Labour ranks at the general election of October 1931.

Labour's recovery owed a good deal to Bevin. With MacDonald now in the Conservative camp, Bevin was prepared unreservedly to support the party – *his* party. He was the power behind the pro-Labour *Daily Herald*. Forming an alliance with left-wing intellectuals, he was founding chairman of the Society for Socialist Information and Propaganda in 1931. He even found his way into the fashionable Easton Lodge gatherings of the socialite Lady Warwick. It was also he who helped remove the pacifist George Lansbury from the leadership of the Parliamentary Party in 1935, with a cruelly effective speech; and it was he who switched the support of trade unionist MPs from Arthur Greenwood to Clement Attlee in the subsequent leadership contest. Either, he decided, would be better than Herbert Morrison, with whom he had recently clashed over whether nationalised industries should be required to have union representatives on their boards. He pointedly reminded delegates to the 1935 conference that the Labour party 'grew out of the bowels' of the trade union movement (and if he judged that the Block Vote at Labour's annual conference should be allowed 'to fall into desuetude', this was with the exception of 'big issues on which the big Unions felt strongly').[28] Not that he was happy with Attlee's performance. Often he would say 'The Party's got no leadership'.[29] In particular he disliked the party's unwillingness to support rearmament. No doubt Bevin's opposition to appeasement owed something to his ignorance of Britain's weakness; but what is without doubt is that it was Bevin, alongside Hugh Dalton, who did most to convince Labour of the need to rearm, and if need be to fight, against Hitler. Bevin was indeed the most important figure in the Labour movement during the 1930s. The Presidency of the TUC in 1937–38 was to be a fitting end to his career.

Continuous over-work had taken its toll. For too many years he had been working 80 hours a week. Back in the summer of 1918 he had had some sort of nervous breakdown; and he had collapsed with nervous exhaustion in December 1922, being laid up for seven weeks. At the end of 1936 there were the first signs of heart trouble, and at the 1937 TUC conference he was obviously in poor health, with a facial muscle that visibly twitched as he spoke. In the summer of the following year he went on a world cruise, preparatory to retirement.

Minister of Labour

Bevin was disappointed by the failure of Neville Chamberlain's wartime government. In 'their heart of hearts the powers that be are anti-trade union,' he wrote in October 1939. 'We do not desire to be invited to serve on any committee or body as an act of patronage. We represent probably the most vital factor in the state: without our people this war cannot be won nor the life of the country be carried on.'[30] He had no such criticism from May 1940, when, on Attlee's advice, Churchill made him Minister of Labour and National Service. Finally the trade unions had been accepted as an estate of the realm.

Britain had to be mobilised for total war. The manpower budget was now more crucial than the financial budget. Bevin therefore had a daunting job. Not only did he have to maximise the total workforce, he had to assess the needs of the armed forces, of war industry and civilian services, and allocate manpower accordingly. Yet, putting aside worries about his health, he accepted the challenge with few doubts about his own ability. Who else could possibly speak for organised Labour? He was Minister of Labour from 13 May 1940, and sat in the War Cabinet from October 1940, until the end of the war. A colleague who observed him judged that Bevin and Churchill 'were the two most forceful ministers with whom I worked ... I am not at all sure that Ernie was not the more ruthless and powerful'.[31] Churchill was certainly aware that Bevin was 'putting his weight about'.[32]

The position he inherited reflected the nature of the 'phoney war' that had now come to an abrupt end. There were still a million people unemployed and the country had not been put on a proper war footing. Bevin immediately called a meeting of 60 industrialists and trade union leaders and asked them to appoint a small Joint Consultative Committee to advise him. He knew quite clearly that he would need the support of both sides of industry in the tasks that lay ahead. He also negotiated 'dilution' agreements. The keynote here was that discussion and agreement preceded action. Bevin had a series of fierce battles with colleagues, especially with Lord Beaverbrook, the Minister of Aircraft Production, over the allocation of manpower. Yet with the British people he was remarkably restrained. Under the Emergency Powers Act of May 1940 Bevin had the power to direct everyone over the age of 16 to perform any act or service, but he realised that civilians would not obey orders in the same way as military personnel. He used his powers of coercion sparingly, sometimes to the chagrin of the Labour left and the Conservative right. To use his own clumsy word, he wished to employ the maximum degree of 'voluntaryism'.

Another feature of his work was his determination to create the conditions in which workers could give of their best in a war that was bound to be long. Hence he not only arranged for the payment of relocation expenses but was responsible for the decasualisation of dock labour and for the provision of canteens and washrooms in factories, as well as for the appointment of medical staff and for better conditions generally. 'Essential work orders' would only be issued to factories that met Bevin's new welfare criteria. His Catering Wages Act, which around 100 Conservatives voted against as socialism by the back door, helped to create better wages and conditions for almost half a million people working in the catering trades. He would force employers to be public-spirited, during and after the war. 'New standards of worker welfare were entrenched,' Robert Mackay has written, 'and the workplace could never be returned to its former crudity.'[33] His characteristic response to the drift from the land was forthright. In the interwar period around 300,000 workers had left the land, and in the first ten months of the Second World War another 70,000 took jobs elsewhere. Bevin decided that farm-workers would be tied to the land – but their minimum wage was to be raised to 48 shillings a week.[34] Real wages in industry increased significantly during the war, by up to 50 per cent, as Bevin insisted that free collective bargaining be retained. He was also sparing in his enforcement of wartime regulations against strikes. In 1944, believing that Trotskyists were fomenting trouble in the mines, Bevin brought in Defence Regulation 1AA, making it an offence, punishable by up to five years in prison, to 'instigate or incite' an industrial stoppage, but wisely failed to enforce it.

The results of Bevin's work can be seen in the degree of mobilisation for war that was achieved. By the middle of 1943 around 50 per cent of the adult working population were in the armed forces or civil defence or were producing munitions. This was a higher degree of mobilisation for war than was achieved in Nazi Germany – indeed it surpassed the record of any other belligerent apart from the Soviet Union – and it included the conscription of women, which Churchill had been loath to introduce.

Yet only 340,000 men and women were directed into war work which they themselves had not chosen.

There were certainly major problems. There were too many strikes, especially down the pits, and absenteeism was also high. Production from the mines did not reach desired levels, even after the conscription of the 'Bevin Boys' (the ten per cent of 18 year-old conscripts who were sent down the mines from December 1943). The wartime Reid report glaringly exposed the inadequacy of British coalmines, but the legacy of ill will that the miners bore Bevin must have exacerbated the situation. Furthermore, productivity in industry was low; and Britain quickly became dangerously dependent on the United States. Anyone doubting the inefficiency of the wartime economy should consult Correlli Barnett's *The Audit of War*. Yet paradoxically the weaknesses of the economy only serve to emphasise the importance of Bevin's wartime reorganisation. As Mackay has written: 'The war exposed the weaknesses of the British economy ... [but] what is remarkable is how well the economy performed. And against the flaws and failings must be set the notable fact that Britain's war economy operated largely with the consent of the mass of the people.'[35] The overall number of days lost in strikes was much lower than in the First World War, amounting to less than an hour per worker per year. The problems the Labour government faced from 1945, which involved a massive reorientation of the economy from war to civilian production, were eased by the efficiency of Bevin's work during the war. He had handled manpower issues well and generally showed a sureness of touch.

Bevin's efforts as Minister of Labour were gargantuan. By the end of May 1940 he felt as though he had packed 50 years' living into a fortnight. Somehow he found the time to tour the country, visit innumerable factories and make well over 300 speeches. He also made an impact in the House of Commons, though he could never sense the mood of the Commons as well as he could that of a TUC conference and sometimes made ill-judged remarks. He played a full role in the government, especially in plans for reconstruction. His pressure for left-wing solutions was, however, seldom appreciated in the party as a whole and he often felt the rank-and-file were being disloyal. He was virulently angry when Labour backbenchers would not endorse the government's line on the Beveridge Report. Relations with colleagues were also under some strain. His opinion of Herbert Morrison remained low, and several times he embarrassed colleagues by scornful, and highly audible, asides when the Home Secretary was addressing the War Cabinet. In 1943 he judged that Morrison would 'be a Tory within five years'.[36] He also clashed bitterly with Shinwell, Bevan and others. Yet he did show a new-found respect for Attlee. He also formed a close alliance with Anthony Eden. In total, it was generally thought by May 1945 that he had made a greater impact on government than any other Labour minister. The *Manchester Guardian* judged

that 'he came out of the war second only to Churchill in courage and insight'.[37]
Even Beaverbrook, his antithesis in so many ways, commented towards the
end of the war that Bevin was 'undoubtedly much the most distinguished' of
Churchill's colleagues in the War Cabinet.[38] Churchill himself, who
'cherished' Bevin above all Labour ministers,[39] offered him the Companion
of Honour, which he turned down on the grounds that he, like countless
others, had only been doing his job.

Inevitably Bevin had become rather out of touch with grassroots
opinion, and he certainly expected Labour to lose the 1945 election, one
reason perhaps why he had been in favour of continuing the coalition
until the defeat of Japan. Labour's great victory was 'the surprise of his
life'.[40] He and his wife had taken a cottage in Cornwall for their holiday.
Instead Bevin was appointed Foreign Secretary and was transported to
the Potsdam peace conference.

Foreign Secretary

One commentator observed after 1945 that 'Attlee is called Prime
Minister, Morrison thinks he is Prime Minister, and Bevin is the Prime
Minister'.[41] This was an unfair reflection on Attlee's leadership of his
government. The 'little mouse' dumbfounded his critics, kept his cabinet
of prima donnas together until Bevan's resignation in 1951, and
occasionally delivered sharp raps on the knuckles, even to heavyweights
like Bevin. Nor would Bevin himself have made a good prime minister.
He was too much the egotist, too given to rages and sulks, too much the
antagonist. When someone said of Nye Bevan that he was his own worst
enemy, Bevin replied 'Not while I'm around, he ain't'. But he would
equally well have said it of Morrison, Shinwell or several others. On the
other hand, there were several intrigues against Attlee and in favour of
Bevin: he could have been prime minister had he coveted the position. It
is to his credit that he did not. He realised that Clem was 'the only man
who could have kept us together'.[42]

After 1945 Bevin was not solely concerned with foreign affairs. For
instance, he took a leading role in industrial relations and was said to
regard the new Minister of Labour, George Isaacs, as merely his deputy.
He was also responsible for effective demobilisation plans. But it was at
the Foreign Office that his ability was fully tested.

Almost the first words Bevin uttered as Foreign Secretary were 'I'm
not going to have Britain barged about',[43] and many have seen him as
one of the most patriotic, constructive and successful of all British foreign
secretaries – indeed perhaps the most successful of the twentieth century.
His success derived first from his realistic appraisal of Britain's relative
weakness (give him greater industrial production, he said, and then he'd

give you a *real* foreign policy), and secondly from his shrewd solution to
the precarious position in which Britain found herself.

According to Alan Bullock and other admirers, Bevin initially hoped that
the wartime alliance with both the USA and the USSR could be maintained.
Left would speak to left. Bitter experience with the Soviets, however, especially
at successive meetings of the Council of Foreign Ministers, taught him
otherwise. Bevin realised before the bulk of his party that Stalin was a threat
to the peace and stability of Europe. In October 1946 he told the Defence
Committee that the Soviet Union was doing all it could 'to bring about the
dissolution of the British Empire' and that, if Britain did not resist, 'all of
Europe would fall under Russian influence'.[44] It may have been economic
and financial weakness which led to the withdrawal of British support from
Greece and Turkey, and the precipitation of the Truman Doctrine of March
1947, but it was Bevin who then seized the initiative and helped transform
Marshall's vague offer of help into Marshall Aid. Most important of all,
according to Bullock, Bevin provided the political will and the creative force
that produced the North Atlantic Treaty Organisation (NATO) in 1949.
When he first sketched out the plan it appeared to a colleague 'vague and
somewhat loose. But the policy ... was there. It was sketched by a man who
knows how things happen and how they are done, who knew a good organiser
does not plan in too much detail, but gives directions to those who have to
attend to details'.[45] At last his grand design was complete. All his life he had
believed that unity was strength. The individual workers, powerless alone,
could combine to resist the depredations of the employer. Now individual
democratic nations could combine to repel the Soviet menace. He had
prevailed upon a United States which might have retreated into isolation to
recognise its obligations to western Europe. The result was the avoidance of
another world war. Events underlined the wisdom of Bevin's policies, so that
even the Keep Left group in the Labour Party were won over. They were
silenced by Stalin's coup in Czechoslovakia (February 1948), the blockade
of Berlin (from June 1948) and the USSR's possession of atomic bombs
(from August 1949).

According to this interpretation, Bevin was himself the master of his
officials at the Foreign Office. According to the revisionist view, however,
these officials, and especially Orme Sargent, the Permanent Under
Secretary in 1946–49, tended to master him. There are other differences
too. Many recent writers insist that Bevin started off with anti-Soviet
prejudices, perhaps stemming from his battles with communists inside
the TGWU. According to Leo Amery's diary of February 1945, Bevin
was 'fed up with Winston over a good many things', including his softness
towards the USSR.[46] He also underestimated the Americans' willingness
to remain in Europe, just as Bullock exaggerates the importance of Bevin's

reaction to Marshall's Harvard speech in June 1947. In short, rather than prevent a third world war, Bevin helped precipitate the Cold War. In addition, he made Britain a client state of the USA and, by excessive defence spending, helped undermine the British economy.

To his critics, Bevin – adopted son of Bristol, that gateway to empire – was an imperialist of the old-fashioned Curzon or Churchill variety, a jingo. After all, he wanted a share of Italy's colonies at the end of the war, he did not want to see India granted its independence, and he had grandiose ideas for the development of British Africa. He told Colonial Secretary Arthur Creech Jones that

> If only we pushed on & developed Africa, we could have U.S. dependent on us, & eating out of our hand in four or five years. The great mountains of manganese are in Sierra Leone, etc. U.S. is very barren of essential minerals, & in Africa we have them all.[47]

Bevin did not easily accept the notion of an Atlantic alliance, with America as the dominant partner. John Kent has argued that his first aim was that Britain should become the equal of the USA and the USSR. Britain would dominate France and then their combined imperial resources should be extensively developed.[48] As late as March 1948 he was telling the Cabinet that 'we should use the US aid to gain time, but our aim should be to attain a position in which the countries of W. Europe would be independent both of the US and the Soviet Union'. Yet his pursuit of African riches, Kent tells us, 'was always a lost cause'.[49]

Small wonder that Bevin, allied with the Chiefs of Staff, fought to resist the retrenchment urged by Attlee, Dalton and Cripps. The Foreign Secretary was determined that Britain should stay in the Middle East. The withdrawal from Palestine he sanctioned only very reluctantly and as a last resort, as a desperate remedy for a desperate disease. It was due to Bevin above all that that conscription was retained and that regular battles were fought each year over defence estimates. Similarly he was determined that Britain should have the atomic bomb: 'We've got to have this. We have got to have this thing whatever it costs ... We've got to have the bloody Union Jack on top of it.'

Bevin's achievements in foreign policy were complex. We exaggerate his power and his clarity if we see him following a straight line that culminated in the signing of the North Atlantic Treaty. Certainly he seems to have exaggerated Britain's strength, or rather to have believed that Britain's reduced power was merely temporary. Similarly, he exaggerated the threat posed by the Soviet Union to western Europe. We should not ask merely, did Bevin dominate his officials or was he dominated by them? Their relations were much more diverse and subtle than these stark alternatives allow. Both played a part in shaping policy. It must be said that at times his language – whether to Molotov or Truman – was remarkably undiplomatic, and Lord Salter has judged that he sometimes used a truncheon when a rapier was needed.[50] On the other hand, plain rather than honeyed phrases do have their part to play in diplomacy. Similarly, Britain's dependence on the United States can be overstated. If some of the judgements of pro-Bevin historians have been simplistic, so are some of the criticisms now levelled against him. Revisionists can revise too far. Who can accept Weiler's argument that Bevin 'isolated the country from Europe for the next twenty years'?[51] Or Barnett's that Bevin was in certain respects 'an altogether disastrous foreign secretary'?[52]

In any overall assessment of the origins of the Cold War we have to admit that the Soviets made far more mistakes than Bevin and the British. It was also Bevin who convinced General Clay of the superiority of an airlift to Berlin over an invasion, even if at the cost of stationing American B-29 bombers with a nuclear capacity in Britain. It should also be remembered that Bevin was inevitably reacting against the failures of British foreign policy in the 1930s. As his Under-Secretary, Hector McNeil, told the Commons in 1946, 'One appeasement in any generation is one too many'.[53] It is no longer possible to depict Bevin as a faultless foreign secretary; but it is still possible to deliver a positive verdict.

Retrospect

Should historians have heroes? Certainly they should not indulge in hero-worship. As Attlee noted, Bevin had a compelling capacity to attract loyalty and affection – from colleagues, civil servants and journalists. But historians must be more detached. Bevin's career was so long, and the events and issues with which he was involved were so complex, that there will always be debate about his stature and achievements. But surely we can no longer accept some of the views of his biographical admirers.

No longer can it be accepted that his egotism was for his class and not himself, or that his arrogance was oddly inoffensive. Try telling that to his victims, and there were plenty of them. Bevin was sometimes a bully and often a good hater, and it must be set to the debit account that he cherished so many animosities. He seems to have been more responsible than Morrison for their long-running feud. He also had a contempt for all 'intellectuals'. And yet, as Kingsley Martin noted, this man, who was at times 'a bulldozer rather than a colleague', was himself in many ways an intellectual.[54]

Nor were his ambitions only for the working classes. Did he really remain a working-class figure all his life, even as he donned a morning coat or dinner jacket and reached for a bottle of 'newts'? It is true that he always retained his working-class accent and phrases, and yet in time there became something a little theatrical about his proletarian ways. He was playing up to his image.

(Was there not a good measure of insecurity at the heart of Bevin's bombast?) Similarly his wife indulged in expensive and excessive shopping experiences abroad in which she would have 'half the contents of the shop ... laid out on the counter for her inspection'.[55] Bevin was also very much a paternalist, who thought he knew what was best for 'his' people.

Bevin could certainly be inconsistent. In the First World War he was against Labour participation in the government; in the Second, he had no such qualms. At one moment in favour of emergency powers for a Labour government, at the next he was against – and he never seemed aware of any contradiction. He was also guilty of anti-Semitic remarks and of colour prejudice.[56]

Revisionism is needed to cut Bevin down to size. We have to strip away the layers of myth that have accumulated around him. But he surely has little to fear from such a process. He was a large and emphatic man who did large and emphatic things; and, despite his clumsy, lumbering appearance, he could also be highly imaginative and creative. Attlee believed that his egotism was that of the artist.[57] He could even 'do' slick. He combined grandiose, even romantic, visions with practical administrative skills of the highest calibre. He has been ill served by those who praise him too much or who exaggerate his qualities.

Bevin called himself 'a turn-up in a million'. He was an immodest man with plenty to be immodest about, but for once he was actually being absurdly modest. He was a turn-up in many millions. If he came close to being an alcoholic in his later years, he was very definitely a workaholic from the moment he entered the trade union movement in 1910 until his death in April 1951. His life was one long grind of work, work worth doing and, on the whole, work well done. He had no real private life, and as a trade union leader, as Minister of Labour and as Foreign Secretary he was crucially involved with important issues. We may vary in our assessments of him, our uncertainty compounded by the fact that he did not keep a diary, produce a memoir or write many private letters. We therefore see him from the outside, obliquely. But surely no one will deny his importance. Here was no member of the Labour 'second eleven'. A case can certainly be made that he exercised a more profound and constructive influence on the Labour movement than any other single figure in the twentieth century. This man of strong, flexible and fertile mind did not pursue a blinkered or irrelevant dead-end 'labourism'. The most remarkable question about Bevin is why he does not loom larger in our political and historical consciousness.

Further reading

The first biography, *Ernest Bevin*, was written by the journalist Trevor Evans (London, 1946): it is the source of much of the information relayed in later books. The next, *Ernest Bevin: Portrait of a Great Englishman* (London, 1952), is similarly by a journalist who admired him, Francis Williams. This too is still worth reading. Williams knew Bevin well and was able to draw on his oral reminiscences. It contains a foreword by Attlee. Alan Bullock has written three volumes of *The Life and Times of Ernest Bevin* (London, 1960, 1967 and 1983), a total of just over 2,000 pages. They are indispensable and, despite their length, compellingly readable. The best up-to-date short biography is Peter Weiler, *Ernest Bevin* (Manchester, 1993). There is a short and provocative essay on Bevin in David Marquand, *The Progressive Dilemma* (London, 1991).

Notes

1. Trevor Evans, *Ernest Bevin* (London, 1946), pp 13–14.
2. Alan Bullock, *The Life and Times of Ernest Bevin*, vol. 1: 'Trade Union Leader 1881–1940' (London, 1960), p xi.
3. Alan Bullock, *The Life and Times of Ernest Bevin*, vol. 2: 'Minister of Labour 1940–1945' (London, 1967), p 193.
4. Alan Bullock, *Ernest Bevin: Foreign Secretary 1945–1951* (London, 1983), p 857.
5. Peter Weiler, *Ernest Bevin* (Manchester, 1993), p 2.
6. G.S. Harvie-Watt, *Most of My Life* (London, 1980), p 58.
7. Ibid, p 134.
8. George Mallaby, *From My Level* (London, 1965), p 188.
9. Lord Moran, *Churchill: The Struggle for Survival 1940–1965* (London, 1968), p 270; Sir Roderick Barclay, *Ernest Bevin and the Foreign Office 1932–1969* (London, 1975), p 44.
10. As Churchill noted, 'everyone has the right to pronounce foreign names as he chooses', and Bevin did so with inimitable latitude. He also regularly murdered the English language.
11. *The Political Diary of Hugh Dalton, 1918–40, 1945–60*, ed. Ben Pimlott (London, 1968), p 405, entry for 30 July 1947.
12. Michael Foot, *Aneurin Bevan*, vol. 2: '1945–60' (London, 1975), p 28.
13. J.B. Priestley, *Postscripts* (London, 1940), p 27.
14. Weiler, *Bevin*, p 35.
15. *Lord Riddell's Intimate Diary of the Peace Conference and After* (London, 1933), p 27.
16. Weiler, *Bevin*, p 10.
17. Evans, *Bevin*, pp 94–5.
18. Francis Williams, *Ernest Bevin* (London, 1955), p 26.
19. Weiler, *Bevin*, p 28.
20. Lord Salter, *Memoirs of a Public Servant* (London, 1961) p 292.
21. Lord Winterton, *Orders of the Day* (London, 1953), p 219.
22. *Political Diary of Hugh Dalton*, p 393, entry for 24–29 May 1947; V. Bonham-Carter, *Daring to Hope* (London, 2000), p 9; Malcolm Muggeridge, *Like It Was*

(London, 1981), p 208.
23. Williams, *Bevin*, p 77.
24. Ibid, p 81.
25. Evans, *Bevin*, p 108.
26. Nick Crowson (ed.), *Fleet Street, Press Barons and Politics* (London, 1998), p 273.
27. Weiler, *Bevin*, p 23.
28. *Political Diary of Hugh Dalton*, p 202, entry for 11 November 1936.
29. Francis Williams, *Nothing So Strange* (London, 1970), p 135.
30. Robert Taylor, *The TUC* (London, 2000), p 79.
31. Lord Butler, *The Art of Memory* (London, 1982), p 11.
32. Moran, *Churchill*, p 270.
33. Robert Mackay, *The Test of War: Inside Britain 1939–45* (London, 1991), p 212.
34. Lord Williams of Barnburgh, *Digging for Britain* (Hutchinson, 1965), p 126.
35. Mackay, *Test of War*, p 230.
36. *Labour and the Wartime Coalition: From the Diary of James Chuter Ede*, ed. K. Jefferys (London, 1987), p 140, entry for 8 July 1943.
37. Bullock, *Bevin*, vol. 2, p 365.
38. *The Second World War Diary of Hugh Dalton 1940–45*, ed. Ben Pimlott (London, 1986), p 798, entry for 23 October 1944.
39. John Colville, *Fringes of Power* (London, 1985), p 550.
40. *The War Diaries of Oliver Harvey 1941–45*, ed. J. Harvey (London, 1978), p 384, entry for 28 July 1945.
41. Evans, *Bevin*, p 210.
42. Leslie Hunter, *The Road to Brighton Pier* (London, 1959), p 26.
43. *The Memoirs of Lord Ismay* (London, 1960), p 403.
44. Weiler, *Bevin*, p 157.
45. *Patrick Gordon Walker: Political Diaries 1932–1971* (London, 1991), ed. R. Pearce, p 186, entry for 9 April 1949.
46. Weiler, *Bevin*, p 146.
47. R.D. Pearce, *The Turning Point in Africa: British Colonial Policy 1938–1948* (London, 1982), pp 95–6.
48. See John Kent, 'Bevin's Imperialism and Euro-Africa, 1945–49', pp 47–76 in Michael Dockrill and John W. Young (eds), *British Foreign Policy 1945–56* (Macmillan, 1989).
49. Ibid, p 70.
50. Lord Salter, *Memoirs of a Public Servant* (Faber, 1961), p 292.
51. Weiler, *Bevin*, p 187.
52. Correlli Barnett, *The Lost Victory* (London, 1995), p 54.
53. J.E.D. Hall, *Labour's First Year* (Harmondsworth, 1947), p 168.
54. Kingsley Martin, *Editor* (London, 1968), pp 49–50.
55. Barclay, *Ernest Bevin*, p 61.
56. See, for instance, Weiler, *Bevin*, pp 75, 90, 170.
57. A.L. Rowse, *Memories and Glimpses* (London, 1986), p 318.

2

Herbert Morrison

Greg Rosen

Herbert Morrison, later Baron Morrison of Lambeth, b.1888–d.1959. Co-founder of the London Labour Party 1913; Leader London County Council 1934–40. MP for South Hackney 1923–24, 1929–31, 1935–45; East Lewisham 1945–50; South Lewisham 1950–59. Minister of Transport 1929–31. Minister of Supply 1940; Home Secretary and Minister of Home Security 1940–45. Lord President of the Council, Leader of the House of Commons and Deputy Prime Minister 1945–51; Foreign Secretary 1951. Deputy Leader of the Labour Party 1945–56. Life peer 1959.

Herbert Morrison was more than once almost leader of the Labour Party. Had he not lost his seat in 1931 he would almost certainly have either beaten George Lansbury to the crown in 1932 or else have replaced Lansbury in 1935. Instead, Lansbury's successor was the relatively junior Clement Attlee. In 1945 there was a good deal of support for drafting in Morrison as leader, though the putative coup was forestalled by Attlee's decision to accept the King's commission to form a government. Until his ultimate failure to succeed Attlee in 1955, and despite his indifferent record in 1951 as Foreign Secretary, Morrison was almost always seen as Labour's leader in waiting – particularly by Attlee who remained as Opposition leader until 1955 largely in order to deny Morrison the succession. The scale of Morrison's defeat in the leadership election of 14 December 1955 (40 votes, against 70 for Bevan and 157 for the victorious Gaitskell) underestimates his continued importance in the Party.

Morrison's subsequent bitterness at being denied the chance to serve
as Labour leader (he had been acting leader and, when in government,
acting Prime Minister during Attlee's illnesses during 1945–55) alienated
him from the victorious Gaitskellites. For them, Morrison's refusal to
continue as Deputy under Gaitskell or formally to support the
'Gaitskellite' Campaign for Democratic Socialism, despite the ostensible
concurrence of views between him and it, was a source of frustration
and resentment. Morrison was also far more interested in bread and butter
issues – delivering a better deal for working people, trains that ran on
time, decent housing, parks, libraries and civic amenities – than the liberal
causes that fired the younger Gaitskellites like Roy Jenkins, Tony Crosland
and David Marquand. Jenkins' memoirs radiate an enthusiasm for
Gaitskell that is simply lacking for Morrison, of whom, 'we had never
thought a great deal'. They characterise Morrison as merely 'a party
machine boss, skilled at his trade, but operating a little below the level
of events'.[1] Indeed, Jenkins and Crosland had been at the forefront of
those urging Gaitskell to stand for the leadership even if it meant
opposing his old friend, Morrison. David Marquand's portrait of
Morrison in *The Progressive Dilemma* is similarly less than sympathetic,
comparing his approach unfavourably with that of the 'adventurous'
Asquith government and depicting the 'Morrisonian consolidators and
their enemies on the left of the party as equally blind' to the 'scope for
radical reform in areas to which the 1945 government had been
indifferent as well as in areas into which it had ventured'.[2]

Morrison was not as reactionary as some have chosen to paint him. He
had been an early and fervent champion of votes for women and continued
to push for reforms such as the right of women to sit in the House of
Lords. Neither was he any more illiberal than most of his generation: his
first speech as a backbencher in over 25 years, on 16 February 1956, served
to announce his conversion to support for the abolition of capital
punishment. It was just that he did not see the liberal agenda as being the
primary purpose of a Labour government. In so doing he was undoubtedly
more in tune with the sentiments of most Labour voters, and potential
Labour voters, than his liberal detractors. In areas where reform might
have had a popular resonance he was not opposed to giving it a try. Thus,
for example, in March 1941, in the face of blandishments from the Imperial
Alliance for the Defence of Sunday that so to do risked the alienation of
the Almighty at a crucial point in the War, he tried and failed to get
Parliament to approve opening theatres on Sunday.[3]

The rise of the former Bevanites under Harold Wilson's leadership of
the Labour Party and their ultimate triumph under Michael Foot and
Neil Kinnock led less to a rehabilitation of Morrison than to the

substitution of Bevan for Gaitskell as the hero of the Labour leadership. Bevan's offer in 1955 to withdraw from the race and let the older Morrison succeed Attlee as leader if Gaitskell would withdraw also was an offer entirely based on expediency. Bevan knew he could not beat Gaitskell, but as Morrison's age would force retirement and a new contest in a few years time, he felt that it might give him a chance to beat Gaitskell in the future. Of Wilson's campaign team in 1963, none apart from the infamous George Wigg had any time for Morrison. Wigg saw Morrison (as indeed he did Wilson) as being the 'unity' candidate. Writing in his memoirs he recalled: 'I had had my fill of the Gaitskell-Bevan brawl. Morrison had defects as leader, some of them serious. Yet he had administrative gifts as good as Bevan's and a down to earth common sense beyond Gaitskell's ken. Above all, his attitude to the job – get on with it – and his basic loyalty to the Movement were qualities which at the time the Party in the House and in the country needed.'[4]

There had never been any particular meeting of minds between Morrison and Foot. For Morrison, Foot was:

> a clever journalist, a man with a sparkling personality, and quite a considerable orator. But he is probably the last man to have more than a negligible influence on the British public... When one watches Michael Foot in his best-known role as a television personality one finds it difficult to believe he has any persuasive effect on the viewers. He gives the impression of what I describe to myself as a kitchen revolutionary; a man who has drifted into the socialist movement from the serene backwaters of a fairly comfortable middle-class environment.[5]

Foot could scarcely have warmed to such a description. Indeed, he regarded Morrison as a 'soft-hearted, suburban Stalin, forever suspecting others of the conspiracies in which he was engaged himself'.[6]

By the time Tony Blair became Labour leader, the London Labour Party had abandoned Herbert Morrison House on Walworth Road and had failed to retain any Morrisonian reference at its new premises. Likewise, the Herbert Morrison Memorial Lecture, organised by the Greater London Council since the late 1960s, disappeared with the abolition of the GLC in the 1980s. When his grandson, Peter Mandelson, gave the Herbert Morrison Memorial Lecture on its revival by the London Young Fabians on 1 November 2000, Morrison had become, said Mandelson, 'one of Labour's forgotten heroes.' Yet as Mandelson, himself a key architect of New Labour, went on to explain, Morrison's impact on the Labour Party and on Britain had been profound:

> Morrison was Labour's first and greatest Leader of the London County Council; the Home Secretary who sustained London through the Blitz;

the dominant figure on the NEC in masterminding Labour's 1945 victory; and the man who as Deputy Prime Minister in the Attlee Cabinet can take more credit than anyone else for driving through that government's domestic and legislative programme. But, first and foremost he was the quintessential political organiser – responsible more than anyone else for building up the London Labour Party. He was not just an office holder in that organisation, from 1915 to 1962, but its dynamic force and inspiration, whether speaking from the Conference platform, his sleeves rolled up at the election HQ or on the dance floor of the Friday night social at the Co-op Women's Guild. He even instigated competitive choir singing among the CLPs![7]

As a strategic thinker Morrison incorporated into Labour's policies and presentation during the 1940s and 1950s a lesson that Labour was all too easily to forget following his retirement and did not fully relearn until the 1990s. As Mandelson put it:

> Throughout his political life my grandfather asserted that Labour should have a broad appeal across the social classes, not because he believed in a mushy centre but because he believed that lower and middle income Britain rely on many of the same things, from universal services to rights at work to safety on the streets.[8]

Morrison argued that not only was there no contradiction in Labour appealing to the skilled in addition to the unskilled, the aspirational as well as the downtrodden, but that it was necessary to do both in order to secure the power to fulfil the hopes of either. He believed, as the rhetoric of today's 'New' Labour would have it, in 'making work pay', believing that, 'everyone will be expected to work. Society will be entitled to say to a person who could work but will not work "neither shall he eat."'[9] He firmly rejected 'the doctrine that any citizen, even a working-class citizen, has an unconditional right to withdraw money from the State without question, query or justification... any Socialist who affirms that is affirming something contrary to the self-respecting and upright principles of socialism itself'.[10]

Morrison's decision, exhibiting a courage that bordered ostensibly upon the foolhardy, to leave his safe seat in South Hackney to contest the hitherto Conservative-held seat of East Lewisham at the 1945 election can best be understood in the light of this strategy. That was why, knowing that his Hackney seat might ultimately disappear under boundary review, he turned down the offer of a safe Labour seat at Deptford in preference for East Lewisham, which not only had never before been won by Labour but had in 1935 a Tory majority of 6,449. As he explained in the press statement announcing his decision:

For many years I have counselled the socialist party that, if it is ever to secure an independent stable Parliamentary majority, it must gain and keep support, not only of the politically conscious organised workers, but also of the large number of professional, technical and administrative workers of whom there are many in East Lewisham. It is because I have confidence in the reasoned appeal the socialist party can make to all sections of the community, manual workers and black coats alike, that I have decided to go to East Lewisham... emphasising by this action my conviction that the soundest socialist appeal is that which is most universal in its scope.[11]

According to Mandelson:

This is as good an encapsulation as any of what Tony Blair calls One Nation socialism and I share it. For me this is far more than about electoral tactics. It's about how social democrats achieve lasting change in society. Take the example of New Labour's relationship with business today. We have sought to take business with us on all our major decisions.[12]

In July 1948, when Labour was girding its loins for the battle to win a working majority to sustain a second full term of office, Morrison reiterated the need 'to take into account the opinions of all sections of the community. Let us not forget the one, two, or more millions of voters, "the floaters" who in the end will in all likelihood determine whether there is a Labour government or not.'[13] For Morrison, the appeal must be, in a favourite phrase, to all the 'useful people' in society, which in his view included even the agricultural workers who lived far from Labour's urban citadels. He also urged that 'the needs of the consumer and the problems of the housewife must be recognised as a real factor in politics, and Party policy and propaganda should take account of it.'[14]

Morrison's strategic insight was in part due to his background. In contrast to most of his colleagues in the higher echelons of the Labour Party during the 1940s and 1950s he was neither the rebellious product of Public School and Oxbridge, usually Oxford, (such as Attlee, Cripps, Dalton, Gaitskell, Pakenham, Pethick-Lawrence, Jowitt, Gordon Walker, Shawcross, Jay, Crossman, Freeman, De Freitas, Mayhew, Younger, Crosland, Tawney) nor a former trade-union official (Bevin, Isaacs, Tomlinson, Robens, Callaghan). Morrison was largely self-taught, having left Elementary school a fortnight after having turned 14, and his activism in the trade union movement was with the National Union of Clerks (later renamed APEX and merged with the GMB in 1989), of which he was from 1910 to 1913 the chair of its Brixton Branch. His involvement was not altogether successful. Despite increasing his branch membership by 75 per cent in his first year as chair, he was forced to resign after opposing a motion from his union at a Labour party conference. But it was here that he learnt that Labour's appeal needed to be broad to be successful.[15]

Morrison's understanding of this need underpinned his success in building up the London Labour Party, both in terms of membership and then as first an independent and then the dominant force on the London County Council. In addition he understood, as John Mackintosh highlighted in a perceptive entry on Morrison for the *Dictionary of National Biography*, 'that more was gained by steady work and preparation, by mastery of the immediate subject and its possibilities, than by all the street-corner oratory which so delighted the older generation of socialists.'[16] In his 1950 election post-mortem memorandum, he was a far-sighted advocate of Labour employing paid agents in key marginal seats to maintain campaign momentum between elections and to maximise Labour's postal vote take-up.[17]

Morrison and his protégés in London were so successful that the Conservatives eventually had to abolish the entire LCC and replace it with a Greater London Council incorporating London's Tory suburbia to regain control of London. Morrison's tenure at the LCC brought the reform of public assistance, the removal of Poor Law officers from hospitals, the construction of a new Waterloo bridge in the face of determined opposition from government and other Conservatives and conservators, the creation of London's 'green belt' and a significant programme of slum clearance, house and school-building. It also coincided with the golden age of his creation, the London Passenger Transport Board, which was responsible for a massive tube expansion and improvement programme incorporating the introduction of improved rolling stock and stations, the widespread replacement of trams by trolleybuses and the electrification of many of the surface commuter lines.

Not only did the achievements of Morrison's LCC demonstrate the practical difference that Labour could make to Londoners, they also provided a badly needed shot in the arm to a Labour Party reeling at national level from governmental failure, the 'betrayal' of Ramsay MacDonald and the subsequent electoral catastrophe of 1931. They showed tangibly to the Party, the activists and the electorate, that Labour government could work successfully. If Morrison ever actually said 'socialism is what a Labour government does,' it was probably to this that he was alluding – that for most voters the reality of socialism as a life experience would be realised through the achievements of Labour in power. As Morrison's biographers Donoughue and Jones put it, Morrison 'always resented the Labour image of good intentions and high principle achieving nothing because of inefficient execution. All government should be responsible, efficient and effective.

Labour government should add idealism, but not at the expense of competence'.[18] His ministerial colleague, Frank Soskice, later Lord Stow Hill, recalled Morrison's yardstick for any policy proposal: 'Will it work? Will it help? Is it fair? What will it cost? How do you do it? What will be the consequences?' Having satisfied himself with these aspects he would urge, 'don't rush it, think about it'.[19]

It was this belief that led to his main breach with TGWU leader Ernest Bevin over Morrison's insistence, as MacDonald's Minister of Transport, that members of his new London Passenger Transport Board should be appointed solely on the basis of ability and that trade unions should not have the right to nominate members *per se* (a dispute which in its origins went back to debates in 1923–24 over the organisation and regulation of London's transport). It was not that Morrison was anti-trade union *per se* (the Transport Salaried Staffs' Association and the National Union of Railwaymen amongst others backed his position on this). However, what Frank Owen dubbed Bevin's 'Corsican concept of public business'[20] meant that the TGWU leader neither forgave Morrison nor forgot. Morrison's position was essentially that the new public corporations had to be well run to secure sufficient long-term public support to prevent the Conservatives undoing what Labour had achieved.

Morrison sustained this approach in the battles on Labour's NEC Policy Committee throughout the 1930s until he was in a position to put it into practice on a wider scale in the nationalisation programme of the 1945 government. Despite carping from syndicalists and others on the Labour left, none of his critics managed to develop a workable alternative plan. As he himself modestly put it, the Bill creating the London Passenger Transport Board, 'was the first major experiment in the socialisation of a complex industry' and, 'provided a blueprint on which all the designs for nationalisation of industries were broadly based'.[21]

Morrison did not seek to nationalise everything for the sake of it: the toffee-shop on the street corner, he was keen to emphasise, need have no fear of a Labour government. There was a widespread belief, however, that planned public enterprise could and would be better run than the bloated and ill-managed private monopolies that had so clearly failed the British economy in the 1930s. Even as people recognised the appalling inhumanities of Stalin's totalitarian Soviet regime, it was nevertheless commonly believed that the proverbial Magnetogorsk produced ball bearings more efficiently than, say, Birmingham. Morrison reassured an American audience in early 1946 that 'the great bulk of our industry will remain private industry and we shall not quarrel with it while it is private enterprise and not private unenterprise'.[22]

The achievements of Morrison's strategy were considerable, ranging from the massive electrification programme, which created the integrated national grid, to the profound improvement in miners' working conditions. He was however to become intensely concerned at the failure of nationalisation sufficiently to improve the efficiency of their industries and to underpin Britain's prosperity. Many of the old managers were reluctant to modernise outdated working practises and equally loath to let outside management consultants interfere, as Morrison urged. His attitude was that of the practical idealist, looking for workable solutions to the difficulties of the hour. Indeed, as Beatrice Webb wrote of him in her diary entry of 14 March 1934, 'He is a Fabian of Fabians; a direct disciple of Sidney Webb's... [He is] the very quintessence of Fabianism in policy and outlook'.[23]

His advocacy of 'consolidation' derived from his Fabian socialism and from his practical political experience. It was not a call for the Party to rest on its laurels but to ensure that the nationalised industries were underpinned by firm economic foundations. In his 1950 post-election Memorandum he explained: 'It is... quite clear that the majority of the electorate are not disposed to accept nationalisation for the sake of nationalisation' and therefore 'it was more important to pay attention to making effective and efficient the existing socialisation rather than to proceed with a further nationalisation programme at the present time'.[24] In his memoirs, Morrison described 'this great experiment of public ownership on an extensive scale', and as it was an experiment, he saw the need for its worth to be proved to guarantee its long-term sustainability. He attacked 'the theory that to condemn imperfections is to condemn ourselves', and asserted that 'Labour has been too unwilling to admit imperfections in existing nationalised industries and to indicate remedies. And the interests of consumers are insufficiently stressed'.[25] The *New Statesman* commented in May 1950 that:

> Herbert Morrison is almost the only Cabinet Minister whose speeches give the impression that he is not too busy to think... he has taken to heart the plain evidence of recent months that the labour programme of public ownership and control in industry needs thinking out afresh.[26]

In later years, Crosland and other 'revisionists' sought to avoid this thorny issue, dismissing economic questions such as the operation of the public and private sectors as distractions from the real issues which were, they believed, increasingly social. Morrison would probably have agreed with the socialist thinker John P. Mackintosh who, though an admirer of Crosland when he entered Parliament in 1966, was a few months before his early death in 1978 to launch a famous attack in the *Scotsman* on the

'basic error' of Croslandism in talking 'endlessly about the distribution
of wealth, its taxation and use for this and that but very little about the
creation of wealth... the central task of justifying and producing a mixed
economy remains'.[27] For Morrison, 'consolidation' was just such an
attempt to address this task.

Morrison was not anti-intellectual. In government he was eager to utilise
the talents of expert advisors, such as the former planning guru of the Political
and Economic Planning think-tank, Max Nicholson. Indeed, his four
Parliamentary Private Secretaries during 1945–51 were all Public School-
educated, middle-class intellectuals, two of whom (Patrick Gordon Walker
and Edward Shackleton) would become Cabinet Ministers, another
(Christopher Mayhew) probably would have done but for Gaitskell's
premature death and the fourth (Stephen Taylor) a Peer and university Vice-
Chancellor. As the Donoughue and Jones biography of Morrison brings
out, far from being anti-intellectual, he surrounded himself with people of
fertile and imaginative minds that he could 'selectively plunder'. In later
years he proved to be entirely comfortable amongst 'all the brainy people
and intellectuals' of Nuffield College, Oxford, having been elected a visiting
fellow in 1947 to write his book, *Government and Parliament*; 'I wouldn't
mind spending my time writing books at a University,' he announced at the
Commons press launch.[28] What frustrated him were the intellectuals of the
left who failed to consider the practical resonance of their ideas. Emblematic
of this is the pointed reference in Morrison's memoirs to the conference
held in Leeds in June 1917 to promote socialist unity and worker-soldier
councils in Britain:

> The effort died a natural death but it established one sharp lesson
> for the Labour politician. When contemplating ventures and shaping
> policies he must ask himself this question: Will it find an echo in the
> minds and hearts of the people? The Leeds conference did not.[29]

Far more than just the 'third-rate Tammany Hall Boss' of Bevan's
caricature, as Leader of the House of Commons, Morrison complemented
an efficiency that pushed over 70 Bills through the Commons between
1945 and early August 1946 with a tolerance of backbench discussion
and dissent that induced considerably fewer revolts than later occurred
under the 'liberal' regime of Chief Whip John Silkin during 1966–69.
The suspension of standing orders during the period of Labour's large
majority, 1945–50, helped defuse revolts on issues like Palestine (on
which Morrison largely agreed with the rebels) and old-age pensions. At
the same time, his systematic establishment of backbench subject
committees (and from mid-1947 of area groups) provided useful forums
for backbenchers to contribute ideas to government. He even organised

the PLP into three rotating shifts in which one of the three could go home and sleep during an all-night Commons sitting. At meetings of the Parliamentary Labour Party it was usually Morrison who put the case for the government and kept the backbench apples on the governmental cart. His role as chair of the NEC Policy Committee for both the 1945 and 1950 elections combined with his weight in government produced an effective working relationship between Government, NEC and Transport House in drafting the manifesto which was clearly lacking in later years after Morrison's retirement. Moreover, much as he enjoyed the role of back-room fixer, he was, unlike a 'Tammany Hall boss,' neither corrupt nor dishonest.

Morrison was regarded as an unusually approachable Leader of the House of Commons by backbenchers, certainly far more approachable than the then Prime Minister, Attlee. Though he had his coterie of devotees and intimates (notably Maurice Webb, Dick Stokes and Hartley Shawcross in Parliament and Jim Raisin at London Labour Party HQ), he never developed the image that was associated with the likes of Ramsay MacDonald, Hugh Gaitskell and Roy Jenkins of being aloof from those outside their particular coterie. Particularly notable was the range of his admirers, from socialist intellectuals like Professor Harold Laski via trade-union loyalists like George Brown and Alf Robens, to the firebrand of the left and heroine of the Jarrow Crusade, 'Red' Ellen Wilkinson, with whom his relationship was particularly affectionate. Despite developing a partiality to whiskey, cigars and the pleasures of the Ivy restaurant, he retained his taste for fish and chips, travelling by public transport and shopping at the Co-op – from whence came all his suits. After a tour of the Northeast in March 1951 he told the *Daily Mail*, 'If you can choose between staying at a posh hotel or at a miner's house in Normanton, you choose the latter'.[30]

Donoughue and Jones wrote that 'there is little doubt that Morrison was the most important single dynamo in the government's machine. The breadth of his responsibilities was perhaps unprecedented in modern government'.[31] In 1951, however, he was to give them up for the Foreign Secretaryship. In hindsight it was a mistake from which his career never fully recovered. For his admirer and protégé George Brown it was because 'he fell victim to the politicians' disease of wanting the best job going in terms of prestige',[32] whether or not his talents or interests were suited to it. The truth is more complex and he had in fact only just turned down the other such prestige post – Chancellor of the Exchequer – on the grounds that 'I listen to Stafford [Cripps] explaining those figures, and I just know I could not do it'.[33] Moreover, it is untrue that Morrison had never before shown interest in foreign affairs. Indeed, on the assumption that Bevin would be heading for the Treasury, Morrison had actually asked Attlee for the Foreign Secretaryship on the formation of the Labour government in 1945.

Morrison's performance as Foreign Secretary is usually depicted as 'comparatively unhappy' to say the least.[34] For the Labour left his greatest crime was an almost Palmerstonian zeal for overseas interventions, such as his threat in the summer of 1951 to deploy Britain's armed forces to defend the Anglo-Iranian Aberdan oil refinery. This was compounded by his advocacy of German rearmament within the context of an anti-Soviet Atlantic alliance, an issue which united the Bevanites of the left with the likes of Hugh Dalton on the right, whose opposition was based on the fact that, as he himself put it, 'I hate all Germans and regard them all as Huns'.[35] The Conservatives tarred Morrison with the brush of his being Foreign Secretary when the Burgess and Maclean Soviet spy scandal exploded and of being hypocritical in his condemnation of the 'war-mongering' stance of the Conservatives over Iran when it was little different from his own. For the Foreign Office itself, his decision on taking office as Foreign Secretary to delegate taking foreign affairs questions to his Minister of State, Kenneth Younger, whilst he took questions on his beloved Festival of Britain, smacked of a failure to take his responsibilities seriously. His decision to take questions on the Festival of Britain again in May that year, instead of the minister responsible, and to attend the eve of Festival dinner on 2 May in London, instead of the Committee of the Council of Europe in Strasbourg, compounded the image of someone who did not have his mind on the job. After Anthony Eden's attack on his failure 'to concentrate' on the 'responsibilities of unparalleled importance' which he bore, Morrison's dismissal of Eden's 'superior view' of the Foreign Office gave the *Daily Telegraph* the opportunity to offer a verdict on Morrison which has haunted his reputation ever since: 'rarely with so few words can a Foreign Secretary have so wilfully raised so many doubts about his capacity for that office'.[36]

The reality was not necessarily as unfortunate as his critics have sought to paint it. Moreover, few of the problems with which Morrison had to grapple as Foreign Secretary were actually of his creation. As Eden generously commented, Morrison was 'desperately unlucky'.[37] Attlee's illness put Morrison in the chair during the Cabinet rows that precipitated the Bevanite resignations, which can hardly have helped him concentrate on his Foreign Office duties. Neither was it his fault that the Burgess and Maclean scandal erupted during his brief period in office nor that, as Kenneth O. Morgan has written, 'the basic futility and failure of Bevin's policy in the Middle-East'[38] chose the summer of 1951 to become so explosively apparent. Morrison was essentially right to agree with the even more hawkish Minister of Defence, Manny Shinwell, that 'Throwing up the sponge' in Iran, from whence Britain derived a third of her petrol, could lead to the nationalisation of the Suez Canal and the collapse of the British Middle-East position.[39] The trouble was that the problem was fundamentally insuperable: despite the bullishness of the Chief of Imperial General Staff, Lord Slim, military intervention was blocked by a Cabinet majority that included Attlee and Gaitskell on the grounds that even if it worked in the immediate sense of protecting the oilfields, it would torpedo Britain's long-term relations with the Arab world. The other options, capitulation or resort to the United Nations, would be represented by Opposition and press as a feeble and defeatist betrayal of Britain's interests and imperial glory. His misjudgement was to overestimate the capacity of the British armed forces to enforce the Middle-East Pax Britannica in much the same manner as Eden did over Suez in 1956. Despite having been regarded as one of the most experienced and knowledgeable Foreign Secretaries of modern times, Eden made the same mistake. Morrison was later to be one of the few senior Labour figures to support Eden's Suez endeavour.

Certainly Morrison lacked a background in foreign affairs, experience in diplomacy and in some cases a knowledge of geography. Worse, for many critics, was that at a time when most of Labour's foreign affairs experts were either pro-Soviet or veterans of the Fabian Colonial Bureau, whose inspirations were decolonisation and the dream that the UN could be turned into something more credible and worthwhile than the old League of Nations, he was neither. His pride in aspects of what he once referred to as the 'jolly old Empire'[40] grated on many of his political colleagues, particularly of the younger generation. This divergence of view is clearly set out in his memoirs where he lambasts his successors for having:

> managed to give the impression that the [Labour] Party is anti-British, and pro-every foreign country, which is an unfair exaggeration. During and after the Suez crisis there was excitement and even hysteria in the Labour ranks. It was doubtless regarded at the time as a highly successful political campaign, but one result was that Labour gave the impression of thinking more of Nasser's Egypt than of Britain, or of France, with a socialist prime minister at the time, or of Labour Israel...[41]

Unpopular though this view may have been across much of the progressive left, in holding it he was undoubtedly closer to the grain of British popular sentiment than many of his detractors.

Like Bevin he was an exponent of realpolitik but in being so he inevitably worked in Bevin's shadow. His reputation within the Foreign Office cannot have been helped by the dim view Bevin would have encouraged his officials to take of his successor. He was, however, probably the only choice: others in the frame like Jim Griffiths, Alf Robens, Hector McNeil, Kenneth Younger and Hartley Shawcross were perceived as of insufficient weight and experience and Bevan was seen as too politically volatile. He had received favourable British press comment on several excursions abroad, in particular to the USA and Canada, after 1945, where he had been regarded as effective in reassuring the American financial community that a British Labour government did not specifically endanger their investments. His official visit to Germany and Austria in May 1951 (he was the first British Foreign Secretary to visit Austria since Castlereagh) was similarly well received. For someone whose posthumous reputation is that he was unable to see beyond the environs of Bow Bells, he lacked the cultivated anti-Teutonic prejudices of Hugh Dalton or Douglas Jay, and it is striking that he became the first senior Party figure openly to back Britain's application to join the EEC (albeit having, as acting Prime Minister during one of Attlee's illnesses, originally opposed it on the grounds that 'the Durham miners won't wear it'). He was also a staunch supporter of Israel – perhaps all the more so in reaction to Bevin – against the depredations of her Arab neighbours. On Korea, his view was considerably more sophisticated than that of many fellow Cold Warriors, combining a determination to stand up to Communist aggression with an understanding of the only long-term solution as being, 'to remove the causes of Communism by alleviating the malnutrition and misery affecting so many millions of people, particularly throughout Asia'.[42]

In Opposition after 1951, Morrison's ability to score runs off the Conservatives on foreign affairs was blunted by his commitment to a bipartisan approach on the fundamentals of policy and Labour's own infighting over its attitude towards German rearmament. Both these factors undermined Morrison's standing and helped the dissenting Bevanites gain ground. By 1951 the Foreign Secretaryship had served to diminish his influence within the Party: Attlee informed Cabinet of his intention to call an election whilst Morrison was at a NATO meeting in Ottawa and he was still sailing back across the Atlantic when Labour's NEC agreed that the manifesto would be drafted by Morgan Phillips in conjunction with Bevan, Dalton and Sam Watson. In 1951 his NEC vote slipped from third place to fifth out of seven, whilst his ally Manny Shinwell was knocked off altogether. In 1952 it was worse: along with Hugh Dalton he was knocked off the NEC by the Bevanite tide, leaving Jim Griffiths as the sole non-Bevanite clinging on in the constituency section of the NEC. Morrison had now lost his key NEC power base and with Attlee's determination to cling on to the leadership until age made it difficult for him to succeed, Morrison's place amongst those who never quite managed to become Labour's leader was secured.

When MPs voted on Attlee's successor in December 1955 they knew that within a month Morrison would be 68 and that another election was four to five years away, by which time he would be over 70. Moreover, his age was beginning to show in his performances at the despatch box and on the conference platform. He was losing the sureness of his touch and at October's annual Labour conference it had been the younger Hugh Gaitskell who had garnered the longest ovation. Whilst a couple of years before, Gaitskell had been one of those urging Attlee to stand aside to let Morrison have his chance to lead Labour into the next election (along with Alf Robens he had actually told Attlee so in 1952), many of Morrison's erstwhile supporters now increasingly looked to Gaitskell as the surest bet to beat Bevan for the leadership and to keep him out for the long-term. Shadow Cabinet member Patrick Gordon Walker, formerly Morrison's PPS and later on Gaitskell's *de facto* chief of staff, confided to his diary what must have been the thoughts of many of Morrison's protégés:

> I have decided to back Gaitskell... I dearly love Herbert... But I have gradually changed my mind... We cannot miss the chance to kill Bevan. If Herbert has the leadership, Bevan will be able to challenge in 3 or four years. That would be fatal for us electorally. Morrison is undoubtedly failing both mentally and physically. He still has deep knowledge of the movement which Gaitskell still lacks. But... in Parliament. His performances of late have been horrible.[43]

Gaitskell was genuinely reluctant at first to stand against his old ally, but in the end he did and won. It is one of the great ironies of history that age having played the crucial role in his final defeat, Morrison went on to outlive both Bevan and Gaitskell.

George Brown, another underrated giant of the Labour movement who ultimately succeeded Morrison as Labour's Deputy Leader and Foreign Secretary, was unduly harsh, if typically blunt, in his verdict that Morrison's 'period at the Foreign Office was a disaster that clouded everything that had gone before'. He was surely right, however, in writing that, 'Looking back beyond these clouds that fell on Morrison at the end of his long political life, one can see him in his true stature.' For Brown, 'Of all those in the Labour movement whom I have known, I rate him as second only to Bevin in terms of political and human greatness.'[44]

Further reading

Lord Morrison of Lambeth published the ghosted *Herbert Morrison: An Autobiography* (London, 1960), which though widely regarded as unrevealing is nevertheless well worth reading. His other writings include the seminal

Socialisation and Transport (London, 1933) and *Government and Parliament* (London, 1954), which he hoped would become the new *Erskine May*. Two volumes of his speeches were published, *Looking Ahead* (London, 1943) and *The Peaceful Revolution* (London, 1949). The best and indeed only full biography of Morrison remains the readable, penetrating and authoritative Bernard Donoughue and G.W. Jones, *Herbert Morrison: Portrait of a Politician* (London, 1973; 2nd edn. 2001). Shorter portraits appear in Kenneth O. Morgan's excellent *Labour People* (Oxford, 2nd edn. 1992), a superb *Dictionary of National Biography* entry (*DNB 1961–70*) by John P. Mackintosh and the lucid but notably unsympathetic 'Herbert Morrison: The Socialist as Consolidator' in David Marquand, *The Progressive Dilemma*, (London, 2nd edn. 1999). Contemporary portraits include Maurice Edelman's *Herbert Morrison* (London, 1948), appear in J.T. Murphy, *Labour's Big Three* (London, 1948) and, by Maurice Webb, in Herbert Tracy (ed.), *The British Labour Party Vol. III,* (London, 1948). Copies of Peter Mandelson's *Herbert Morrison Memorial Lecture* (1 November 2000) are available from the London Young Fabians via the Fabian Society.

Notes

1. Roy Jenkins, *A Life at the Centre* (London, 1991), pp 111 and 83.
2. David Marquand, *The Progressive Dilemma* (London, 1999 edn.), p 108.
3. Bernard Donoughue and G.W. Jones, *Herbert Morrison: Portrait of a Politician* (London, 1973), p 309.
4. Lord Wigg, *George Wigg* (London, 1972), p 177.
5. Lord Morrison of Lambeth, *Herbert Morrison: An Autobiography* (London, 1960), p 322.
6. Michael Foot, *Aneurin Bevan*, Vol. II: '1945–60' (London, 1973), p 288.
7. Peter Mandelson, *Herbert Morrison Memorial Lecture* (London Young Fabians, 1 November 2000).
8. Ibid.
9. *Forward*, 11 September 1937, cited in Donoughue and Jones, *Morrison*, p 184.
10. *Hansard, Parliamentary Debates*, col. 664–7, 23 May 1946.
11. *The Times*, 10 January 1945, cited in Donoughue and Jones, *Morrison*, p 336.
12. Mandelson, *Morrison Memorial Lecture*.
13. *Forum*, July 1948, cited in Donoughue and Jones, *Morrison*, p 443.
14. Morrison Memorandum for Joint Meeting of NEC and Ministers, 19–21 May 1950, cited in Donoughue and Jones, *Morrison*, p 455.
15. Donoughue and Jones, *Morrison*, p 21.
16. John P. Mackintosh, 'Morrison', *Dictionary of National Biography* (Oxford, 1979), p 769.
17. Memorandum for Joint Meeting, May 1950, cited in Donoughue and Jones, *Morrison*, p 456.
18. Donoughue and Jones, *Morrison*, p 395.
19. Donoughue and Jones, *Morrison*, p 477.
20. Frank Owen, *Daily Express*, 10 March 1951, cited Donoughue and Jones, *Morrison*, p 345.

21. Lord Morrison, *Autobiography*, p 119.

22. *Daily Telegraph*, 11 January 1946, cited in Donoughue and Jones, *Morrison*, p 378.

23. Cited in Donoughue and Jones, *Morrison*, p 190.

24. Memorandum for Joint Meeting, May 1950, cited in Donoughue and Jones, *Morrison*, p 456.

25. Lord Morrison, *Autobiography*, pp 329–31.

26. *New Statesman*, 6 May 1950, cited in Donoughue and Jones, p 457.

27. *Scotsman*, 10 April 1978, cited by Greg Rosen in 'John P. Mackintosh: His Achievements and Legacy', *Political Quarterly*, 70, 2, 1999, p 216.

28. *Manchester Guardian*, 29 April 1954, cited in Donoughue and Jones, *Morrison*, p 528.

29. Lord Morrison, *Autobiography*, p 69.

30. *Daily Mail*, 5 March 1951, cited in Donoughue and Jones, *Morrison*, p 467.

31. Donoughue and Jones, *Morrison*, p 348.

32. George Brown, *In My Way* (London, 1972 edn.), p 238.

33. Lord Plowden interview, cited Donoughue and Jones, *Morrison*, p 466.

34. Anthony Eden, *Full Circle* (London, 1960), p 320.

35. Hugh Dalton diary, August 1951, cited in Kenneth O. Morgan, *Labour in Power 1945–51* (Oxford, 1984), p 430.

36. *Hansard*, 9 May 1951 and *Daily Telegraph*, 10 May 1951, cited in Donoughue and Jones, *Morrison*, p 491.

37. Lord Avon interview, cited in Donoughue and Jones, *Morrison*, p 509.

38. Kenneth O. Morgan, *Labour People* (Oxford, 1992 edn.), p 157.

39. Cited in Morgan, *Labour in Power*, p 468.

40. *Daily Telegraph*, 11 January 1946, cited in Donoughue and Jones, *Morrison*, p 378.

41. Lord Morrison, *Autobiography*, p 328.

42. *The Times*, 3 July 1950, cited in Donoughue and Jones, *Morrison*, p 463.

43. Robert Pearce (ed.), *Patrick Gordon Walker: Political Diaries 1932–71* (London, 1991), p 227.

44. Brown, *In My Way*, p 239.

3

Hugh Dalton

Stephen Howe

(Edward) Hugh (John Neale) Dalton b.1887–d.1962. Labour MP Peckham 1924–29; Bishop Auckland 1929–31, 1935–59. Member of National Executive 1926–27, 1928–52; chair of Finance and other subcommittees; party spokesman for foreign affairs 1935–40. Minister for Economic Warfare 1940–42; President of the Board of Trade 1942–45; Chancellor of the Exchequer 1945–47; Chancellor of the Duchy of Lancaster 1948–50; Minister of Town and Country Planning 1950–51; Minister of Local Government and Planning, 1951.

Almost nobody in the past century's British political life has exercised such influence for so long, without ever becoming Prime Minister or party leader, as did Hugh Dalton. And almost no senior politician has so consistently pursued a set of high principles, nor been so loyal and so unselfishly helpful to his or her party and friends.

These may be thought perverse judgements: for every account of Hugh Dalton agrees on two things. First, that he was never entirely successful in anything he did, was indeed always just a little worse than the best – and that this resulted from some deep flaw of character, from insecurity and emotional immaturity. Second, that the armour he built to protect that vulnerable core of his being made of him a deeply unpleasant character, unlovable and unloved: a schemer, bully, manipulator and petty tyrant. He had no real friends: only people he could use, or those younger men who could use him, and through whose successes he could experience vicarious triumph. His marriage was purgatorial, and throughout its later years a sham. Dalton, on this near-consensually held view, was not only a deeply unpleasant person but almost a monster, who escaped being truly sinister only because of the hint of absurdity that hung over much that he did or tried to do.

Certain images and phrases recur time and again in memoirs, journalism, and academic studies: Dalton pacing 'like a caged panther', his 'eyes blazing with insincerity'; Winston Churchill's 'keep that man away from me'; Sir Frederick Leith-Ross's 'I can only deal with one shit at a time'; Beatrice Webb seeing the undergraduate Dalton already as 'a subtle wily man'; an older Dalton in a Commons dining room, eating peas off his knife to embarrass a young Tory MP at whom he snarled as a 'little suburbanite'.

Then there are the more obviously absurd images: Keynes's mocking nickname for him of 'Daddy Dalton'; or Chuter Ede complaining that in Cabinet 'I addressed my colleagues as if I were the Archdeacon addressing the junior clergy'.[1] We have Hugh instructing the young Roy Jenkins in the importance of expressing matiness towards elderly trade union MPs – and misremembering the name of the man he demonstrated this on.[2] We encounter a youthful Tony Benn – whom Dalton thought of as, at least potentially, one of his protégés – contrasting him with Bevan. 'Dalton – saturnine, wicked, amusing, intellectual, roguish; Bevan open, honest, good-humoured, and devastating.'[3]

The hostile or sneering judgements should not be taken at face value – but they cannot be entirely dismissed. On some levels, Dalton was quite literally second-rate. At Eton, he was an 'Oppidan', not a more prestigious 'Colleger'. At Cambridge, he stood always in the shadow of his more handsome, charismatic and popular friend Rupert Brooke. He was not elected to the Apostles, and failed to achieve either a First or Presidency of the Union. Applying for his first proper job, at the London School of Economics, he was only the selectors' second choice – the first being Clement Attlee. As an academic economist, he worked hard and was respected, but was never in the first rank. In Attlee's governments, he was one of the 'Big Five' with Clem himself, Bevin, Cripps, and Morrison – but probably the least powerful of the five, fifth among equals. As Chancellor, he presided first over dynamic expansion and sweeping reform, but then over crisis and retrenchment, before falling victim to his own indiscretion and overconfidence. In the ensuing years of inner-party conflict, his inveterate scheming – even if it was almost always on others' behalf, not his own – made him widely distrusted. Dalton was very good at many things, but never the best.

Yet alongside this, there is a remarkable array of achievements to be recorded. In the 1930s, he was the most important architect both of Labour's economic and of its foreign policies. In the 1940s, he was an immensely energetic, determined and effective member of the War Cabinet and then a powerful, able, if not of course entirely successful Chancellor. Through the 1950s, he helped, guided and influenced a group of younger men (they were, it has often been noted, all men) who included many of Labour's future leaders and its most creative post-war thinkers. Posthumously, his memoirs and diaries have come to be seen as probably the most revealing single source on the British political life of his era.

As to Dalton's character, behaviour and personal relationships, here too a strong plea in mitigation and partial defence can and should be entered. If he seemed emotionally cold, then – the cliché is true, and important – Englishmen of his generation and background were expected to be so, and were raised and trained in ways that made it difficult and unusual to be anything else. His marriage was clearly more affectionate, companionate – and more important to him – than the stereotypes suggest. His diaries, despite their general reticence on intimate things, record too many expressions of happiness with Ruth, and of his debts to her, for one to doubt that. When apart from her, as he was during the middle period of the war, he was clearly more prone to depression, and felt the stress of office more intensely, than at other times. When, in 1952, he described her as a '*wise* political wife', it may not have sounded very intimate – but it was, from Dalton, very high praise.[4]

As to friendship, if Dalton in later life truly had no soul-mates among his contemporaries, it must be remembered that he suffered the fate of many Englishmen of his generation; that of losing so many of his early friends in the First World War that an emotional gulf was left which could never again be filled.[5] Increasingly, as the years went by, close friendships with younger people – mostly aspirant or apprentice Labour politicians – were a partial substitute. The gap in age and status meant that few of these could be truly relationships of equality, and indeed both Dalton and others sometimes referred jokingly to such young associates as his 'poodles', but some were very far from being merely links of patronage and clientage. No such instrumental, or intellectually unequal, partnership could have allowed encounters like that with Anthony Crosland in 1951, when Crosland suggested to Dalton's face that all the people he had admired or who had influenced him were second-rate minds.[6] Nor could it have evoked anything like Dalton's extraordinary, confessional, self-revealing letter to Crosland a few months earlier.[7] And if there was, as has so often been speculated, an element of latent homosexuality in some of these partnerships, then surely the only oddity is that, even now, some supposedly liberal writers still appear to think that somehow discreditable.

Yet in seeking to question some of the nastier stereotypes about Hugh

Dalton, one cannot without dishonesty or silliness bend the stick all the way back. Denis Healey comments that he had learned how to deal with people like Dalton from previous experience with a superior officer during the war: a Colonel universally known as 'Basil the Bastard'.[8] Hugh was, outwardly, a hard man, not only bad-tempered, arrogant and overbearing but also with a deep, disturbing streak of cruelty in him. In his First World War diaries, the story is told of Italians using a captured Austrian soldier as a human firework: binding him to a stake and forcing a bomb into his anus.[9] Dalton does not record this by way of an observation on the horror of war, or a meditation on man's beastliness to man: for him, this is a funny story. Twenty years later, early in the Second World War, he was pleased to hear that the French had sacked 15 generals, but wished they could have been shot as well.[10] For those who believe, with Judith Shklar,[11] that cruelty is the worst thing people can do, the judgement on Dalton must be harsh. Cruel in a different way was his diary 'obituary' on Ernest Bevin. 'The surprise is that he didn't die sooner. He had been no use, physically or mentally, for some time.'[12] As a first reaction to the death of a man he had worked with so closely for over 20 years, this is astonishingly callous. More mundanely, even the long country walks which he so loved had a competitive and aggressive element, with Dalton eager always to prove that he could go further and faster than his younger guests.

Richard Crossman, recording Dalton's visit to his hospital bed in 1952, saw both sides:

> [T]here was Hugh Dalton to bring one the point of view of a man who stood with a cloven hoof in each camp and an unkind word for all – though that's not fair, because to his own young men, including me, he's really affectionate.[13]

And Denis Healey, surely the most perceptive of all Labour's modern autobiographers, wrote that:

> There was a deep insecurity and sadness at the root of his being... His capacity for human feeling withered, though he tried to revive it by a series of sentimental attachments to younger men. Many politicians attempt to develop a persona for public show. With Hugh Dalton the persona came to replace the personality. Yet despite his gargantuan weaknesses, Dalton was a seminal force for good in the Labour movement for over forty years.[14]

Dalton was born near Neath in Wales in 1887, but raised almost entirely at Windsor. His father John Neale Dalton, already 48 when Hugh was born, was Canon there and personal tutor to the royal princes, including the future King George V. Canon Dalton remained personally close to and influential on the Royal family throughout his life: but it was not an unstrained relationship. Dalton was strict, if not downright harsh, towards his royal pupils. Their later view of him mingled gratitude and resentment, and as we shall see, the Windsors came to regard the Canon's son with outright and politically damaging dislike.

Hugh's was thus a strange childhood, intimate with but of course not accepted as an equal by the Royal family: apparently spoiled, and already gathering a reputation for bullying bad behaviour which never after left him. The aged Queen Victoria supposedly thought him a 'horrid little boy', and his much-abused younger sister Georgie certainly concurred.[15] Yet reaction against such an upbringing surely also helped produce one of Hugh's more attractive attributes: his lifelong, passionate egalitarianism. He attended St George's Choir School at Windsor, then Summerfields preparatory school and Eton. He went up to King's College, Cambridge in 1906, studying economics and mathematics.

Hugh's attachment to Cambridge always remained intense – and bittersweet, since so many of his friends there had died young in the 1914–18 war. Revisiting in 1929, he reflected 'Cambridge is the most beloved place in the world, and its youth the most attractive. As this gap of years slowly widens between me and them, in their eternal replenishment, my heart softens to them more and more'.[16] His social circle at King's mingled aesthetes and aspirant politicians, grouped in a College debating club named the Carbonari and in the University Fabian Society, and centred round Rupert Brooke. The all-pervasive intellectual influence among them was G.E. Moore's *Principia Ethica*, published in 1903, with its doctrine that the pursuit of love, beauty and knowledge (very much in that order) was the highest thing in life. In economics, although Dalton was for a time tutored by Keynes, the latter (only four years his senior) seemingly never had a very high opinion of him, while Hugh for his part never became a convert to Keynesian theory, either in his academic work or his policies as Chancellor. Politically, the young Dalton seems to have moved very quickly from the vague Tory Democracy and pro-imperialism of his schooldays to Fabian socialism. He was not so unusual in being an early, upper-middle class convert to Labour; but unlike almost all other such converts in never having been a Liberal. Nor, unlike most of them, was he ever a pacifist or an anti-colonialist.

After leaving Cambridge, Dalton first studied – briefly and without enthusiasm – for the Bar, but then shifted back to economics, undertaking a doctoral thesis at the LSE. Published in 1920 as *Some Aspects of the Inequality of Incomes in Modern Communities*, it remained the most technical and academically specialised of all his writings, but also – obviously enough – had a clear political message to push.

Dalton's academic work was interrupted by war service in 1914–18: but that service was also a formative experience for him. Initially drafted into the rather humdrum activities of the Army Service Corps behind the Western Front, he transferred to the Royal Artillery, and his battery was among the British units sent to 'stiffen up' the rather shaky efforts of their Italian allies. When the Italian front collapsed under an Austrian-German assault at Caporetto in October 1917, Dalton was caught up in the ensuing chaos, but displayed marked bravery (for which he was decorated) and subsequently wrote an account of the retreat which, in its evocative power, almost matches the more famous picture of Caporetto in Ernest Hemingway's *A Farewell to Arms*.[17] The experience of command, and the knowledge that he had proved his physical courage under fire, no doubt helped create the image of forceful self-assurance he always later carried – though as we have seen, contemporaries often suspected that behind this façade always gnawed a worm of self-doubt.

Returning to the LSE, he simultaneously built a substantial academic reputation and began his pursuit of a parliamentary career. His book on *Inequality* was followed by a major, closely related article in the *Economic Journal* and a textbook on *Principles of Public Finance*.[18] He was appointed lecturer and then Reader at the LSE – but came under criticism for spending ever less time there, as he searched for a parliamentary seat. After several unsuccessful contests, he won Peckham in south London in 1924 – but became embroiled in bitter disputes within the local party. It is hard not to sympathise with him at this time. Although we only have Dalton's side of the story in any detail, it would seem that his main local critic, party Agent Ernest Baldwyn, was motivated by a near-obsessive personal malice against the MP.[19] He was relieved to move, in 1929, to a safer seat with a more pliable local party, Bishop Auckland in County Durham.

He had meanwhile been stricken by private tragedy. He had married Ruth Hamilton Fox in 1914, and their daughter Helen was born three years later. It is clear that there were difficulties both with the marriage and with the care of Helen: far less clear exactly what those difficulties were, or why Helen was placed in a residential nursery home for at least part of her infancy. Yet if Hugh and Ruth had not loved their daughter, they would surely not have been so entirely devastated by her death from meningitis in June 1922. If the early deaths of so many friends had left one hole in Hugh's heart, the loss of Helen produced another, perhaps greater emotional void. Seven years later he recorded in his diary that 'of Her, for fear of tears, I never speak'.[20]

Dalton's success in his new Durham constituency coincided with the formation of MacDonald's second Labour Government. He became a junior Minister at the Foreign Office, under Arthur Henderson. His main responsibilities were with the international Disarmament Conference which Henderson initiated. It was work to which Hugh was passionately committed, as his book *Towards the Peace of Nations* (1928) had already testified – though his diaries of the time also record his scorn both for many of his ministerial colleagues and for the diplomats with whom he worked.

In Labour's 1931 electoral disaster, Dalton was among the majority who lost their seats. This had great long-term significance for him as for many others, since the handful of Labour figures who survived the slaughter, including Attlee, seemed far better placed to shape the party's direction and form its leadership than those who were temporarily in the wilderness. He believed himself that, but for this blow by fate, he would have become leader of the party (though simultaneously, he denied having ever aspired to that role). Yet even without a parliamentary seat until 1935, Dalton's influence was great in these years: perhaps, in the long view, greater than at any other time. On the party's National Executive and its Policy Committee, and especially as chair of the Finance and Trade Subcommittee, he not only oversaw the reshaping of Labour's economic thinking, but acted as crucial patron and stimulus to a group of mostly younger people who collectively gave the party – for the first time – a coherent and credible medium-term strategy for economic management. Several of these came together in the semi-clandestine 'XYZ Club' which involved Labour supporters in the City and Fleet Street, others in the New Fabian Research Bureau (though Dalton's view of the latter, which he felt was dominated by impractical left-wingers under G.D.H. Cole's influence, soon became scornful).

Much of this new thinking was summarised in Dalton's 1935 book *Practical Socialism for Britain.* He himself thought that the achievements of the Attlee governments were 'most surprisingly close' to the blueprint set out in that book.[21] His biographer, Ben Pimlott, echoes the judgement. Though not as elegantly argued as Douglas Jay's *The Socialist Case* (1937), nor as innovative in its economic thinking as Evan Durbin's *The Politics of Democratic Socialism* (1940) – both Jay and Durbin were among Dalton's earliest 'poodles' – it was perhaps the most comprehensive and important statement of Labour's new ideas.

Just as important was Dalton's influence on Labour foreign policy in these years. As the party's chief foreign affairs spokesman from 1935 – when he returned to Parliament – he argued persistently, passionately and in the end successfully for Labour to adopt an anti-appeasement, pro-rearmament stance, spurning the pacifist tendencies previously so pronounced within the party and symbolised by the ageing but generally beloved George Lansbury. Together with Ernest Bevin, Dalton's was the key role in producing that change: but if Bevin's brutally effective demolition of Lansbury at the 1935 Party Conference was the crucial public moment of transition, Dalton's more quietly tenacious efforts at persuasion were in the long run more significant. Yet even he, like so many contemporaries, initially found much to admire in Mussolini (whom he met in 1932),[22] dangerously underestimated Hitler and saw little merit in arguments that Britain should – if only out of self-interest – aid Republican Spain in the 1936–39 Civil War. Nor was his judgement in Labour's internal affairs quite impeccable: he backed Herbert Morrison against Attlee in the 1935 leadership contest (later his opinion of Morrison was to become very low but, like so many others, he underrated Attlee from start to finish), and some of his attacks on Stafford Cripps and the Labour left seemed pointlessly immoderate and provocative.

Yet Dalton's efforts, more than any other's, made it possible for Labour to enter Churchill's wartime coalition in 1940; while the work on economic planning he had done or sponsored through the 1930s meant that the Labour ministers in that coalition had – quite unlike their predecessors in 1924 or 1929 – some coherent idea of what to do with their new power. Dalton himself was placed in charge of the Ministry of Economic Warfare – or as Churchill mischievously dubbed it, the Ministry for Ungentlemanly Warfare. It seemed a post ideally suited to the man who delighted in being thought ungentlemanly, an outlet for his conspiratorial tastes as well as his organisational drive – and his hatred for all things German. Yet he clashed with several colleagues, most seriously with Minister of Information Brendan Bracken. Bracken was certainly not Dalton's match in energy or intellect, but Churchill was mysteriously fond of him (so much so that some, however absurdly, believed Bracken must be the great man's secret, illegitimate son). The conflict was 'resolved' by Dalton being moved to the Board of Trade in February 1942. He resented being thus shifted away from the 'sharp end' of prosecuting the war effort. Yet here too his powers were great and wide-ranging. Probably his most important measure was the Distribution of Industries Act, creating a structure of incentives and pressures for businesses to relocate to depressed or underdeveloped areas. This innovative basis for an interventionist regional economic policy, though watered down under post-war Conservative governments and later still substantially supplanted by European Union regional development policies, was another of Dalton's most lasting achievements.

Dalton's drive for more planning and more controls faced Conservative opposition within the Cabinet and from backbenchers – as with his proposal to introduce coal rationing in 1942. Tories and coal-owners saw it, quite rightly, as a first step towards nationalisation. This was just one instance of the conflicts, both within and between parties, which persisted beneath the surface appearance of wartime national unity: Dalton's war diaries provide probably the most intimate and revealing portrait of those conflicts available.

In 1945 Dalton hoped, indeed expected, to become Foreign Secretary in Attlee's government – and indeed it was Attlee's intention too that he should take that post. But here it appears that one of the rare modern instances of direct Royal intervention in British domestic politics took place. The detail remains unclear, but it seems that King George VI urged strongly that Bevin, not Dalton, be placed in charge of international affairs.[23] It seems, too, that the King's personal animosity toward Dalton was the crucial factor. Hugh Gaitskell, in conversation with the King in 1951, clearly had the latter's deep dislike for Dalton confirmed to him, and that it 'really goes back to the Windsor days when Hugh Dalton's father was tutor to King George V, and apparently very like HD in having a loud voice and bullying manner'.[24] Hugh went to the Treasury instead.

Dalton's years as Chancellor were probably not the period of his greatest real influence: that distinction surely lies with his policy-making role in the later 1930s, and he later half-jokingly said that 1947 was 'not one of my good years'.[25] But they were the apex of his official career, and the most controversial time in all its span. He entitled the third volume of his memoirs *High Tide and After*; and 1945–7 was clearly that moment of high tide, both for him and for his party.

Initially, he pursued a boldly expansionary policy, based on low interest rates and egalitarian tax reforms. He made sure the money was available for family allowances, for the new National Health Service, for greatly increased education and regional development spending and for a massive (if in the event feebly executed) scheme of council house building. He managed all this, and sustained near-full employment, while actually cutting the overall tax burden. He pursued the hostility to inherited wealth which he had first expressed in his 1920 book on inequality, increasing death duties at the higher levels. He nationalised the Bank of England. His public and parliamentary performances radiated confidence, indeed arrogance – in a way that aroused the Opposition benches to blind fury, and was intended to do so. He was, as Pimlott says, 'the most socialist Chancellor of the Exchequer Britain has ever had'.[26]

Yet problems mounted. The low interest policy aroused intensifying criticism, as did the 1946–7 winter fuel shortages (which were, of course, hardly Dalton's fault; though also perhaps not quite so much Manny Shinwell's as the Chancellor furiously insisted). A major issue of Government stock – inevitably nicknamed 'Daltons' – in October 1946 was a notable failure. Above all, everything Dalton did had in the background a ticking time-bomb: the American insistence, as a condition for their post-war loan to Britain, that sterling be made fully convertible in 1947. As the deadline approached, an air of impending crisis mounted – and, as is the way with these things, the prophecies of disaster threatened to become self-fulfilling. Many have argued subsequently that the obvious, indeed the only, way to square the circle was to cut hard at Britain's overseas, mainly defence-related, commitments. Indeed Dalton argued this at the time: to no avail. Assumptions, or pretensions, of global power remained unassailable, even as the Attlee government began to dismantle the Empire. Dalton had been a youthful enthusiast for Empire. In the 1930s, he seemed indifferent to it (*Practical Socialism* contains just a couple of hundred words, of notable blandness, on colonial questions). As Chancellor, he felt no moral qualms about raiding the colonies' financial reserves to help bridge the 'dollar gap'. A little later, he was to speak of the subject Empire's peoples in nakedly racist terms. But he was a realist. If he had had his way, Britain's global role would have been wound down far faster, and probably less painfully, than it was – and there would have been no 'independent' British nuclear weapons programme.

The August 1947 convertibility crisis, when it finally came, was just that: a crisis, not a catastrophe. But neither the government's radicalism, self-confidence and popularity, nor those of Dalton himself, ever fully recovered from it. His last months as Chancellor were anticlimactic: deflationary in policy terms, subdued in personal ones. In November, just minutes before introducing an emergency autumn Budget, he did in a moment of careless indiscretion what more recent Chancellors do deliberately and routinely: 'leaked' a few details to a journalist. It would certainly not be a resigning matter today (one often wonders what *is*); and even by the higher standards of the 1940s, it was something which a less battered Minister, with more of his Premier's confidence, could have hoped to survive. But Dalton's stock had fallen sharply since the spring, and he had to go. Allegations that he had behaved improperly over planning applications, and over the offer of a company directorship, though unproven and clearly at least in the main untrue, further damaged both his reputation and his morale. Although he returned to government the following year, and successively served as Chancellor of the Duchy of Lancaster, Minister of Town and Country Planning and of Local Government and Planning, all were obviously second-division posts. He remained a powerful voice on economic policy, and in shaping the government's arm's-length attitude to European cooperation, but as Pimlott puts it: 'Before, he had been a history-maker... Afterwards, he was a politician.'[27]

The rest, inevitably, was decline – first in his public profile, then in his party standing (he lost his National Executive seat in 1952, victim of the 'Bevanite' upsurge in the constituencies), finally of his mental and physical powers. He was himself keenly, almost self-laceratingly aware of the last. Determined not to carry on in politics until senility crept in, determined equally to practice what he preached in making way for youth, he tried also, by his public statements on the issue, to embarrass Shadow Cabinet colleagues – some of them considerably older than he was – into following his example. Unsurprisingly, few did so.

Not all that he did in his last active political years seemed so principled. His own highest priority and greatest pleasure, that of encouraging and guiding younger colleagues, giving a kick-start to promising political careers, aroused – as we have already seen – mixed feelings then and since. His aspirations to be a peacemaker between Bevanite and 'revisionist' camps within the party were interpreted by some (as the remark by Crossman quoted above suggests) as mere duplicity. His schemes to get rid of Attlee and to promote various desired successors could only reinforce such impressions. From 1952 onward he spent much time on his three volumes of memoirs, and much also recuperating from a series of illnesses and accidents. In March 1959, most ominously, he suffered a stroke. Although he accepted Gaitskell's offer of a life peerage in 1960, this was mainly, he said, so as to keep in close touch with young friends 'down the corridor'. His health continued to deteriorate through 1961, with heart trouble, sciatica and something at least close to senile dementia. Hugh Dalton died on 12 February 1962.

Dalton's career was shaped throughout by two crucial formative influences, two great passions, and two abiding interests. The influences were his family background and his Cambridge days; the passions egalitarianism and patriotism; the interests economic planning and international relations.

Family background made him distinctively, indeed noisily, 'upper middle class', but in an unusual way. The Daltons did not belong to the intellectual and professional 'alternative Establishment' which provided so many prominent recruits to Labour: Stracheys and Crippses, Benns and Foots. They were attached, rather, to the very core of the 'real Establishment', House of Windsor and Anglican Church. Closely, but uneasily attached: Hugh's father as Canon and royal tutor was poised between being a true member of that inner circle, and being merely part of its servant class. The family was neither aristocratic nor rich. Nor did Hugh ever become personally wealthy. Yet his background was privileged in ways that marked him throughout his life: most obviously in accent and mannerisms, but also in more substantial fashion. It enabled him – or so he thought – to be easily censorious of those Labour figures like Ramsay MacDonald who seemed seduced by aristocracy: 'My friends, I say, are poorer and simpler people'.[28] Yet he clearly regretted that there were 'only' three Old Etonians on the Labour benches when he

first entered Parliament, as against dozens among the Tories opposite.[29] The
patrician air often served him well. Or so, again, he believed: 'I think that
one reason why our people liked my speeches was because I treated the
Tories, and Liberals too, with a slightly contemptuous self-confidence.'[30]

If childhood made him 'Establishment', Cambridge made him an
'intellectual'. No label was more widely, variously – and often pejoratively –
thrown around in Labour circles, from the party's foundation until at least
the 1960s (its subsequent disappearance is an intriguing minor sociological
phenomenon). Dalton himself noted that some used it to mean anyone
with a public school and university education. Within this remarkably vague
and inflated category, what kind of 'intellectual' was Dalton?

He was always, very distinctively, a party intellectual. After his early,
more purely academic books he never wrote anything that was not
intended very directly to influence and help Labour. In the 1930s he
kept 'his' groups of economic policy thinkers sharply distant from the
various cross-party circles then operating on rather similar lines, like the
Next Five Years group. With the (partial) exceptions of those academic
works, *Inequality* and *Public Finance*, Dalton's thought was not 'his own',
but the party's. It is both difficult and fruitless to evaluate his thinking
except in relation to Labour's policies and inner debates. This obviously
distinguishes him sharply from even the most politically engaged of
'classic' intellectuals – a Du Bois or a Sartre, even a Keynes. By some
definitions, then – those like Edward Said's which make stubborn
independence of mind central to what defines the category – Dalton
was not really an intellectual at all, except in that peculiar Labour sense.[31]

Egon Wertheimer surely had Dalton among those in mind when he
wrote of middle-class converts to Labour that:

> The scholarliness characteristic of the Continental intellectual is not
> highly prized among these gentlemen. Their distinguishing feature
> is a strong and often rather artificially cultivated will to power that
> in certain circumstances might be turned to the advantage of the
> oppressed and injured, but never for a lost cause.[32]

Certainly Dalton was utterly unabashed about his determination to use
to the full all the power he could gather – but always, he insisted, for
some higher, unselfish end.[33]

His was also, in some evident ways, a narrow intellect. His cultural
and literary tastes, like his philosophical influences (above all G.E. Moore)
were clearly formed in youth and shifted or broadened little, if at all,
thereafter. His diaries almost never note him, in later life, reading non-
political literature. An exception was the weekend of 14–15 October
1939, when he read, or it seems, in every case *re*read, Euripides' *Trojan*

Women, Masefield's *Gallipoli*, Rupert Brooke – and one of his own earlier books![34] Thinking about retirement, the valedictory verse he summoned to mind was from Herbert Trench and W.E. Henley – poets popular, again, in Dalton's youth and, deservedly, not since.[35] So far as Hugh had a 'secret planet', a hinterland of cultural passions such as that which Denis Healey has so brilliantly evoked in his own case,[36] it was indeed secret, rather small, static and in later life almost fossilized.

Yet it is evident that had his intelligence not been focused so narrowly and in such partisan fashion, he could not have had the kind of impact that he did. His work in the 1930s – both his own writing, and that which he sponsored and organised – was dedicated single-mindedly to giving Labour a programme for government. Thus it would both again become electable, and know what to do when elected: the fiascos of 1924 and 1929–31 need never be repeated. In doing this, he not only harnessed serious resources of financial and planning expertise to Labour's policy-making – for the first time – but also brought such experts into effective co-operation with both parliamentary party and unions. He was obviously delighted to quote in his memoirs a friend's judgement, that he had devoted much of his political life to 'closing the gap' between middle class leaders and trade unionists.[37] This was true, and crucial for the party's future.

However we choose to judge Dalton's purely cerebral powers, there can be no doubt that his own high estimation of them, and correspondingly low view of almost everyone else's, damaged him more than any of his other failings. Yet, astonishingly, he refused to recognise this trait in himself. In 1942, Christopher Mayhew told him that, had he suffered fools more patiently, he might have become Prime Minister. Dalton replied:

> For many years, I tell him, I exercised the most tremendous control,
> even in the presence of the greatest fools. Only recently have I allowed
> myself the luxury of showing some of them – and by no means all of
> them even yet – what I think of them.[38]

He made the same rather surprising claim about his patience and self-control in not criticising colleagues rather earlier, in a 1935 letter to Kingsley Martin.[39] And in 1953, yet again, he mused: 'I am amazed at my tolerance, through so many decades, of so many dullards.'[40]

All this is unattractive, even silly. Yet it remains true that Dalton's friends and allies, at any one time and on any particular issue, were nearly always cleverer than their opponents – and this includes his temporary dalliance with the Bevanites over German rearmament. That does not mean that they, or he, were always right; but he had a sure eye for quality, for political intelligence and talent.

The twin passions or guiding principles across his career were egalitarianism and patriotism. About the sincerity of the former there can be no doubt. It motivated his initial conversion to socialism, his earliest and most important academic writing and much of his activity in the 1930s. In *Practical Socialism*, although he repudiated the idea that a classless society required absolute equality of incomes, he placed a drive for equality of opportunity at the heart of all his arguments. Both there, and in almost all his actions as Chancellor, his personal enthusiasm for expanding social welfare and educational opportunity, for a more progressive taxation system, and above all for attacking concentrations of inherited wealth, did not falter. Near the end of his life, he worried whether Gaitskell really meant to change British society – and noted that 'Poor old Morrison', for instance, didn't really want to do so.[41] Dalton did desire fundamental change; and did as much to make it possible as any British politician before or since.

It has been suggested that 'for Dalton, socialism was a kind of revenge... In his case, the tired Tory jibe that egalitarianism is about levelling down rather than about levelling up contained a distinct element of truth'.[42] Yet although aspects of his personal manner might seem to support this claim, neither his own writings nor his policies as minister do so. The charge might stick more fairly to his successor as Chancellor, Stafford Cripps. Unlike Cripps, Dalton was no Puritan or ascetic. Above all, his case for greater equality was a moral one:

> Why is social equality desired by Socialists? Because Socialism means comradeship, and comradeship means social equality. Because great inequality is both unjust and ugly. Because it gives cake to a few, while many lack bread. Because it breeds servility, wastes talent, and restricts the sources of initiative and leadership.

Finally, because it makes a mockery of freedom.[43]

Even so, his was an egalitarianism very much of his time, and with its striking limits. It did not extend fully to issues of gender, and certainly not, as we shall see, to ones of race. His fierce hostility to inherited wealth did not seem to extend to institutionalised forms of inherited *privilege*. Whatever the discomforts of his and his family's relationship with the House of Windsor, he was certainly no republican. In *Practical Socialism* he had called the House of Lords 'a blot on British democracy', and supported proposals that it be replaced by a nominated (significantly, *not* directly elected) second chamber.[44] Yet he never later, as Minister or elder statesman, showed any enthusiasm for such measures – and, of course, at the last entered the Lords himself. Indeed on constitutional questions in general he was among Labour's reactionaries, and contributed greatly to the party's general conservatism on such questions between the 1930s and the 1990s.

In his later years, almost all his 'poodles' came from prosperous backgrounds and were Oxbridge graduates. George Brown was almost the only exception – and Dalton's diaries record that class was more than once the occasion for uncomfortable scenes from Brown, and even more from his wife Sophie, in their dealings with Hugh.[45] Dalton was not a social – as opposed to intellectual – elitist, but certain traits of his upbringing could never be shaken off. Jennie Lee was to charge that Dalton's class background made him unable to see the need for two lavatories in each of the millions of new council houses that Attlee's government was pledged to build: 'He had not sympathy or imagination enough to bridge the gap.'[46]

Hugh Dalton was, then, a genuine but in some ways limited kind of egalitarian. What kind of patriot was he? The question would not have occurred to him: or not in the sense that all politicians today must be conscious of it, in the wake of decline, decolonisation and devolution. In his writings, he tended to use the words 'English' and 'British' interchangeably (for instance in the opening lines of *Practical Socialism*). He almost literally never wrote or said a word suggesting awareness of Scottish, Welsh, or even Northern Irish distinctiveness or special problems. His account of a brief ministerial visit to the last in 1944 breathes the classic English politician's condescension and incomprehension: 'This is "loyal" Ulster, and I don't doubt that it is all most sincere, even, as by tradition, most fanatical.'[47] His was not, however, an 'imperial' or 'Greater British' patriotism. Except in his earliest youth, he showed no enthusiasm for the idea of Empire as a vehicle for social progress; an idea far more widely held than is often now remembered, and uniting the Tory Democrats and Liberal Imperialists of Dalton's childhood, the Webbs and many other Fabians, and the 'Empire Socialists' of the 1920s. In both *Towards the Peace of Nations* and *Practical Socialism*, he gestured towards the importance of closer ties with Canada, Australia and New Zealand – but it was a mere gesture.

For all his lifelong engagement with foreign policy, he was never truly an internationalist of any kind. He had real affection for some foreign peoples – the Poles, the Italians, later the Israelis – and once sanctimoniously declared that 'all foreigners are comrades'.[48] But not only was he among the most anti-European of all senior figures in the 1945–51 governments, not only do all his writings on inequality fail even to mention questions of inequality between rather than within nations, but across his whole career both his intellectual influences and his literary passions were near-exclusively Anglo-Saxon. In this, too, he was not untypical of his background and generation.

The same might perhaps be said of his racism, though to 'excuse' the latter in that way is probably too lenient on a man who could routinely describe a local doctor as 'a Buck Nigger',[49] or who could record his refusal to take on the Colonial Secretaryship thus: 'I had a horrid vision of pullulating, poverty stricken, diseased nigger communities' and more revealingly still, 'all the silliness and emotion about the black man who married a white typist'.[50] The latter allusion is to the marriage of Seretse Khama to Ruth Williams, which was viciously opposed by white African settler opinion and by South Africa – pressures to which Attlee's government shamefully capitulated. The affair rightly evoked great moral passion among many of Dalton's colleagues – but, evidently, not at all from him. At a 1952 Cambridge Labour Club speech, he praised Queensland as a 'White Man's Country', evoking righteous indignation from some of the students.[51] Later, as on a visit to Brazil, he seemed distastefully obsessed with delineating the 'racial types' he encountered there.[52] On the other hand, the suggestion by Harold Laski's biographers that certain remarks by Dalton qualify him as an anti-Semite rest on far too slender evidence for a conviction, when set against numerous friendly personal relationships and indeed Dalton's pro-Zionism.[53]

How, then, should we judge Dalton's legacy and achievement, after the fog of anecdotes and personal animosities has been cleared? His accomplishments, flawed but very substantial, as Minister and party spokesman in both economic and international affairs, have been sketched. It can be argued, though, that his greatest importance was a longer-term intellectual one: that his influence, direct or indirect, pervaded all serious social-democratic thought within Labour until at least the 1980s, including that of the men and women who split the party to form the SDP in 1981.[54] If so, it was again little acknowledged by those who followed in his steps. All the major 'revisionist' statements, from Crosland's *Future of Socialism* to Hattersley's *Choose Freedom* or the 1980s writings of Roy Jenkins, Shirley Williams and David Owen, either did not mention Dalton at all, or had the most cursory of references – and even the latter were mostly allusions to his record as Chancellor, not to his writings. Crosland's major work, indeed – and despite the enormous encouragement that Dalton had given him in the writing of it, as in his whole earlier career – almost damned with faint praise. Dalton's *Practical Socialism* was described as just one of 'a number of non-analytical works of a practical reformist nature' which 'dealt essentially with short-term problems, and contained no long-run analysis of the future of capitalism'.[55]

The influence, then, must be sought less in print than in Dalton's activities as patron of aspirant younger party leaders and thinkers. In some of the personal-political relationships of his later life, though, there was not only inequality and instrumentality – trading intimacy for patronage – but a disconcerting absence of thankfulness among the recipients of his help. At different points in the 1950s Dalton assiduously – and in retrospect at least, rather implausibly – urged the merits first of James Griffiths, then of Alfred Robens as the next Labour leader. Neither man seems to have shown much gratitude. Griffiths' memoirs have the briefest and most dutiful of praise for aspects of Dalton's ministerial record, but not the faintest hint of personal warmth.[56] Even those of Dalton's protégés who did succeed, Gaitskell and Callaghan, fail to evince any fondness towards him.[57] Douglas Jay's memoirs stand almost alone in breathing personal affection as well as respect for the man.[58] But then, Dalton himself said 'I always discourage' gratitude from others.[59]

Hugh Dalton's own description of his adolescent physical attributes could also be taken as a neat summary of his intellectual characteristics and of his impact on Labour's evolution: 'Weight rather than pace; endurance; low cunning.'[60] They were all qualities Labour needed, in its years of consolidation during the 1920s, of recovery in the 1930s, of triumph in the 1940s and of reappraisal in the 1950s. Hugh Dalton was at the heart of all those. As anti-appeaser, as ungentlemanly warrior, as ruthlessly effective planner and reforming Chancellor, he served country as well as party well. On leaving office in 1951, he reflected that: 'I have stuck to politics, because it has been fun, and because it is a drug, and because it has seemed to be a means of doing a lot of good.'[61] Few people, apparently, thought that Hugh Dalton was a good man. But most recognised that he was, in truth, a man who did a great deal of good.

Further reading

All discussion of Dalton stands in the shadow of Ben Pimlott, who not only wrote, in his *Hugh Dalton* (1985), one of the greatest of modern British political biographies, but edited Dalton's *Second World War Diary* (1986) and *Political Diary 1918–40, 1945–60* (1986). In his *Labour and the Left in the 1930s* (1977) and numerous 'satellite' essays – some collected in *Frustrate their Knavish Tricks* (London, 1994) – Pimlott also provides some of the surest guides to the various intellectual and social worlds in which Dalton moved. Among shorter biographical sketches and assessments, outstanding is David Marquand, 'The Progressive as Bounder' in his *The Progressive Dilemma* (1991).

Dalton's own memoirs remain compelling – if not, naturally, always entirely reliable – sources: *Call Back Yesterday*, *The Fateful Years* and *High Tide and*

After (London, 1953, 1957 and 1962). Of his other writings, *Towards the Peace of Nations* (London, 1928) was clearly his own favourite, but *Practical Socialism for Britain* (London, 1935) has probably been the most influential. For the Cambridge of Dalton's youth see Robert Skidelsky, *John Maynard Keynes Vol. 1: Hopes Betrayed 1883–1920* (London, 1983) and Paul Delany *The Neo-Pagans* (London, 1987). On the 1930s rethinking of Labour economic policy and Dalton's part in it, the key study remains Elizabeth Durbin, *New Jerusalems* (1985). For Labour during wartime, Paul Addison, *The Road to 1945* (London, 1975) and Stephen Brooke, *Labour's War* (Oxford, 1992). The Attlee governments have, of course, been very well served by modern historians and biographers: almost all the major studies cast important light on Dalton's role.

Notes

1. *High Tide and After* (London, 1962), p 419.
2. Ben Pimlott, *Hugh Dalton* (London, 1985), pp 445–6.
3. Ruth Winstone (ed.), *Tony Benn. Years of Hope: Diaries, Papers and Letters 1940–1962* (London, 1994): entry for 8 February 1951, p 139.
4. Ben Pimlott (ed.), *The Political Diary of Hugh Dalton, 1918–40, 1945–60* (London, 1987): entry for 24 July 1952, p 596.
5. See for instance *Call Back Yesterday* (London, 1953), p 102; *Political Diary*: entry for 30 October 1951, p 567.
6. *Political Diary*: entry for 7 February 1951, p 500.
7. Letter of 25 November 1950, partially reproduced in Pimlott, pp 590–1.
8. Denis Healey, *The Time of My Life* (London, 1989), p 78.
9. Unpublished diary entry for 11–14 July 1917, quoted in Pimlott, p 93.
10. Ben Pimlott (ed.), *The Second World War Diary of Hugh Dalton* (London, 1986): entry for 26 May 1940, p 22.
11. Judith Shklar, *Ordinary Vices* (Cambridge, Mass, 1984), see pp 8–9.
12. *Political Diary*: entry for 14 April 1951, p 530.
13. Janet Morgan (ed.), *Backbench Diaries* (London, 1981), pp 124–5.
14. Healey, *The Time of My Life,* p 78.
15. Pimlott, pp 14–15.
16. *Political Diary*: entry for 7 December 1929, pp 79–80.
17. *With British Guns in Italy* (London, 1919).
18. London, 1922 – revised and republished several times until 1954, and widely translated.
19. Pimlott, pp 166–71.
20. *Political Diary*: entry for 26 July 1929, p 61.
21. *Fateful Years* (London, 1957), p 59.
22. *Political Diary*: entry for 30 December 1932, pp 172–4.
23. Pimlott, pp 408–22, seeks to disentangle the conflicting accounts and clear the murk. Dalton's own account is in *Fateful Years*, pp 474–5, and *High Tide*, pp 8–14.
24. Philip M. Williams (ed.), *The Diary of Hugh Gaitskell 1945–56* (London, 1983): entry for 4 May 1951, pp 249–50.
25. *High Tide*, p 5.

26. Pimlott, p 452.
27. Ibid, p 551.
28. *Political Diary*: entry for 5 September 1931, p 155.
29. *Call Back Yesterday*, p 33.
30. Ibid, p 159.
31. See Edward W. Said, *Representations of the Intellectual* (London, 1994).
32. Egon Wertheimer, *Portrait of the Labour Party* (London, 1929), pp 132–3.
33. See for example *Fateful Years*, p 325.
34. *Fateful Years*, p 283.
35. *Political Diary*: entry for October–November 1951, p 559.
36. Healey, *My Secret Planet* (London, 1992).
37. *Fateful Years*, p 110.
38. *War Diary*, p 371.
39. Reproduced in Martin, *Editor* (London, 1968), p 173.
40. *Political Diary*: entry for 27 February 1953, p 604.
41. *Political Diary*: entry for Mid-October 1954, p 634.
42. David Marquand, 'Hugh Dalton: The Progressive as Bounder', in his *The Progressive Dilemma* (London, 1991), p 85.
43. *Practical Socialism*, p 320.
44. *Practical Socialism*, pp 71–81.
45. See for example *Political Diary*: entry for 3–14 April 1958, pp 687–9.
46. *My Life with Nye* (Penguin edn. Harmondsworth, 1981), p 187.
47. *War Diary*: entry for 4–6 January 1944, p 696.
48. *Political Diary*: entry for 24 June 1929, p 58.
49. *War Diary*: entry for 29 April 1945, p 856.
50. *Political Diary*: entry for 27 February 1950, p 472.
51. *Political Diary*: entry for 11 November 1952, p 602.
52. *High Tide*, pp 396–407.
53. Isaac Kramnick and Barry Sheerman, *Harold Laski: A Life on the Left* (London, 1993), pp 206–7.
54. For one version of this argument, see Radhika Desai, *Intellectuals and Socialism: Social Democrats and the Labour Party* (London, 1994). Bill Rodgers' early parliamentary career was one of Dalton's last successful exercises in patronage and wire-pulling.
55. Crosland, *The Future of Socialism* (2nd edn. London 1964), p 2 & n.
56. James Griffiths, *Pages from Memory* (London, 1969).
57. James Callaghan, *Time and Chance* (London, 1987); Philip Williams, *Hugh Gaitskell* (London, 1979), esp. pp 96–100.
58. Douglas Jay, *Change and Fortune* (London, 1980), p 62.
59. *Political Diary*: entry for 6 April 1955, p 663.
60. *Call Back Yesterday*, p 26.
61. *Political Diary*: entry for 10 November 1951, p 570.

4

Stafford Cripps

Keith Robbins

Sir Stafford Cripps, b.1889–d.1952. MP for East Bristol 1931–50; South East Bristol 1950. Solicitor-General 1930–31. Expelled from Labour Party 1939; re-admitted 1945. Ambassador to the Soviet Union 1940–42. Lord Privy Seal and Leader of the House of Commons 1942; Minister of Aircraft Production 1942–45. In Attlee's administration served as President of the Board of Trade 1945–47; Minister for Economic Affairs 1947; and Chancellor of the Exchequer 1947–50.

With his country at war, and no immediate occupation having presented itself, an independent MP left London at the end of November 1939 on a transcontinental journey. His initial destination was Karachi and, for this purpose, after journeying through France, an airliner was boarded at Naples in non-belligerent Italy. This 50-year-old traveller did not return to his home country until the beginning of May 1940. He arrived just in time to hear and take part in the two-day debate on Norway and to realise, a few days later, as a result of the German attack on the Low Countries and France, that the plight of his country was grave indeed. It comes as no surprise to learn from his speech in the Commons that he considered the Prime Minister, Neville Chamberlain, 'unfit to carry on'. Even so, it was probably some surprise to the speaker that Chamberlain's majority fell sharply and that, in the ensuing crisis, Winston Churchill emerged as Prime Minister. Yet the bearing of these developments on his own political prospects was not self-evident. The new Prime Minister did not appear likely to require his services and, for his part, the new Cabinet no more corresponded to what was needed than did its predecessor. The fact that Labour men in the persons of Clement Attlee as Lord Privy Seal and Arthur Greenwood as Minister without Portfolio were now in the War Cabinet made little difference, from his perspective. No call to enlist his services as a 'Labour leader' could have been expected in these circumstances. Some kind of leader he might yet be, but as things stood he was not even 'Labour'. Churchill had cronies with loose party affiliations around him but they were generally of a sybaritic disposition. This outsider would not qualify on that score.

Sir Stafford Cripps, the global traveller, had been expelled from the Labour Party in January 1939. If there had been a General Election in 1939/40 he might well have lost his parliamentary seat. There would in all likelihood have been a Labour candidate standing against him in Bristol East, the seat he had held since first entering the Commons in January 1931. His parliamentary career might only have lasted for eight or nine years. He could have perhaps expected a footnote in the political history of the 1930s, which might have characterised him as a distinctive, if somewhat exotic, backbench figure. He would scarcely have merited a place among 'Labour's second XI'. Even in a war that was still phoney in 1939, it was hardly likely that a 'leader in waiting' would choose quite this moment to leave his country and seek eastern promise on a trip of indefinite duration. In the early months of 1940, indeed, when Cripps was mysteriously fact-finding in such places as Bombay, Calcutta, Rangoon, Chungking, Hong Kong, Shanghai and Tokyo, and then finally across the United States, there were those who had already written him off. If they had known that he had been given the opportunity, they might have joked that Cripps would have more chance of making a place for himself in history as Chiang-Kai-Shek's industrial supremo – a post the Generalissimo unexpectedly but unavailingly offered in Chungking – than he did in British politics in London.

There was, however, another episode in this exotic eastern journey that indicated that this unusual figure was not as much 'out of the loop' as other observers might have supposed. He appeared, after all, to be able to fix up interviews with people who mattered in a manner not customary amongst Bristol MPs without ministerial status: Jinnah, Gandhi (in India) and Chiang Kai-Shek (in China) among them. In addition, the Soviet mission in Chungking – from where Chiang Kai-Shek was conducting the war against the Japanese – proved willing to facilitate a somewhat testing flight to Moscow. The independent MP had a two-hour interview in the Kremlin with the Soviet Foreign Minister, Molotov. It was not a secret encounter to be kept from the British government. Cripps sent a report of his impressions to the Foreign Secretary, Lord Halifax, though this did not prevent the Foreign Office from regarding his short presence in Moscow as untimely. His visit to the United States was also not without importance. When he spoke, in the 'Norway' debate in the House of Commons in May, part of his contribution had been to convey the impression, on the basis of his personal encounters, that 'American opinion' favoured a change of government. He therefore appeared to speak as one with authority and to possess a certain global stature. If so, however, it was problematic on what that authority was based and what, if anything, it portended. That was the nature and the problem of the man. He was exceptional – at this juncture a one-man band – a categorisation which suggested either disaster or triumph, but little in between.

Stafford Cripps was not a safe and solid Labour man with an artisan's pair of hands to prove it. He had not plodded his way through party ranks to higher things through exemplary ward service. He had not ploughed a constituency furrow. It was not until 1928, when he was nearing 40, that he even joined the Labour Party. Two years later, when an awkward and unexpected vacancy in the position of Solicitor-General occurred, Cripps agreed to fill it although, unusually, he did not yet have a seat in the Commons. Fortunately, on the death of the sitting Labour member, Cripps was adopted for Bristol East and comfortably won the ensuing by-election in January 1931. He thus became an MP only a couple of years after declaring his allegiance to Labour. He then served modestly in an administration which had always lacked an overall parliamentary majority and which, in the event, was to come to an end in the ensuing August crisis. Looking back from 1940, therefore, it was only for a few months that he had held office and then only in a junior and specialised capacity. Thereafter, perhaps permanently, the crisis which engulfed his party in 1931 prevented him from gaining any broader ministerial experience.

Yet, unlike other Labour stalwarts and aspirants who fell in the 1931 General Election and did not regain their seats in 1935, Cripps survived as MP for Bristol East. That very fact was of great significance. It catapulted him inevitably into a public position simply by virtue of being a survivor in a parliamentary party shattered, for the moment at least, by apostasy or defeat. George Lansbury, the only survivor on the Labour benches of MacDonald's Cabinet, was the new leader of the party, but he was 40 years older than Cripps. Attlee had been in the Commons since 1922 and was six years his senior. If and when Lansbury stood down, it suddenly looked as though one or other of these two public-school men might assume the leadership of the party. As things stood, they seemed the obvious lieutenants. All of this presupposed, however, that normal expectations might prevail, that is to say that after recovering from the shock of 1931 Labour would resume its upward march, gain in due course a parliamentary majority and form a new government which would in turn resume 'normal service'.

However, it was just such a presupposition that now seemed in question to Cripps. Were not the issues that confronted the country systemic? Now was no time for Labour to be thinking about tinkering and fine-tuning. In a word which did not suffer from under-use, there was now a 'crisis' of a comprehensive political/economic character. By the time that Labour had recovered from the shock of 1931 and was capable of resuming its upward path, the deepening crisis of capitalism might itself have precipitated a total change in the assumptions on which parliamentary government rested. Cripps thought that there might be a takeover of power by elements who would ensure that Labour would never achieve power 'under the rules', rules which would be likely to be bent by repressive and reactionary forces. It was an analysis along these lines which appealed to someone who was himself undeniably a son of 'the Establishment' and whose own legal career had until this point been advanced within its assumptions and conventions. Radical rejection of parental Conservatism on the part of a new generation is not unknown, in this or any other decade. What is unusual in the case of Cripps is that he did not have to stage a domestic revolt. His father, eminently and outwardly an 'Establishment' figure, had already vigorously journeyed ahead of him into the ranks of Labour.

Stafford Cripps, the youngest son of Charles Alfred Cripps and his wife Theresa (née Potter, sister of Beatrice Webb, née Potter), was born in their town house off the Fulham Road in west London in 1889. His grandfather, Henry William Cripps had been a distinguished ecclesiastical lawyer. The substantial country home of his parents was at Parmoor in Buckinghamshire. After Winchester and New College, Oxford, (institutions which had also been attended by his father) Charles Alfred Cripps had been called to the bar at the Middle Temple. His subsequent legal career was very lucrative. Between 1895 and 1914 he was a Unionist MP and held prominent legal offices in the dioceses of York and Canterbury. He was created Lord Parmoor in 1914. A decade later, however, he was sitting in the first Labour Government as Lord President of the Council – joining his wife's brother-in-law, Sidney Webb. He shared the leadership of the Labour Party in the House of Lords with Lord Haldane. He also possessed special responsibility for League of Nations affairs – about which he had been an enthusiast ever since the idea had been mooted during the First World War. He was again Lord

President and Leader of the House of Lords from 1929 to 1931. His house at Parmoor frequently saw gatherings devoted to various progressive causes in pursuit of political and religious ideals. It could be said, therefore, that from the very beginning Stafford was part of a 'connexion'. However, when his childless aunt, Beatrice Webb, commented in her diary on the entry of her nephew into the Commons in 1931 she remarked that he was the only one of her 155 nephews and nieces who might become a big figure in public life. It was clearly not enough merely to belong to a politically-connected clan. There had to be a personal spark and, in her opinion, Stafford had it. He would go far, though his one handicap, she noted, was his poor health.

Following family tradition, Stafford had been sent to Winchester for his schooling – his father was a governor – and imbibed its traditions without undue difficulty or dissent. In the eyes of his headmaster, he was a thoroughly good fellow. His next step, however, broke with family convention in two respects. He decided to read for a degree in chemistry (rather than law or a humanities subject) and to study not at New College, Oxford – though he could have done – but at University College London under Sir William Ramsay, a Nobel prize-winner in the subject. He matriculated in 1908 and worked with considerable success in the laboratories in Gower Street, though he strayed from them in his final year to become President of the Student Union. Nationally, however, these were not years characterised by political torpor, and the young student played his part in 1910, unavailingly, in trying to ensure that his brother joined his father as a Unionist MP. Neither succeeded. The following year, precipitately so both sets of parents believed, Stafford married Isobel Swithinbank. She was the potential beneficiary of a substantial fortune. Cripps, however, felt no disposition simply to contemplate a comfortable life of country idleness. He had already decided to follow in his father's footsteps at the Bar and that link seemed certain to open up wide legal opportunities, even more so since his scientific background could be put to exceptional use in technical cases.

The advent of war in August 1914 interrupted what appeared likely to be a smooth legal ascent. The Parmoor household was not enthusiastic for war, though it accepted the honourable advocacy of a fellow Wykehamist who was Foreign Secretary. Stafford would have enlisted but was rejected by the army on medical grounds. Instead, for a time, he helped with supplies at Boulogne. Later, his scientific training seemed to make him an ideal person to be involved with munitions manufacture and he found himself at Queensferry in North Wales. The administrative responsibilities that came his way taxed his strength. His health mysteriously and completely broke down. There were months when he could scarcely walk. Suffering from a debilitating colitis, but not yet 30, he was henceforth always concerned about his health. His dietary obsessions, much remarked upon subsequently by his enemies, stemmed from this time. His father, now Lord Parmoor, put him on the waiting list for membership of the Athenaeum and hoped that the return of peace would enable his son to return to the Bar and pick up a career which had begun so promisingly. And, in the early 1920s, Stafford did regain both strength and enthusiasm for legal work. In his conduct of a succession of cases in these years he displayed a mastery of technical detail and a consummate ability to argue a case. He was aided too by a remarkable memory and he gave the impression that he believed his own arguments. The public brilliance, however, was not achieved without private industry and self-discipline. His only weakness seemed to be an addiction to tobacco. His income mounted steadily and his wife had come into her substantial inheritance. In 1927 he became the youngest KC and his legal career seemed destined to go from strength to strength.

In retrospect, in view of what subsequently happened, it has sometimes been portrayed as merely a necessary prelude to the political career that surely beckoned. There is no firm evidence, however, that Cripps consciously groomed himself for such a transition. Outside the law, the only political activity to engage him stemmed from the interest, which he shared with his father, in the contribution the Christian Churches might make to world peace. Unless they played their part in overcoming hatred and enmity, not only would the cause of Christianity itself suffer, but the world would also sink into a state of chaos and barbarism. The way of Christ was contrasted, in a way which might seem simplistic, with the way of the politician. Certainly, Cripps was happier talking to his old headmaster, now the Bishop of Oxford, about such matters than engaging in actual political activity. Together, they expressed much optimism about the new League of Nations. Stafford acted as treasurer to the British section of the World Alliance for the Promotion of International Understanding through the Churches. His Christian convictions were powerful. They still suggested to him that politicians had much to answer for because of the way in which, by their addiction to intrigue and diplomacy, they created misunderstandings, hatred and fresh wars. Sadly, however, by the middle 1920s it had already become apparent that the rivalries of Europe were not readily overcome by the admirable resolutions of the World Alliance.

It was perhaps inevitable that a 'brilliant young lawyer' was just the type of man that the Labour Party needed at this juncture. Certainly Herbert Morrison thought so and sounded him out. Initially, Cripps resisted. He was more interested in the Church than in politics. However, disappointed by the attention given in the Church Assembly to the status of Charles I, King and Martyr, he came round to the view that it was as a Christian politician that he might make his contribution. His formal adherence to the Labour Party did not flow from a deep reading in politics and economics which had resulted in a conversion to 'Socialism'. He felt a concern for 'the oppressed classes', and sought their welfare, but viewed them benevolently if somewhat distantly from his large town house near Hyde Park. Soon, when some of his new party comrades came to stay with him at his home in the Cotswolds, they were a little surprised to find him punctilious in dressing for dinner. Cripps explained that he came into the party with his habits formed. He saw no reason to change them.

There were, therefore, both at this point and in the future, aspects of his circumstances and make-up which left him lonely in a band of brothers, though loneliness could have its political advantages. Tributes to his intellectual capacity were readily forthcoming from those who had witnessed him in court. In fact, however, there was no subtlety in his handling of ideas or profound grasp of contemporary political, social and economic developments. He was happier in expressing undoubted truths with uncomplicated conviction – such as that the world needed a religious purpose – than in unpicking their content. It perhaps comes as no surprise, therefore, to learn that, at this juncture, his only claim to fame as an author rested on his updating of his father's esteemed contribution to ecclesiastical law, *Cripps on Church and Clergy*.

Such was the unlikely background of the man who came to be popularly portrayed, after 1932, as the leader of the 'Labour Left'. Initially, with Lansbury and Attlee, he was one of the triumvirate which led the rump of 46 Labour MPs. Given the National Government's massive majority, however, the orthodox 'shadowing' of an administration was neither practicable nor enticing. What was more important to Cripps was to establish that Labour was radically different so that the electorate would be presented with an unambiguous choice between the parties of capitalism and the party of socialism. 'Gradualism' was dead. One step was no longer enough for Cripps; it was what had hitherto been conceived as the distant scene of Socialism that now needed to be brought forward. Purposive planning would require a wholesale change in the machinery of government. Naturally, the socialist revolution would be in the interests of the people as a whole. At this juncture, the speed with which Cripps espoused new ideas might either be painted as an indication of the fertility of his mind or its proneness to quackery. He admitted that he lacked any knowledge of economics but did not see this as any obstacle to advocating one of the current fads for currency reform with enthusiasm.

The energy and vitality Cripps was displaying upset some colleagues whose lives had been spent in the service of the party. The diet of unadulterated idealism which Cripps offered was both inspiring and wearying in circumstances in which the Labour Party was a bruised creature, uncertain of its direction and vulnerable to factionalism. Where did its internal balance of power lie as between the parliamentary party, the national executive, the trade unions and the party machine? Still himself very new to its inner dynamics, Cripps spoke his mind with scant concern as to the consequences for the party's harmony. Moreover, unlike others, he possessed money and was willing to use it to buttress causes in which he believed. That was particularly the case with the Socialist League, which began as a propaganda body designed to ram home the claim that the last days of the liberal economic order were at hand. Cripps came to chair this body. In its ranks were intelligent men who supposed that some kind of 'smash' was imminent. On various occasions, Cripps elaborated on the 'emergency measures' and 'general protective controls' which would be necessary. He and his associates gave the impression that it was pedantry to worry about 'freedom of speech' or to be alarmed by the degree of dictatorial power that would evidently be necessary. The portrayal of class-conflict owed little on his part to personal experience or sociological sophistication. All of this activity was no doubt what Beatrice Webb had in mind when she supposed that the fate of the Labour party was in the hands of her nephew. The task of building up 'a more sincere Socialist party' was a far more difficult one than had confronted any other leader in Great Britain for a hundred years. Did Stafford have the intellect and the will to do it?

Stafford had both but even so he did not succeed. His 'all or nothing' approach alienated more prosaic and pragmatic figures both in the party and in the trade union movement. Alleged specialists in the art of political judgement, such as Hugh Dalton, let it be known that Cripps completely lacked it. Walter Citrine, TUC general secretary, lamented that Cripps uttered such irresponsible drivel. The press focus on the 'dictatorship' issue was harming the party's recovery, even though Cripps himself stated that a dictator was the last thing in the world that he wanted to be. Even so, in the social polarisation that Cripps was encouraging, there appeared to be the possibility that the country would see a battle between a 'Socialist dictator' (Cripps) and a 'Fascist dictator' (Mosley). That both Cripps and Mosley were products of Winchester College gave the prospect of such a choice a certain piquancy, but there was little chance that either would possess major electoral attraction. The prospect that Cripps would succeed Lansbury was therefore alarming in important party circles, though it could not be denied that he had attracted some devoted acolytes. Bevin let it be known that the great trade union movement was a little suspicious of theories advanced by middle-class gentlemen. In these circumstances, therefore, it was inevitable that Cripps was at the centre of most of the disputes which bedevilled the party in this period, the twists and turns of which cannot be elaborated here. The controversies were sharpened by the divisions that arose as the international situation darkened. On a variety of occasions Cripps made statements, either at party conferences or elsewhere, which indicated that it would be folly to give any kind of support to the National Government in foreign policy. British workers should never again be duped into a war supposedly to 'save democracy'. If Britain were to be pushed into a 'capitalist war' he hoped that the workers would revolt. It was not even certain that Socialism would be suppressed in the event of Britain being conquered by Germany. He told armaments workers that it would be wrong to put the arms machine under the control of their class opponents. If they refused to make munitions the capitalists would be helpless. That was the framework he brought to these issues, though, as events unfolded, it could admit various tactical shifts. Rarely, however, did these precisely coincide with the formal evolution of Labour Party policy. The policies advocated by the Socialist League in its 'Unity Campaign' had caused endless friction with other elements in the party climaxing in its disaffiliation and dissolution in 1937. Further dissension arose, however, because of Cripps's advocacy in 1938–39 of a Popular Front. The knives could no longer be sheathed. Expulsion from the party came in January 1939 and he failed to reverse the verdict in a last speech to the party conference in May. He did not accept conditions offered in September for rejoining. It seemed, at last, that a dedicated maverick was being sent out into the political wilderness where he belonged. In practice, however, the wilderness meant the agreeable Mediterranean, where Cripps took his family on a two-month cruise.

The fact that Cripps was granted a two-hour interview with Molotov in 1940 during the course of his global tour therefore comes in one sense as no surprise. He shared with his aunt an ability to discern in the Soviet Union a new civilisation, though he was not a Communist and stated that he had reservations about certain aspects of its development. He had been highly critical of the failure to cement an alliance with Moscow in 1938–9. With the outbreak of the war, he was firmly of the view that the Soviet Union held the key to its outcome. Therefore, when there was a need to try to establish better relations in May 1940, Cripps's general political stance seemed to make him the ideal person to send as ambassador – though there were more sceptical observations from those who thought that he had an excessive belief in his own capacity to influence the Kremlin. He received an assurance from Churchill that it was indeed the British desire to treat the Soviet Union as a friendly neutral – notwithstanding the signature of the Nazi-Soviet Pact in August 1939. He reached Moscow in June 1940. His period in the wilderness had proved short-lived. A new and very different phase in his career was about to begin.

He was his customary energetic and enthusiastic self in trying to achieve a rapport with both Molotov and Stalin but found the going heavy. It appeared that the Soviet-German alliance could not be undermined, though Cripps personally was prepared to recognise the Soviet control of the Baltic states which he supposed would be well-received by the Soviets and might make feasible a British-Soviet non-aggression pact. Such notions, however, were not well received in the Foreign Office. In turn Cripps became frustrated by the prejudices that he believed to be entrenched there. For his part, his first-hand contact with Soviet society left mixed impressions. He could not but believe that the underlying intentions of the regime were laudable and, by contrast, held to the view that there was something rotten at the heart of British civilisation. However, he could not avert his eyes from certain cruelties and an underlying brutalism. Nevertheless, he used every opportunity open to him to try to prise the Soviet Union and Germany apart. It was a dispiriting and lonely situation and at times he doubted his own underlying conviction that, despite appearances to the contrary, there was a fundamental hostility between Berlin and Moscow. His own position remained somewhat anomalous. There were suspicions in London, by no means without foundation, that he exceeded his instructions and improvised unhelpfully. There were particular problems posed by the possibility of a German attack on the Soviet Union. Cripps seemed to think it diplomatically helpful to let it be known that Britain might come to some kind of arrangement with Germany to end the war. Intrigue was rife and he could not get near Stalin. He was summoned back to London in June apparently under suspicion all round. He was singled out for criticism from the Kremlin for peddling the absurd notion that war impended between the Soviet Union and Germany. And, when the invasion did come, his attempts to bring Moscow and London to some kind of collaboration were singled out as a pretext for the German action. Yet, despite the strong suspicions about his political judgement that also existed in London, somehow he contrived to emerge from this complex diplomatic imbroglio as a kind of hero.

It was Cripps who was hurriedly sent back to Moscow in the new situation to see if a fresh basis of trust could be established. He brought with him a small British military mission. No one could tell for how long the Soviet Union would be able to resist. Cripps urged the fullest possible support in a context in which Britain and the Soviet Union were now 'co-belligerents'. The fullest possible support was not possible but Beaverbrook, new Minister of Supply, came to talk to Stalin. Cripps was unhappy and seemed virtually to share the belief for a time – urged also by German propaganda – that Britain was prepared to fight to the last drop of Russian blood. He wanted to come home because he believed his usefulness was at an end. Churchill was in no hurry to see him return. The Prime Minister had certainly pledged himself to supporting the Russian people but his underlying hostility towards Soviet Communism had not disappeared. From his perspective, the substantial upsurge of public support for the Soviet struggle after June 1941 was alarming. By the end of 1941, when Cripps was finally allowed to return to London, new political prospects opened up if he tried to capitalise on this sentiment. Additionally, the Japanese attack on Pearl Harbor in that same December, brought capitalist America into the war. It remained to be seen how Cripps positioned himself if he aspired once more to the *de facto* leadership of the British left. A broadcast and speeches he made on his return had an immediate impact as he stressed the need for total commitment – with the Soviet effort as the crucial exemplar. The war was clearly going badly in North Africa and South-East Asia. Cripps, the maverick outsider, had to be incorporated.

The immediate development was his entry into the War Cabinet as Leader of the Commons and Lord Privy Seal, a step which excited the press and upset some Labour MPs. The gossip was that he was the coming man, a point of view which the Conservative backbencher, Cuthbert Headlam, was not the only one to find rather ridiculous. It was undoubtedly the case that Cripps was a very clever lawyer, he wrote in his diary, but he had done nothing to warrant such a belief. He might turn out to be a leader 'but whether he is to become leader of the Conservatives or of the Labour lot I really cannot venture to prophesy'.[1]

Only a few months passed, however, before Cripps's career lurched in another direction. Churchill announced in the Commons in early March 1942 that Cripps had agreed to go to India to find out whether the Cabinet's proposals for a new Indian constitution would be acceptable to all parties. Some suspected that it was an attempt by the Prime Minister to discredit him – if the mission failed. To send someone who could not be accused of being an Imperialist had an obvious logic at a time when the war in East Asia made it imperative to keep India 'loyal'. Cripps was the nearest approach to a British Gandhi. India, he was to say, would have self-government – when the war was over. From the Congress standpoint, however, some tangible movement was immediately necessary on the part of the British government. That centred on the defence portfolio and in essence the task before Cripps was to reconcile Congress aspirations in this regard with the firm British need to maintain overall military control. The Viceroy, Lord Wavell, did not enjoy the presence of this interloper on his patch. As in Moscow, so in India, Cripps readily came to the conclusion that he could ride his instructions on a loose rein. Churchill was not to be budged beyond a certain point. It soon became apparent that the 'Mission' would not succeed and Cripps came home after three weeks. If it had succeeded, he would undoubtedly have scored a triumph, but in the event its failure did him little political harm – blame could be placed elsewhere.

In the months that followed, Cripps undoubtedly posed a 'challenge' to the Churchillian regime but it was of an idiosyncratic and, in the end, insubstantial kind. Some suspected in May 1942 that there would be a move to replace Churchill by Cripps in about six months. They asked themselves whether he was seeking simply to place himself in the position in which his advice to Churchill became dominant or was he cultivating Conservatives with a view to the succession? Was his radicalism going into cold storage for the duration of the war? Why was he so interested in the machinery of government? Perhaps the fact that he had no party behind him was an advantage, perhaps not. So the speculation continued. Cripps himself, in the face of further British setbacks in North Africa came increasingly to the view that the government would not last, or at least that he should not last in it. In a testy exchange of memoranda, Churchill scorned ideas Cripps put forward for a war directorate. Would the acrimony end in a spectacular parting of the ways? In the event, however, Cripps did not resign and the time to challenge, if it had ever existed, passed. He had by no means been alone, in the summer of 1942, in his criticisms of the way the war was being run, but by the end of the year, after Montgomery's success at El Alamein, Churchill appeared to regain his stride. MPs who had earlier fancied Cripps's chances now sagely wrote in their diaries that they had never thought them very great. Observers on all sides of the House found him a great enigma. There must be some flaw in a man who wanted to spend so much time with the Archbishop of Canterbury. He had energy and eloquence but somehow his considerable individual attributes did not 'add up'. Cripps himself, as he was being out-manoeuvred by Churchill, lamented that he never seemed able to team up with anyone.

Cripps was in eclipse but still a significant figure. He left the War Cabinet to become Minister of Aircraft Production, in which post he remained until the end of the wartime coalition in May 1945. There was no doubting the importance of the role and he brought to it his customary energy and application. As a 'proper minister' for the first time, he could not avoid being drawn deeply into all the issues which surrounded the

maximisation of aircraft production at this juncture. How was efficiency
best secured? What kind of public-private partnership was necessary?
Although now in a vastly more important position than he had been in
the First World War, he was again a kind of manager. He resumed the
persona of a scientifically-trained technocrat, preoccupied by pressing
issues of resource allocation and less concerned with their more far-
reaching ideological implications. That did not mean, however, that he
modified his assumptions about what 'the State' and 'planning' could
deliver in areas of policy far beyond the technicalities of aircraft
production. Even so, even subsequent writers sharply critical of these
assumptions in their critique of British wartime production have detected
elements of unexpected pragmatism in his everyday decision-making.
And the Minister for Aircraft Production worried about bombing. A
more detailed evaluation of his performance cannot be attempted here.
Suffice it to say that he emerged from the war with what might be called
'ministerial credibility', something which he had hitherto lacked. Yet he
still seemed a puzzling figure to some parliamentary observers and the
duality in his make-up remained unresolved. Cuthbert Headlam, for
example, observing Cripps on a tour of aircraft production centres in
the North-East, glowingly approved the little speeches he made, but that
did not stop him thinking the minister 'a strange, aloof creature'. He
was a freak and not a person who would ever be a controlling force in
political life. In addition, unfortunately, he had a blue nose.

It would be a mistake, however, to suppose that the latter part of the
war had turned Cripps into a desiccated technocrat who paused merely
to eat nuts. He still held to his underlying vision of transformation and
progress, even if, temporarily, a period of discipline, self-sacrifice and
austerity was required. Indeed, in speeches up and down the country, he
expressed a Christian vision that impressed even those who did not think
Socialism should be its inevitable accompaniment. Cripps said things
with a conviction that matched him for the hour. He spoke his mind
with a freedom that was the product of his continuing detachment from
party politics and gave him a stature and standing which was as
distinctive, in its own way, as Churchill's. It was, however, a position
only made possible by the exceptional circumstances of war and coalition.
If he was to continue to hold a significant position in British public life
when the end of both came in sight he would have to rejoin the Labour
party. In February 1945 the prodigal son came home, though not all its
senior figures, mindful of the past, eagerly prepared whatever vegetarian
alternative existed to a fatted calf. And when the electorate gave Labour
its great election victory, there was no doubt that Cripps would play a
significant part in the ensuing administration.

One of the 'great offices of state' would not come his way, at least not immediately. From his perspective, however, there could scarcely be a more central role at that particular juncture than to become President of the Board of Trade – the post to which Attlee warily appointed him. In effect it enabled him to carry on with many of the issues in which he had been previously engaged. He had to preside over the transition of industry from war to peace in a context of great difficulty and uncertainty. How could Britain pay its way? How could higher production be achieved? His own views had been somewhat modified. Whereas once nothing less than total nationalisation would have sufficed, he now appeared to favour a planned economy certainly, but a mixed one.

Before these issues received his full attention, however, India once more called. He was sent in the spring of 1946 to lead a small Cabinet Mission to try once more to find an agreement amongst the various Indian parties on a federal structure which would keep the country together. Once again Cripps found himself immersed in tantalising negotiations that seemed to make some progress but then faltered. Once again, his own self-confidence in his capacity to effect a breakthrough was both admired and distrusted. After three months, he once again came home to report the failure of a mission. This time the effort had sapped his strength significantly. It was reported that he had become so emaciated that his clothes seemed to be draping a skeleton. Cripps had not, in the event, been the man to 'solve' the Indian question, though he would dearly like to have done.

Those who worked with him on this occasion, as he grappled with the problems before him, were constantly struck by his dedication and seemingly endless capacity for work. That remained true of all those who worked with him on domestic matters thereafter. His insistence, moreover, that economic progress was not a 'technical' matter but one which required the engagement of the whole person was striking, if, for some, disconcerting. In one of the numerous addresses he gave in the early post-war years, collected under the significant title *God in Our Work* (1949), he claimed that Britain's industrial morale was low because a merely materialistic, self-centred outlook on work could not suffice. The stimulation of a patriotic war, with its call for self-sacrifice in a wider and nobler cause had gone and, in his judgement, nothing had yet taken its place. It was his deepest conviction that it was through human relationships, and not through monetary payments, that a sense of friendship, justice and co-operation was created. Such a stance had its impact, though perhaps a diminishing one. It was not agreeable to be reminded by him that the American loan was running out. The continuing shortages, rationing and other restrictions were not what the people supposed would be their lot once the war had come to an end. Even evidence that Cripps unexpectedly shared a Churchillian penchant for cigars could not shake off Opposition charges that he was the embodiment of joyless austerity. And, sadly, his physical frame, never robust, became ever leaner. He was working himself to death, as indeed it seemed that he had been bent on doing ever since manhood.

The fuel crisis of the winter of 1946–7, in severe weather conditions, raised questions about the competence of the government. In the summer of 1947 there was a run on the pound when (temporarily as it turned out) sterling became fully convertible with the dollar. Cripps again saw himself as the national saviour but his attempt to have Bevin replace Attlee as Prime Minister – with the corollary that he himself would have overall economic responsibility within the government – failed. Bevin did not want the job. Ironically, however, Attlee appeared to offer Cripps the job he really wanted. In September 1947 he took on the new post of Minister of Economic Affairs. The press interpreted this appointment to mean that Sir Stafford had become 'economic overlord' but this was a perception shared neither by the Prime Minister nor the Chancellor of the Exchequer, Dalton. There was much ambiguity about Cripps's role and ample opportunity for conflict with the Treasury. In reality, without a department of his own, his hand was far less strong than many supposed and the attractions of implementing 'co-ordination' would diminish. However, these matters were not put to the test for long. In November 1947, after casually revealing the contents of his budget to a journalist shortly before delivering his speech to the House of Commons, the Chancellor of the Exchequer, Dalton, was forced to resign. Cripps was the only man who could succeed him. He did now become the 'economic supremo' but in the event it was to be for slightly less than three years. He resigned from office in October 1950 after months of sharply deteriorating health. Six months later he was dead.

There is, therefore, an element of tragedy about this final phase in his career. As has been rightly observed by Edmund Dell, he reached the summit when his health meant that he was not capable of exercising effectively the powers of a Chancellor. The problems that were still before him would have taxed men in the prime of physical condition. He remained committed to the National Health Service, but its costs moved inexorably upwards. Cripps was determined to hold down consumption – what he called in 1949 'the last in his list of priorities' – on the supposition that expanded production could go into exports. The Marshall Aid Programme after mid-1948 substantially eased his problems – though it would expire in 1952. He brought the compilation and implementation of the annual Budget to a new peak of supposed significance. He tried hard to distinguish between 'totalitarian' and 'democratic' planning but the balance between 'Socialism' and 'a Free Society' which he now struck did not always commend itself to more left-wing colleagues. He was not inclined to the view that Britain should become heavily involved in new and more integrated economic and political structures in western Europe. He believed that Britain was still in some sense an imperial power.

However, while there were many international developments which necessarily impacted on economic policy, one problem which was Cripps's central responsibility came into sharp focus. In May 1949 he had publicly declared that devaluation was not on the government's agenda. However, his younger junior colleagues, particularly Gaitskell and Jay, believed that it would be a positive step. Eventually, reluctantly and with a sense of defeat, Cripps announced on 20 September that the pound would be devalued by one-third and would stand at $2.80. Devaluation was not in itself something to celebrate. What mattered were the measures that accompanied it and the extent to which opportunities for export were seized. There were those who thought that, having made this announcement, Cripps should resign but in fact for a few months his health revived somewhat and he was determined to carry on. That inevitably brought him into the heart of the discussion about the timing of a general election in 1950. He refused to have a pre-election Budget (due in April), arguing that he would be accused of vote catching. There were fears about how the economy would behave in 1950 and Cripps was amongst those who believed it would be right to go early. There were damaging arguments about nationalisation. Particularly afterwards, those who had favoured a summer election knew that they had been right. Labour had squeezed home in February with a small majority. Cripps had played an energetic part in the campaign – and had been particularly singled out for attack by the Tories. The outcome ensured that he remained in the frontline. The Budget he framed for April became, after all, a pre-election Budget – for an election which would be unlikely to be long delayed – but it was his last. Then there was the question of Britain and the Schuman Plan – which proposed the pooling of the coal and steel resources of France and Germany under a supra-national authority – together with the fresh problem of the Korean War to deal with, but Cripps was exhausted. He could not go on.

There has been no simple verdict on Cripps. For some, by the time of his resignation he had demonstrated, in the words of Maurice Shock, the possession of the 'capacity, command and courage that go to make a great minister'. But, while conceding that his reputation as Chancellor remains high, Edmund Dell argues that it is the reputation of a man who said the right things rather than did the right things. Just what would have been the 'right things' for the British economy in 1947–50, however, remains contentious, perhaps inevitably. Ten years earlier, few would ever have supposed that it would have been Cripps that commanded its height, or at least was under the illusion that he did so. That in itself is a measure of the extent to which a man who had been written off as a brilliant but unstable and erratic operator had matured, through the extraordinary circumstances of war, into a Labour elder statesman. Even so, perhaps he died a disappointed man for there had been moments when he had thought that his country and his party had need of him as leader. In that, he was mistaken.

Further reading

In addition to the 2002 biography by Peter Clarke, Simon Burgess, *Stafford Cripps: A Political Life* (London, 1999) and C. Bryant, *Stafford Cripps: The First Modern Chancellor* (London, 1997) are the most recent studies and largely replace E. Estorick, *Stafford Cripps: A Biography* (London, 1949) and C. Cooke, *The Life of Richard Stafford Cripps* (London, 1957). There is a sketch by Maurice Shock in K. Robbins (ed.), *The Blackwell Biographical Dictionary of British Political Life in the Twentieth Century* (Oxford, 1990). Edmund Dell considers Cripps as Chancellor of the Exchequer in his *The Chancellors: A History of the Chancellors of the Exchequer, 1945–90* (London, 1996). Two particular episodes in Cripps's career (Moscow and India) can be studied in more detail in G. Gorodetsky, *Stafford Cripps' Mission to Moscow, 1940–1942* (Cambridge, 1984) and in N. Mansergh (ed.), *The Transfer of Power 1942–47, Vol. 1: The Cripps Mission, January to April 1942; Vol. 7: 23 March–29 June 1946* (London, 1970, 1977) and R.J. Moore, *Churchill, Cripps and India, 1939–45* (Oxford, 1979). A. Cairncross, *Years of Recovery: British Economic Policy 1945–1951* (London, 1985) and K.O. Morgan, *Labour in Power 1945–51* (London, 1984) provide a general context. Cripps himself published *Can Socialism come by constitutional means?* (London, 1934), *The Struggle for Peace* (London, 1936) and *God in Our Work* (London, 1949).

Note

1. Stuart Ball (ed.), *Parliament and Politics in the Age of Churchill and Attlee: The Headlam Diaries 1935–51* (London, 1999), p 298.

5

Aneurin Bevan

Kenneth O. Morgan

Aneurin (Nye) Bevan, b.1897–d.1960. Labour MP for Ebbw Vale 1929–60. Editor of Tribune *1942–45. Minister of Health and Housing 1945–51; Minister of Labour 1951 (resigned from Attlee's government). Labour Party Treasurer 1956; Deputy Leader of the Labour Party 1959.*

Nye Bevan is firmly established in the socialist pantheon as a hero of Labour. This is not surprising. Like Keir Hardie, he built up a rare charismatic reputation as evangelist, orator and prophet of workers' power. Not only was he a prophet, he was also a great constructive pioneer. His National Health Service remains, 50 and more years on, a symbol of social solidarity. What is far more surprising is that Nye should have become in time a hero for New Labour. At a great event in Congress House in November 1997, to mark the centenary of his birth, the memory and legacy of Bevan were hailed not only by old Bevanites like Michael Foot and Barbara Castle, but also by Gordon Brown. New Labour's iron (or at least prudent) Chancellor passionately lauded Bevan as the model of the social democratic faith.

More remarkably still, Tony Blair has repeatedly placed Bevan in the great line of Labour succession along with Clem Attlee, Ernie Bevin and all the saints who for their labours rest – alongside also old liberal heroes like Lloyd George, Beveridge and Keynes. Nye, the scourge of the capitalist ruling class, has become a pivot of the Progressive Alliance. In a foreword to Geoffrey Goodman's centenary celebration of Bevan, *The*

State of the Nation, Tony Blair acclaimed not only Bevan's 'ideas and personality and rhetoric', not only his managerial skill in creating the National Health Service, but also his call for 'passion in action' as embodied in Bevan's political testament, *In Place of Fear*. Tredegar's class warrior had become a hero of the Third Way, embraced by the establishment. By contrast, his old enemy, the revisionist Hugh Gaitskell, was out of favour as an elitist and an anti-European. Edmund Dell's fiercely critical posthumous account of the labour movement, *A Strange Eventful History*, almost contemptuous of Gaitskell and Tony Crosland for the muddle-headedness of their attempt to blend socialism and democracy, found words of favour for the visionary and inspirational qualities of Nye Bevan. Meanwhile, Patricia Hollis's biography of Jennie Lee in 1997 saw this stormy petrel of the ILP far left acclaimed as a great minister who had promoted the arts and established the Open University.

Commentators lost few opportunities to contrast Nye Bevan's 'passionate parliamentarism' and the Bevanite 'legitimate left' in the 1950s, with the anti-parliamentary extremism of the Bennites and 'hard left' in the 1980s. Asked in 1980 what Bevan would have thought of the hard left then, Harold Wilson briskly replied 'Nye wouldn't have been seen dead with that lot'. Aneurin Bevan, it seems, has been reinvented as a mainstream patriot, who defended Britain's manufacture of nuclear weapons, and whose National Health Service represented social citizenship, everyman's idea of what it meant to be British. His disciple, Neil Kinnock, seems to have reached the same view, as have the tabloid press. The ultimate marginal radical has been transplanted into the centre ground.

Is this justified? Is this reinvention of Nye credible, or is it yet another example of a dissenting radical going legitimate in hindsight? British political history is full of instances of people seen as extremists in their day becoming licensed rebels over time. It happened to Keir Hardie and Michael Foot; Tony Benn seems on the verge of suffering the same fate. Bevan was never an establishment figure. Even the Tories whose company he enjoyed were offbeat mavericks like Beaverbrook, Bracken and Randolph Churchill. He was the most hated, as well as the most idolised, politician of his time. A product of the socialist cauldron of South Wales in the early twentieth century, he was a ferocious critic of the conventional capitalist wisdom. Baldwin, Chamberlain, even Lloyd George, were savaged. He was, along with Cripps, expelled from the parliamentary Labour Party for advocating a Popular Front in 1939, and almost was again in 1944 for unfraternal attacks on Ernest Bevin and the unions. The Bevanites were accused by the party right of treachery and fomenting civil war. In 1955, he was expelled again, and almost terminally, for anti-party and anti-union activities, Attlee's prudence and the whims of individual union members of the Labour National Executive saving him at the last. The later reconciliation with Gaitskell was always a shotgun marriage.

Even his record as architect of the National Health Service led him into trouble. His enemies denounced him as the 'Minister of Disease', a 'Tito from Tonypandy' (deliberately mispronounced and also inaccurate, since Bevan actually came from the equally alliterative Tredegar). His fateful remark when launching the NHS at Manchester in July 1948 that the Tories were 'lower than vermin' became a defining moment in Britain's equivalent of the class war. He received abuse, packets of excrement addressed to the resident of 'Vermin Villa', a kick in the pants in White's from a deranged landowner, appropriately named Strangeways. The hero of Labour's grassroots became the most hated man of his time. By contrast, Benn or Scargill were the darlings of the halls.

And yet this stormy petrel does seem, from the vantage point of half a century later, a far more centrist, or at least less extreme, politician than contemporary journalists and political critics would allow. Bevan's later embrace by New Labour in its fullest Mandelsonian efflorescence may be less surprising. From his emergence as a serious politician in the 1920s, he usually chose the mainstream, even if under protest. Not for Nye, with his restless urge for power (even if 'you always saw its coat-tails disappearing round the corner'), the parochial ILP impotence of Jimmy Maxton and the Clydesiders. (Indeed, many of the latter, including John Wheatley, Minister of Health in 1924, and Tom Johnston, wartime Secretary of State for Scotland, came to forsake the wilderness as well.)

Bevan grew up in the class turmoil of South Wales in 1910–26, between the Tonypandy riots and the General Strike. Those were the stormy years of the Plebs League and the Central Labour College evangelising in the valleys; of industrial rebels like Noah Ablett and Arthur Cook; of the 'betrayal' by Lloyd George over the Sankey Commission's proposals for nationalisation of the mines in 1919 and the climbdown by fellow unionists of the Triple Alliance on Black Friday (15 April 1921); of the titanic coal strikes of 1921 and 1926, and the poverty and unemployment, wage cuts and mass victimisation by the coal-owners that resulted. This was capitalism raw and in crisis. Born in 1897 and sent to work in the mines in 1911 (when Tredegar itself was briefly ablaze not just with strike militancy but apparently anti-Semitic attacks on local properties), the young Bevan imbibed a rich variety of philosophies. He read the romance of Jack London, the revolutionary ideas of the German Joseph Dietzgen and the American Daniel de Leon, the Marxist texts of the social science tutorial classes run by the Central Labour Colleges in the valleys. He was excited by the quasi-syndicalism of the Rhondda-based Plebs League and its Marxist missionaries, Will Mainwaring, Will

Hay and particularly the charismatic ideologue, Noah Ablett. They produced that passionate pamphlet, *The Miners' Next Step*, published by the Unofficial Reform Committee at Tonypandy. The young Bevan's ideas centred on direct action by the miners themselves. His views crystallised in his years at the Central Labour College in London in 1919–21, a workers' seminary for other young socialists like Jim Griffiths, Morgan Phillips, Ness Edwards and the Communist novelist, Lewis Jones. This was a more formative phase in Bevan's ideological progress than his own later, rather languid, account was to suggest. He appeared the prototype of the young industrial rebel, focusing on direct action at the point of production to win for the workers the surplus value that was rightfully theirs for the fruits of their labour. In 1926 he fought shoulder to shoulder with his comrades in the pit. His work as disputes agent for the miners confirmed for him the deep injustice of the benefit system and the wage cuts that afflicted those miners not thrown out of work.

But it is highly relevant that these years still kept Bevan somewhere within the mainstream. The miners' strike of 1921, even more the general strike of 1926, confirmed for him the sheer futility of industrial struggle doomed to defeat by well-prepared coal-owners, and the anti-strike apparatus, civil and military, assembled by their allies in government. For all his bitter anti-capitalist rhetoric, Bevan foreswore strategies such as the Minority Movement linking up the Miners' Federation rank-and-file with Communist allies, which attracted the support of a far-left fellow agent like S.O. Davies. Still more did he reject the path which took another colleague, Arthur Horner, into the *cul de sac* of the Communist Party, about to enter its extreme form of Stalinist sterility. While Bevan never wholly abandoned the mirage of industrial direct action (using it to goad the official TUC leadership during the war and to contrast the centralism of nationalisation after 1945 with the more vibrant message of workers' democracy), by the mid-1920s he was essentially an orthodox parliamentary socialist. He became a member of the Tredegar UDC as early as 1922; he worked on the Tredegar Medical Aid Society (which influenced his ideas on the NHS after 1945); in 1928 he became a member of the Labour-controlled Monmouthshire county council as councillor for Ebbw Vale. To complete the process, his friend Archie Lush, a fellow participant in the local Query Club, began a private campaign to subvert the local MP, the passive Evan Davies, and a very rare form of re-selection took place. It turned out to be deselection since the miners balloted strongly in favour of Bevan and in 1929 he was easily returned as Member of Parliament for Ebbw Vale. He remained its representative for the rest of his life. A decade of experiment convinced him that it was in the parliamentary method, the conquest of power in Westminster, that the workers' route to democratic socialist freedom ultimately lay.

Bevan began as an angry MP of the left. His remarkably controversial maiden speech on the coal industry featured a ferocious attack on the great figure of Lloyd George – 'better dearer coal than cheaper colliers' – which shook that veteran, perhaps as an uncomfortable echo of his own youthful onslaughts on Joe Chamberlain during the Boer War. Bevan was foremost, along with the Clydesiders, in denouncing the second Labour government under Ramsay MacDonald, and even more in condemning MacDonald's perceived treachery in forming the National Government with the Tories and Liberals in August 1931.

More bizarrely, the eloquent young Welshman fell into strange company. He became friendly with the Marxist intellectual, John Strachey. Through him, he briefly followed the lead of Sir Oswald Mosley with his call for corporate planning, public works, tariffs and revival of the home market. More personally, he was taken up with Lord Beaverbrook and hobnobbed socially with such intimates as Brendan Bracken, who derided him as 'Bollinger Bolshevik, Ritzy Robespierre and Lounge-lizard Lenin'. This stylish bohemian seemed far removed from the austerity of his native mining valleys. It was noticeable that in the House Bevan less frequently moved amongst the South Wales Labour MPs, many of them elderly union officials of limited cultural sophistication compared with Bevan himself.

Yet he always remained anchored within the Labour movement, never joining diversionary movements like the Socialist League. This was a constant source of passionate debate with his wife, Jennie Lee, a Marxist who kept to the ILP fringe until 1944. Bevan affectionately chided her as 'his Salvation Army lassie', who preferred the sanctity of a political nunnery, cherishing the 'virginity' of her pure little sect when it disaffiliated from the Labour Party in 1932 rather than the broad church of the British labour movement. In South Wales, this was a bleak time of mass unemployment and the means test, of the harsh operations of the Unemployment Assistance Boards, of wage cuts and hunger marches and fights with the police, of the stay-down stoppages at Nine Mile Point, Abertillery, inspired by syndicalist direct action in the Asturias. Bevan toyed with a variety of approaches, including a bizarre idea for setting up Workers Freedom Groups as a kind of local defence militia. In 1937 he joined the Unity Campaign associated with Sir Stafford Cripps, and condemned by the Labour Party hierarchy.

But he was generally housed within the Social Democratic tabernacle, never a permanent sectarian. When the international crisis built up in the later 1930s, Bevan called for a united nationwide response. From the standpoint of the Popular Front, which indeed was to lead to his expulsion from the parliamentary Party, along with Cripps and George

Strauss in 1939, his fundamental cry was always for a broader unity. In the columns of *Tribune*, on whose editorial board he sat from 1937, becoming editor in 1941, his approach was patriotic as well as socialist. Certainly he was no pacifist. Earlier than many, he called for armed resistance to fascism, starting with the rescue of the Popular Front government in Spain. He condemned Munich, on the distinctive grounds that it represented a crisis for the ruling capitalist class. In *Tribune*, he became, remarkably in the light of later events, an advocate of the view that Winston Churchill should be brought into a restructured government. In March 1938 he passionately backed up a powerful speech by Churchill calling for resistance to the dictators. 'The time has arrived to assert the power of the free democracies against Hitler,' Bevan wrote, even though Churchill's sympathies for Franco's uprising were a serious mark against him.

During the war, Bevan appeared most removed from mainstream Labour views. He rejoined the parliamentary party almost immediately, but then embarked upon a prolonged campaign of opposition to many of the policies of the Churchill coalition. In the wartime years, Bevan moved from bit player to enjoy top billing as the 'squalid nuisance' of Churchillian oratory. He was remarkably effective in challenging the coalition's strategic decisions, in calling for a Second Front to assist our Russian allies rather than prop up the empire in north Africa, in condemning carpet bombing by the RAF as ineffective as well as inhumane, in exposing anti-Communist diversions like involvement in the civil war in Greece. At home, he denounced the coalition, as Laski and others on the left did, for obstructing the advent of socialism. His anonymous tract *Why Not Trust the Tories?* (1944) laid waste the policies of a Tory-run government on social welfare, employment and industrial planning. Equally, he condemned Labour ministers for setting their socialist convictions aside and missing a unique opportunity of revolutionary social change. He refused to criticise wartime strikes and stoppages by some miners and other trade unionists, and attacked the great Bevin and 'jaded, irresponsible, cynical trade union leaders' for imposing penal restrictions on the right to strike and for general attacks on civil liberties. These led to a great crisis in May 1944 when union leaders tried to throw him out of the party altogether. Bevan was certainly amongst those (Orwell in *The Lion and the Unicorn* was another) who saw the war as 'a radical moment', a unique opportunity for social transformation.

But Bevan always sought revolution via the ballot box and the parliamentary approach. He saw the war years as having made free institutions, especially the Commons, even more powerful as an instrument of the popular will. *Why Not Trust the Tories?* was a passionate affirmation of free assembly, ending with his much-loved evocation of Colonel Rainboro' of the Levellers proclaiming his egalitarian message at the 1647 Putney debates amongst Cromwell's army. At the height of his alleged extremism as an enemy of the consensus, he always saw democracy as his essential strategy for change. It was never likely in 1944, with victory in Europe in sight and even Jennie Lee on the verge of rejoining the Labour Party, that Bevan would favour the impotence of exclusion. He would never opt for the gesture politics of the 'beloved rebel' Jimmy Maxton. On the contrary, after penning a grudging apology which kept him in the Labour fold, he stood for the first time for the National Executive constituency section and was elected, coming fifth out of seven. From then on, he had a crucial power base within the party structure. He bent his efforts to striving for a Labour victory and to shoring up Labour's own plans for post-war reconstruction, unlike what he saw as the pallid alternatives of the Coalition, with its Keynesian nostrums for full (or fuller) employment when peace returned. As such, he caught the attention of Attlee as a dynamic force who ought to be accommodated somewhere in a Labour government. Bevan was indeed one of the very few Labour leaders who foresaw the popular uprising that would sweep Churchill ignominiously out of office in July 1945. As he had long prophesied, the overwhelming force of mass democracy could be harnessed to destroy the capitalist order for all time. Bevan, unexpectedly sent to the Health ministry to put the proposed National Health Service into effect, would carry that process forward.

As a minister in the Attlee government, at least as long as he remained at Health until January 1951, Bevan was a remarkable success. More than almost any other minister, he could point to a record of great legislative achievement which permanently transformed the face of British society. But he was effective in large measure because he went with the grain of political realities. He was a broadly centrist minister most of the time who caused no great trouble for his colleagues. Compared with later Labour ministers such as George Brown or Tony Benn, Bevan was the model of loyalty. His National Health Service, marked by years of deadlock with the British Medical Association and particularly its key officials, was a triumph of relativist philosophy. At times, Bevan lost his temper as well he might, in denouncing the BMA representatives as 'a small group of politically poisoned people'. They, and especially the serpentine Charles Hill, erstwhile 'radio doctor', violently replied in kind. Later on there was 'vermin'. But he always left leads open. In the end, his ability to persuade and beguile, notably the Royal Colleges and Lord Moran of the Physicians, 'corkscrew Charlie' to his intimates, was decisive.

The National Health Service was only roughly conceived when Bevan became a minister, and the early key decisions were all essentially his. Donald Bruce, his PPS, has written of how his charm and passion won the devotion of his civil service staff from Sir Wilson Jameson downwards. The broad concept of a service financed from general taxation and freely available at the point of delivery had been enshrined in Beveridge during the war. Bevan's most radical innovation was to take the hospitals into national ownership and control. This led to fierce opposition from Herbert Morrison and Chuter Ede, backed by Greenwood, Alexander and Tom Williams, who wanted control to remain in the hands of the local authorities. At the key Cabinet on 20 December 1945, Bevan just managed to get his way with the support of the venerable Lord Addison, himself a former medical man of great authority as well as the first Minister of Health in 1919, and, most crucial of all, the personal backing of Attlee. Bevan argued that local authorities lacked the resources to take over the voluntary hospitals and only central control could ensure a properly national service effective in all parts of Britain. He just carried the day. But this was also the accepted view of men like Arthur MacNalty, the Chief Medical Officer, who had backed proposals in the *Economist* during the war for regional organisation and ultimate nationalisation. As Charles Webster's account makes clear, Bevan's proposal reflected the most effectively argued solution among the technocrats, which was also open to the least political objection from the personnel within the health service.[1] It was the least speculative approach open to him. Whether indeed it was more appropriate than local control, experiment and accountability has been much contested by specialists in public health from that day to this, although Professor Webster himself evidently supports Bevan's view.

In other key respects, Bevan's health service was steeped in concessions. Of course, he made compromises galore with the doctors, and acknowledged bitterly that he 'stuffed their mouths with gold'. He retained private practice in full, and 'pay beds' in the hospitals. He never looked like conceding a fully salaried medical profession. The final settlement, negotiated via Moran and Webb-Johnson of the Surgeons, made the state element only a small part (£300) of doctors' remuneration. Limits were waived on specialists' fees and the appeal procedures for doctors coming before NHS tribunals were reformed to meet the criticisms of general practitioners. The sale of practices was indeed ended, but £60m was provided to compensate GPs for the change. A process of two-tier health provision, with the basic national system left under-funded and circumvented by privately funded medical schemes run by BUPA and others, was already underway.

The NHS, so widely acclaimed at the time and subsequently a talisman of faith for the once-critical doctors themselves, was a skein of compromises which greatly disappointed some on the left. Radicals like Dr Stark Murray of the Socialist Medical Association, a pioneer body which had helped put the idea of a national health service on Labour's programme in the first place in the early 1930s, were left in dark disillusion. His colleague, Dr Somerville Hastings MP, was more positive, though he too became a critic in time. The SMA felt that the opportunity for creating a really national remodelled health service had been lost. In particular, their own cherished scheme for neighbourhood health centres had been largely set aside. The SMA ended up as a marginalised and largely ineffective pressure group. It was in marked contrast, for instance, to NALT, the Labour teachers' group, who felt that the government's educational policy gave them a platform from which to promote the cause of multi-lateral or comprehensive schools. Bevan's creation is commonly attacked from the right for its financial provision. This led to a succession of supplementary estimates from 1949 and rows between Bevan and Cripps over the possibility of imposing charges for medical prescriptions. But it should be emphasised, too, how the historic achievement of this socialist minister was equally assailed at the time as a sell-out to rich specialists and private practitioners, almost a betrayal of the values of real socialism.

In other aspects of his role as a minister, Bevan again found that his socialist aspirations were hemmed in. His policy on housing, successful in building 1m new homes, far more so than was often acknowledged, was relatively traditional. Here, he left the initiative firmly in the hands of the local authorities, and rejected proposals for more challenging policies such as a new Housing Corporation, put forward by Douglas Jay and others. Here, too, socialism would have to be put on the back burner. While Bevan concentrated on the public provision of council housing for rent, and severely restricted housing for sale, he was forced to recognise the desire for home ownership as well. He was also compelled to mirror the pattern of the existing class system, for instance in creating special categories of better housing stock to minister to the needs of middle-class managers. On the other hand, Bevan's insistence that local authority housing should be marked by high standards of construction and minimum levels of comfort for council house tenants sees him at his most imaginative and most generous.

Elsewhere, Bevan was not a troublemaker. He liked neither Ernie Bevin nor a Cold War foreign policy. Bevan especially disliked what he saw as a violently anti-Jewish policy in Palestine. On the other hand, the realities of international tension between the West and Stalin's Russia stirred Bevan as powerfully as other ministers. For all his residual anti-Americanism, he was not and never had been a fellow traveller. His anti-Communism, if only on libertarian grounds, was beyond doubt. The rape of Czechoslovakia and especially Stalin's attack on the socialist experiment in Tito's Yugoslavia powerfully influenced Bevan's responses. He was a strong champion of NATO coming into being, even while insisting that it was progressive policies and ideas, not armaments, that would defeat Communism in the end. On the Berlin blockade in 1948–49, Bevan was one of the hawks, not least because of the Social Democrat base in West Berlin itself. He called for Allied tanks to drive a route through the Soviet zone to West Berlin so that its population could receive food and essential supplies. Most striking of all, Bevan raised no protest when news came out almost accidentally that Britain was manufacturing nuclear weapons. Indeed, he would have favoured this policy, if only to ensure that the Americans alone did not control a nuclear arsenal directed against the Kremlin. Not for Bevan the quasi-pacifist evasions of Labour foreign policy that had paralysed the party throughout the 1930s, even beyond Munich. He endorsed Britain's atomic bomb, its worldwide defence network based on military conscription, and all the arms budgets until the fateful new policy of early 1951. Britain's socialist middle way needed to be defended against all comers. No mirage of 'a socialist foreign policy' here.

At home, Bevan was well content with the main thrust of policy-making under Attlee. He supported, of course, the policy of nationalisation, and fought strongly alongside Dalton and (surprisingly perhaps) Bevin for iron and steel to be kept on the list in late 1947. But, as an old syndicalist of Plebs League days, he recognised that industrial democracy, let alone any form of workers' control, were casualties of a stern centralism, and that public ownership should be made to work better, including for consumers, before it was blithely extended. Bevan went along with the remainder of welfare legislation, even if it reflected the centrist liberalism of Beveridge, for instance through compulsory contributions, rather than egalitarian socialism. He backed up Ellen Wilkinson in basing educational change after 1945 on the selective grammar schools. In practice, for all his rhetoric, Bevan like Herbert Morrison was in effect from 1948 an advocate of consolidation, making the foundations more secure before pushing on to the next phase of the socialist advance. At the Dorking colloquium in May 1950, Morrison and Bevan virtually voiced the same conclusions at that transitional moment.

Elsewhere, too, Bevan was markedly more circumspect, or perhaps simply more loyal, than, say Benn in the later 1970s. He did not lend support to backbench revolts against the government on domestic or external issues, even when they often included Jennie Lee and close friends like Michael Foot, his successor as editor of *Tribune*. He used with advantage his links with old fellow-miner, fellow Central Labour College student and fellow Welshman, Morgan Phillips, the supreme *apparatchik* in Transport House. For a time *Tribune* came perilously close to being an organ of the party faithful.

Nor did Bevan encourage dissent at party conference. This later champion of the left-wing constituency rank and file slapped down critics at the 1947 conference who wanted him to change policy over tied cottages at the behest of the grass roots. Solidarity was crucial, and so was discipline. No 'emotional spasms' here. Imperiously, he kept clear of the party Liaison Committee as well. In 1949 he endorsed the expulsion of the fellow-travelling far-leftists, Platts-Mills, Hutchinson, Solley and Konni Zilliacus from party membership. They were guilty of disloyalty and anti-party activity. Zilliacus, Bevan told Huw T. Edwards, 'had passed the bound of all reasonable toleration'. Equally he strongly condemned industrial rebels, notably unofficial strikers in the docks and gas industry. Bevan had no difficulty, on the Cabinet Emergencies Committee in 1948–49, in supporting the use of troops to break strikes. He gave his backing to the Attorney-General, Hartley Shawcross, in exploring legal weapons to be used against stevedores encouraging disaffection in the London docks. Britain's socialist experiment should not be imperilled by the self-indulgence and indiscipline of a minority, a view faithfully mirrored by Barbara Castle 20 years later during the debates on *In Place of Strife*. This was also Bevan's own approach during his ill-starred three months as Minister of Labour in January–April 1951. Never, down to Gaitskell's budget proposals at that time, did Bevan openly oppose his own government's domestic policies. Even the necessary retreats in the period 1948–50 – rationing, a wage freeze, devaluation of the pound (which Bevan vigorously defended on socialist grounds in a memorable speech in the Commons) – were all defensible. In any event, they were the work of the new Chancellor, Sir Stafford Cripps, an old ally from Popular Front/*Tribune* days before the war, and a fellow victim of expulsion from the party in 1939.

It is not his record in the Attlee government but rather the way he left it that is largely responsible for Bevan's later reputation as an irreconcilable of the far left. In an historic episode, Bevan clashed furiously with the new Chancellor, Hugh Gaitskell, initially about the scale of his proposed £4,700m rearmament programme for 1951–54, and then fatally over the charges to be imposed on the health service to help pay for it. After announcing, almost casually, in a speech at Bermondsey on 3 April that it was a resigning matter of principle, he left the Attlee Cabinet on 22 April, along with Harold Wilson – not hitherto a dissenter but a critic of the arms programme on economic grounds – and the lesser figure of John Freeman. Bevan's disastrous resignation speech included bitter criticism of Gaitskell (whom Michael Foot in *Tribune* compared to the traitor Philip Snowden back in 1931, the ultimate comparison in terms of Labour mythology). A 'party within a party' (so-called) came into being, with its own manifesto *Keep Left* in July 1951, and the Bevanites were born. Labour lost the 1951 general election, plunged into four years of civil war and gained a long-term reputation for being divided and unelectable that lingered on into the 1990s when the advent of New Labour put paid to it for good and all. Bevan, at first, was the figure held to blame.

Clearly, resignation in such circumstances indelibly stamps a politician as a divisive, perhaps destructive, force. The moderation of most of Bevan's conduct in the years 1945–50 was forgotten. Gaitskell and Dalton freely compared their former colleague to Mosley, even to Hitler. A series of ministers, Attlee, Gaitskell, Dalton, Gordon Walker, Shinwell and others, spread the total untruth that Bevan had previously voiced no concern at the new rearmament programme. Bevan was accused of the same mixture of semi-detachment and psychological instability attributed by Downing Street to Peter Mandelson when he resigned, 50 years later in January 2001. Others claimed that Bevan had no problem of principle at all but was consumed by personal jealousy of Gaitskell, a public school upstart who had only entered the Commons in 1945. 'He's nothing, nothing, nothing,' Bevan exclaimed, though Gaitskell was hardly more conciliatory for his part. Indeed, Bevan felt a real sense of grievance towards Attlee, never the best premier in promoting or removing ministers, when Gaitskell was pushed into the Treasury in place of Cripps in October 1950, followed by the promotion of Morrison to the Foreign Office in place of Bevin in March 1951, where he was to make a derisory impression. Bevan, denied promotion to the two key posts by Attlee, was given little in return. He was not moved on to the Colonial Office in February 1950, apparently because of his excessive sympathy for black Africans, while his move to the Ministry of Labour was at best a move sideways to a post held without distinction by the elderly George Isaacs for the past five years. After Bevan's glorious achievements at Health, Attlee had given him a curmudgeonly and grudging reward. He reacted with years of quarrelsome behaviour, which Barbara Castle attributed in part to the male menopause.

But this is not why Bevan resigned, and it would be unfair towards both him and Gaitskell to lay the main emphasis on personal jealousies. Bevan resigned not because he was an extremist, not because he suddenly cast considerations of loyalty to the winds, but because Gaitskell's budget raised grave issues that went beyond previous policies, and because on those issues it was Bevan, not Gaitskell, who was demonstrably right. Contrary to what appears in some later memoirs, Bevan had twice declared at length in Cabinet that Gaitskell's proposed rearmament programme was impractical and unaffordable. On 1 August 1950, while supporting the Anglo-American position in resisting the North Korean invasion of the south, Bevan condemned the then £3,600m programme. On 25 January 1951, just after Attlee's talks with Truman in Washington had led to a massive increase in Britain's rearmament burden to £4,700m, heavier per capita than in the United States itself, Bevan argued at length and in detail that it was quite impractical. He offered major economic objections – the effect on exports and inflation, the bottlenecks in supplies, the disruption of labour, the crucial shortage of machine tools. Gaitskell did not seriously contest them, but in effect argued that Britain had no option but to back America to the hilt. It was the supposed Celtic firebrand Bevan who offered careful economic arguments, the supposed rational economist Gaitskell who spoke as a politician, underpinned by emotion. Bevan steered clear of financial controversies in a fine Commons speech of 15 February defending British involvement in Korea. But it was well known that he opposed the arms programme, and that helping to finance it by imposing charges on dental and ophthalmic areas of the health service would be a resigning matter for him.

Other ministers did not help. Possible allies like Griffiths, Tomlinson, even perhaps Dalton, drifted away. Attlee was ill at a crucial moment, leaving the Cabinet in the hands of Morrison, Bevan's arch-enemy. Attlee's letter from his sickbed, unhelpfully and unhistorically comparing Bevan's actions with Lord Randolph Churchill's impetuous and politically fatal resignation from the Salisbury government in December 1886, made matters worse. The crisis could have been avoided. The gap between ministers was the pathetically small sum of £13m (£23m in a full year). Many tried to bridge the narrow gulf – the aged Lord Addison, the dying Ernest Bevin, lesser ministers like Robens, Stewart and Callaghan. But, almost fatalistically, the majority willed Bevan to leave them, and he did. His resignation did not show him up as a fellow-travelling extremist. What it showed was that the inexperienced and highly-strung Gaitskell, for all his statistical expertise, had got his sums fatally wrong. Indeed, his one and only budget in 1951 was financially inadequate as well as politically disastrous. It discouraged investment and failed to address inflation. When Churchill returned to power in late October, he took Bevan's side. The arms programme was proved by Ian Bancroft and other civil servants to be quite impractical; they were scornful of Gaitskell's calculations. Labour's original arms programme was cut by Churchill by over a third and phased over four years, not three. They were all Bevanites now, it seemed. But the outcome was disastrous for Bevan's career and long-term reputation, and perhaps for his party as well.

The years of internecine controversy while in opposition between 1951–55 have also been taken to prove Bevan's radical departure from the middle ground. It was a painful period, which did great harm to Labour's standing, with the venerable Attlee in his last phase unable to turn back the tide. But again a careful assessment of Bevan's record may lead to a revision of the conventional wisdom. His dissent was fierce and consistent – but on foreign and defence policy only. On domestic matters, Bevan and Gaitskell, both of them democratic socialists who favoured nationalisation and greater equality, were never far apart. Although Bevan received a great boost from his strength on the constituency section of the National Executive, where 'Bevanites' filled six out of seven places, the great debate was fought out primarily within the parliamentary party. The constitutional assumptions of Bevan and Gaitskell were basically the same. There was intense personal bitterness, and rhetorical broadsides from Gaitskellites and Bevanites alike. But they did not necessarily emanate from Bevan. Indeed, it was his followers like Foot and Castle who were the main protagonists. Wilson and later Crossman had moved to more centrist positions long before 1955. Bevan himself, however, seemed to keep his distance from his followers. 'Surtout je ne suis pas Marxiste', Karl Marx is supposed to have said. Bevan, almost a proletarian Gaitskellite in excellent disguise, might have observed that, above all else, he was no Bevanite.

The great debates were almost wholly about foreign affairs. These were years when, especially after the death of Stalin in 1953, coexistence and conciliation seemingly gripped the international mind. Churchill himself called for summit diplomacy between the great powers (amongst whom he naturally included Britain) but failed to push his old wartime friend 'Ike' in this direction. There were strong arguments for trying to build a new consensus around peaceful coexistence, for moderating the arms race by going slow on the hydrogen bomb, certainly for not slavishly following the Americans in encouraging Chiang Kai Shek and taking belligerent postures towards Communist China, which shrewd observers believed had only limited congruence of view with the Soviet Union in any case. There were at least grounds for rational debate, but reason was set aside, not least by an impassioned and ageing Bevan himself. For a third time in 1955, he was almost expelled by the comrades, and this time it would have been three strikes and out.

Yet Bevan in these years was still cleaving to the broad centre-ground of the party. Nothing confirms this more strongly than his volume *In Place of Fear* (1952), taken to be a supreme testament to the Bevanite outlook at this time. It is certainly a fascinating book, if distinctly disjointed, really a series of essays written over a period of many years. But it is also very far from being an extreme book, any more than the original Keep Left tract, *One Way Only*, in July 1951 had been unusually radical with its pleas about the shortage of raw materials, overseas aid and world poverty. *In Place of Fear* is a civilised, qualified statement of the socialist case for parliamentary democracy. It expressed a view of socialism rooted in its time, with nationalisation central to it, but that was standard prior to Crosland's *Future of Socialism* in 1956. It is open to criticism on many fronts, not least for its unrealistic assumption that world trade patterns in no way 'limit the application of socialist policies to the British economy'.[2] Indeed the economic argument of the book, neither Keynesian nor Marxist, is somewhat rudimentary.

But the main thrust of Bevan's argument concerns applications, and here it is immediately recognisable within the mainstream Labour tradition. Financially, there is a strong commitment to public expenditure, Labour's main mantra down to 1997 and far from lost thereafter. Public spending was the essential tool to remove the injustices of an unequal harsh society; the NHS was financed from general taxation, not by a poll tax. Politically, the essential route to socialism was the parliamentary one, 'government by discussion'. As Jennie Lee later wrote, Bevan wrote as a 'passionate parliamentarian', albeit one who felt empirically in terms of relativities. Parliamentary socialism was the route to power, the essential road to the New Jerusalem. And emotionally and morally, Bevan saw democratic socialism as a vibrant creed with values of its own, libertarian, pluralist, the creed of the Levellers and Tom Paine and Bevan's favourite philosopher, the Uruguayan Jose Enrique Rodo. Socialism would never be drowned in the linguistic obscurities of the later Third Way. It was clearly delineated, it had its own lineage – and it was great fun. Not for Bevan the austere joyless desiccation of the Webb-Cole tradition, which Crosland was shortly memorably to denounce. Bevan's own honeymoon would be spent in sunny Torremolinos, not like the Webbs investigating trade societies in Dublin. *In Place of Fear* is the testament of a humane libertarian, never a work of dogmatic extremism. It retains all the poignant magic of the socialist classic.

Bevan's location in the mainstream was finally confirmed in his last phase. After Gaitskell's election as party leader, there was a reconciliation. Bevan, with his record of disaffection and exclusion, never had a chance of succeeding Attlee. Attempts to discern a possible victory route via secret electoral deals with his old enemy and rival for the leadership, Herbert Morrison, are unconvincing. Bevan, though, was still inspirational in party and country, with an international reputation

through his friendships with such as Nehru, Nenni, Djilas, Ben Gurion
and Mendès-France. Gaitskell wisely brought him into the Shadow
Cabinet as Colonial spokesman in February 1956. He had little time to
make much of an impact there, though one revealing episode came that
April when Bevan, along with George Brown, led the way in challenging
Nikita Khrushchev over the treatment of Soviet dissidents. Bevan's anti-
Communism was fully confirmed. No-one would have doubted it had
they read Bevan's trenchant attacks on Soviet suppression of east European
social democracy in his foreword to young Denis Healey's *The Curtain
Falls* back in 1951. Khrushchev sneered that if these were the Labourites,
he was for the Conservatives. At the time of Suez, while Bevan strafed
Eden and Selwyn Lloyd with ridicule for their humiliating failure over
the invasion, people noted that he seemed more measured than Gaitskell
in condemning the government. Maybe this was Bevan the old Zionist,
friend of Israel, and secret patriot.

As shadow foreign secretary, he and Gaitskell worked together well enough
in trying to probe for alternatives to break the sterility of the cold war. Both
took up the cause of 'disengagement' in central Europe, notably the Polish
Rapacki plan for a nuclear-free zone in central Europe, including in time
perhaps a reunified, if disarmed, Germany and the return of the Oder-Neisse
territories in the East. In general, Labour with Bevan as its spokesman
maintained its traditional pro-NATO stance, with little sympathy with the
emergent European Common Market at this stage. Kenneth Younger
speculated that had Bevan become Foreign Secretary in 1959 or in 1964 he
would have been a relatively orthodox, even right-wing anti-Communist
practitioner of power, but this seems an exaggeration.

The most dramatic instance of Bevan's orthodoxy, the one that caused
most pain to friends and disciples, came at the 1957 party conference.
With opposition growing against British nuclear weapons, and the
Campaign for Nuclear Disarmament due to come into being at Easter
1958, Bevan emotionally defended the possession of nuclear weapons.
Britain should retain them as a bargaining counter. It should not send a
Labour foreign secretary 'naked into the conference chamber'. Other
countries wanted Britain to retain nuclear weaponry, at least for the
immediate future, if only to act as a counter to an unpredictable, capitalist
United States. A moralistic gesture by Britain to give up its own nuclear
stockpile, whatever other nuclear powers would do, would be futile and
pointless. It would have no effect on the thermo-nuclear weapons
remaining in the hands of other countries, nor would it slow down the
progress of a nuclear arsenal in coming states such as China. Unilateralism
would be simply 'an emotional spasm', the negation of the politics of
power, of real politics in the living world about which he had lectured

Jennie Lee in her 'nunnery' so often in the past. Later on, the arguments of both sides seemed questionable. Both pro- and anti-bomb factions laid heavy emphasis on the illusion of Britain's moral influence in the world. Bevan himself became uneasy when pressed by Frank Cousins on whether Britain would engage in 'first use' of the bomb, or whether having the bomb was compatible with non-testing. In the end, he and Gaitskell came up with the half-formed notion of the 'non-nuclear club' just before the 1959 general election. But from the standpoint of Bevan's wider role in the movement, his rejection of unilateralism was highly symbolic. In a supreme crisis, he threw himself behind the leadership, behind a tradition of British participation in world collective security, which had been Labour's watchword since 1939. His friends and allies in CND could never move him from that, though it was perhaps fortunate for Bevan that his premature death spared him Labour's supreme agony over unilateralism in 1960, a purgatory that endured until the leadership of Michael Foot a generation later.

Bevan's occupation of the centre, even right-wing ground, in defence policy made him more than most a force for unity. In 1959 he became deputy party leader. His status emerged dramatically in the party conference of October 1959 just after a humbling electoral defeat at the hands of Macmillan's Tories. The conference was preceded by Gaitskell announcing, on no clear evidence, that Labour's defeat was due in part to Clause Four in the party constitution, which committed the party to unending nationalisation. This produced uproar in the ranks. Once again Gaitskell was compared with MacDonald and Snowden, the traitors of 1931. Bevan, now in the early stages of cancer, strode gallantly to the rescue. He had already been important in getting the party to accept *Industry and Society*, a document in 1957 which argued the case for a mixed economy and warned against rigid models of nationalisation. Like others on the British left, he recognised the need for an updated form of socialism, attuned to modern circumstances, with an emphasis on social equality and strategies for economic growth. In the 1959 party conference, he saved Gaitskell's bacon with a brilliantly evasive speech, which aimed to reconcile the views of Gaitskell and Barbara Castle over public ownership. He quoted Lenin on the need to capture 'the commanding heights of the economy'. He cited Euclid as evidence that two things equal to a third thing were equal to each other. Unity was preserved; the Clause Four issue disappeared for another 35 years. It was all due to Nye the great moderate and compromiser. His far less abrasive Welsh colleague, Jim Griffiths, continually referred to himself as a reconciler, as did a younger Welshman, Cledwyn Hughes. So they both were. But, in the key crisis, Nye was the greatest reconciler of them all. A few months later cancer killed him.

On his election as leader in February 1963, Harold Wilson took his ex-Bevanite colleagues over to the wall to toast the portrait of Nye, the man who ought to have been leader instead. But Nye Bevan was not Labour's lost leader, and his mantle was an elusive, ambiguous garment. He could never have led the party, given his record of dissent and expulsion, and his usually bad relations with the TUC. Attlee's avowal in 1952 that Bevan should have 'had the leadership on a plate' may be doubted given Attlee's steadfast refusal to give the younger man any significant promotion. But Bevan still remains a giant in Labour's Valhalla – yet a giant as much of the centre ground as of the left. Throughout his career, he cleaved to the majority view on domestic politics, foreign policy and the nature of democracy.

Does he then deserve his emerging role as an icon for New Labour? His socialism was of his time, conceived within a very different global economy and a polarised class structure. To speculate counter-factually, he would never have accepted the Thatcherite creed of a market-driven, 'flexible', deregulated economy, which Labour retained after 1997. On the other hand, he would have welcomed anti-poverty measures like the minimum wage and child poverty programme, and Gordon Brown's 2002 budget to revive the NHS. He might have come around to devolution for all his lifelong opposition to Welsh separatism. In 1959 he reluctantly endorsed a Welsh Office being put in Labour's manifesto, while no-one who heard his moving address at the Ebbw Vale *eisteddfod* in 1958 could doubt his passion for the Welsh identity and culture. Other policies might have puzzled an old member of the National Council of Civil Liberties. One could, though, imagine an updated Nye, like an older Neil Kinnock, coming to accept the social thrust of a European Union with the prospects of working more closely with social democratic comrades in Europe, east as well as west. New Labour still has its socialist ingredient, however well disguised. Within it, Bevan and his Health Service, convey the essence of the idea of community, of a commitment to public service, a measured incremental socialism that 'made one freedom safe by adding another to it'. So Tony Blair's enthusiasm for the 'solidarity, social justice and co-operation' embodied in Nye's philosophy is not so bizarre. Sceptic, pluralist, visionary, Aneurin Bevan was a socialist for all seasons, who belongs to the ages. A latimer for the oldest, finest values of all, he may take his appointed place in the world of the new.

Further reading

Bevan left few private papers of significance. Important speeches of his are published in Charles Webster (ed.), *Aneurin Bevan on the National Health*

Service (Wellcome Unit, Oxford, 1991) and Peter J. Laugharne (ed.), *Aneurin Bevan: A Parliamentary Odyssey*, Vol. I: *Speeches at Westminster, 1929–1944* (Liverpool, 1996) and Vol. II: *Speeches at Westminster, 1945–1960* (Liverpool, 2000). Other first-hand material, to be treated with care, appears in the published diaries of Dalton, Gaitskell, Crossman, Castle and Benn. Bevan himself wrote relatively little, other than in *Tribune* from 1937, but his tract for the times, *Why Not Trust the Tories?* (London, 1944), written under the pseudonym 'Celticus', and especially his sparkling collection of essays, *In Place of Fear* (London, 1952) embody many of his political and social ideas. Of the biographies, Michael Foot's *Aneurin Bevan* (two volumes, London, 1962 and 1973) is passionate, partisan and a classic of political literature. It was abridged and edited in one volume by Brian Brivati (London, 1997). John Campbell, *Nye Bevan and the Mirage of British Socialism* (London, 1987), is sympathetic but suffers from largely ignoring the background in South Wales, and its attacks on socialism, written from the standpoint of the SDP (which imploded in the year Mr Campbell's book appeared). Instructive essays by politicians and academics appear in Geoffrey Goodman (ed.), *The State of the Nation: The Political Legacy of Aneurin Bevan* (London, 1997), a centenary tribute with a significant foreword by Tony Blair. Dai Smith, *Aneurin Bevan and the World of South Wales* (Cardiff, 1993), which covers several other themes, is a vivid evocation of Bevan's background in the Welsh valleys. The founding of the NHS is magisterially covered in Charles Webster, *The Health Services since the War*, Vol. 1 (HMSO, London, 1988). More general treatments appear in Kenneth O. Morgan, *Labour in Power, 1945–1951* (Oxford, 1984); Peter Hennessy, *Never Again: Britain 1945–1951* (London, 1992); and John Stewart, *'The Battle for Health': A Political History of the Socialist Medical Association* (Aldershot, 1999). Mark Jenkins, *Bevanism: Labour's High Tide* (London, 1979) was a pioneering study in its day. Essays on Bevan include those by Kenneth O. Morgan in *Labour People: Leaders and Lieutenants, Hardie to Bevan* (Oxford, 1987, new edition, 1992) and in Paul Barker (ed.), *Founders of the Welfare State* (London, 1985), reprinted in *idem, Modern Wales: Politics, Places and People* (Cardiff, 1995). Bevan's marriage to Jennie Lee is illuminated by Lee's autobiography, *My Life with Nye* (London, 1980) and Patricia Hollis's brilliant *Jennie Lee* (Oxford, 1997).

Notes

1. Charles Webster, 'The Birth of the Dream', in Geoffrey Goodman (ed.), *The State of the Nation* (London, 1997), p 118.
2. Aneurin Bevan, *In Place of Fear* (London, 1976 edn.), p 51.

Part II

The Era of
Wilson and Callaghan

6

Roy Jenkins

David Lipsey

Roy Jenkins, later Lord Jenkins of Hillhead, b.1920. He married Jennifer in 1945; three children. MP for Central Southwark 1948–50; for Stechford Birmingham 1950–76 and for Glasgow Hillhead 1982–87. Minister of Aviation 1964–65; Home Secretary 1964–67 and Chancellor of the Exchequer 1967–70. Deputy Leader of the Labour Party 1970–72, he resigned over Europe. Home Secretary again from 1974–76, before leaving British politics to become President of the Commission of the European Union 1977–81. A founder of the Social Democratic Party in 1981, its leader and then Liberal Democratic leader in the House of Lords. He became Chancellor of Oxford University in 1987. From 1997 to 1998 he chaired the Independent Commission on the Voting System.

Of the three 'nearly' men of Labour politics in the 20 years after 1964, Roy Jenkins came by far the closest to becoming prime minister. Denis Healey, Renaissance man and barroom bruiser in one, came within 10 MPs' votes of succeeding Callaghan as leader in 1980 and was certainly popular enough with the public. But Healey was a loner, lacking the patience for party management, and ultimately therefore unlikely to have been able to unite the party to win. Tony Crosland, who might well have won that election had he not died in 1977, might by then have been a unifying figure. But even if he had preserved his health and will, it is hard to believe that he could have transcended the collective madness which then engulfed the Labour Party. By the early 1980s, the crown for which the three had long contended was a hollow one, offering only the travails of opposition.

Roy Jenkins, by contrast, was twice close to being prime minister: in 1968–69, as Harold Wilson faltered, and in 1982, when his new party, the Social Democratic Party, was soaring up its parabola. He also mounted a perfectly respectable bid for the leadership in 1976, following Wilson's resignation. Though in the end well beaten by Jim Callaghan, he comfortably beat both Healey and Crosland.

Of his three opportunities, Jenkins himself thinks he came closest in 1968–69. His success as Chancellor was widely contrasted with Wilson's haverings as prime minister; and his claque in the Parliamentary Labour Party (PLP) and the press was in good voice. He may not have been as close to success as he at the time thought; indeed, his real chance may have been his last one, in the 1980s. Be that as it may, to be so often so near to the actual job is to have come a great deal closer than his rivals, who came near only to becoming leaders of the Opposition.

In the process, Jenkins accumulated some comforting consolation prizes. He held two of the three major offices of state – Home Secretary and Chancellor – with distinction, though never the job for which he was at least equally well fitted, Foreign Secretary. He became President of the European Commission, though he was not perhaps quite as distinguished in that role. He started a new party, and steered it to a permanent home with the Liberal Democrats. Even in his later years, he was able to establish himself as a mentor to a young prime minister, and produce what was generally recognised as an extraordinary report for the Blair government on electoral reform.

In addition, had he achieved nothing in politics, *Asquith* and, much later, *Gladstone* must be accounted among the great political biographies of the century; and the nascent *Churchill* may join them. Taken in the round, Roy Jenkins achieved more than most of the prime ministers he aspired to replace: certainly more than Harold Wilson, probably more than James Callaghan. He is an advertisement for the virtues of 'nearly'.

Origins

Like Hugh Gaitskell, the Labour leader who died suddenly in 1963, Roy Jenkins was thought of in some circles as a snob, more attracted to duchesses than horny-handed sons of toil. Unlike Gaitskell, however, there was nothing in his origins which made him so. Indeed, had he chosen to, Jenkins could perfectly well have established himself as the Keeper of the Cloth Cap in the Labour Party on the basis of his father's impeccably working-class credentials. Admittedly Arthur Jenkins became a local figure of high esteem, a member of parliament and a junior minister. But he began as a union man in the proudest of British labour organisations, the mineworkers. He even served a short little-talked-of period in prison as a result of intervening, to preserve the peace, in clashes between the police and miners during the lock-out that followed the 1926 general strike; and being arrested and convicted for his pains.

Unable to blame his widely-respected father for Jenkins' alleged snobbery, some critics have turned on his mother, Hattie, whom Jenkins admits was 'from a background several steps up in the valley social hierarchy... from that of my father.'[1] But Leo Abse, the amateur psychologist and Labour MP largely responsible for this charge, is not a reliable witness. Certainly Jenkins himself says: 'If I developed a certain taste for still grander grandees of liberal outlook, the inheritance came, in my view, more from him than from her.' And perhaps still more they came from his time at Balliol, a self-regarding Oxford college where he went after a run-of-the-mill grammar school education. In any case, anyone who knew Jenkins in later life would bear witness that what at first blush seemed like snobbishness and aloofness had its roots in a real and enduring streak of shyness.

Unlike Healey and Crosland, Jenkins had a relatively cushy war. He was not shot at. A lot of training, providing opportunity for a lot of reading, was followed by a period at Bletchley, code-breaking. Though Jenkins complains that this was a most arduous task which gave him headaches it did not perhaps have quite the character-moulding effects of frontline service. Thus, though in the case of Crosland and Healey, their early disposition to be pro-Europeans can be ascribed to personal experience of the horrors of continental divides, Jenkins' similar disposition cannot be explained in the same way. It was a passion, nevertheless, that went deeper for longer with Jenkins than with either of the other two.

Jenkins did not find a winnable seat for the 1945 general election, but in 1948, he was established in parliament, for the disappearing seat of Central Southwark. He was then chosen for the reasonably safe and permanent seat of Stechford in 1950. No notable or character-forming occupation intervened between 1945 and 1948. Indeed, he may perhaps be regarded as the first of the modern breed of full-time politicians, that is to say, the breed that has not had any strong formative experiences in adult life save politics. Only once did Jenkins seriously consider leaving the trade: in 1963 when he was offered the editorship of the *Economist* newspaper. At first he was 'surprised, flattered and excited'. But it did not take much by way of encouragement as to his prospects under a future Labour government from Harold Wilson to dissuade him: and Jenkins later became sniffy both about the newspaper and the seriousness of his flirtation with it.

Within this, however, there were periods when Jenkins was more,

and periods when he was less, engaged with politics. Journalism and
writing were important to him in the long gap between coming into the
House and Labour's eventual return to office in 1964. It was easier too
to be involved during Gaitskell's leadership, when that brave, romantic
man was Pied Piper to the Labour right; harder after his death. Even
under Gaitskell, however, Jenkins was less dedicated to the organisational
work to which his friend and rival Crosland devoted himself. Perhaps
the origins of the long evolution of relations between the two so that the
friendship became less obvious than the rivalry lay in their positions
respective to Gaitskell. Certainly Crosland later in life could be
incandescent at the various attempts by the Jenkinsites to establish their
man's claims to be Hugh Gaitskell's natural heir.

Jenkins as hero

The death of Gaitskell was a huge personal blow to the radical right of the
Labour Party. But it did not necessarily harm their careers. Jenkins backed
George Brown for the succession despite his temperamental unsuitability
for the job: Dick Crossman describes at length in his diaries a conversation
of mutual incomprehension with Jenkins where the younger man found it
'surprisingly difficult' to explain his antipathy to Wilson.[2] But Wilson,
who understood very well that he had to keep a potentially fractured party
together, was not exactly punitive. After the election, Roy Jenkins was
made Minister of Aviation, with a department of his own, though not a
seat in Cabinet. He handled an interesting portfolio, which included the
near-cancellation of Concorde, with skill. What mattered more, he was a
parliamentary performer and it may well be his triumph in replying to an
early vote of censure – in those days, the House would be packed for such
occasions, which were reported extensively in the press – which gave him
a long-term career advantage over his rivals.

The rivalry remained. First blood went to Jenkins, who had a
department of his own, while Crosland was No. 2 to George Brown at
the ill-fated Department of Economic Affairs. Then, in a piece of
breathtaking chutzpah, in 1964 Jenkins turned down a vacancy for a
Cabinet job at Education, which went to Crosland. Jenkins naturally let
it be known that he had refused. He got the reward he was playing for
when Frank Soskice had to resign as Home Secretary.

Through the Thatcherite 1980s, Jenkins' tenure of the Home Office
was much criticised: this was the birth, so the resurgent 'Moral Right'
claimed, of the 'permissive society'. Given the Beatles, pot and mini-
skirts, it is doubtful that any Home Secretary could have held back the
tide of permissiveness, though plenty would have tried. But the sheer
illiberalism of pre-1964 Britain is hard now to credit.

Though, thanks to a Jenkins bill as a backbencher, theatrical censorship had gone, this was still a society that was, like the governments that had ruled over it, pleasure-hating, penal-minded, mono-racial and homophobic. It was Jenkins' good fortune to be (in the words of his biographer, John Campbell) 'a classic example of the right man being in the right job at the right time'.[3] It was an opportunity he exploited with skill and verve. In the face of a department more tradition-bound and more regulation-oriented than any in Whitehall, it was a huge achievement.

Abortion law was reformed, the bill, admittedly, introduced by a Liberal backbencher, David Steel, but going through only thanks to Jenkins' support. Homosexuality was legalised between consenting adults. Jenkins defined the terms of the debate on race for a quarter of a century with his famous definition of integration: 'not as a flattening process of assimilation but as equal opportunity, accompanied by cultural diversity, in an atmosphere of mutual tolerance'. The 1968 Race Relations Bill, outlawing discrimination, followed, under Jenkins' successor. Corporal punishment in prisons was ended; legal aid improved.

But the notion that Jenkins was a pure permissive is wide of the mark. For example jury trials were reformed to allow majority verdicts, so that criminals could less easily nobble them. This was pushed through despite opposition from Britain's deeply conservative legal profession (though in 2000 Jenkins himself joined the lawyers' lobby to resist Jack Straw's proposals as Home Secretary to restrict the right to jury trial). The organisation of the police was rationalised. The 'sprung alibi', whereby defendants could produce an alibi at the last minute in court giving the prosecution no chance to rebut it, was banned. Jenkins, therefore, emerges as a radical even more than a liberal Home Secretary, prepared to bring about change, and to take on vested interests in doing so.

Being walked out on by the Police Federation, being taken to task following the escape from prison of George Blake, a spy: these were politically difficult moments for Jenkins. He saw them through with inner toughness, reinforced, as he admits in the Police Federation case, by a very large drink. But he avoided what would for him have been the worst test of nerve: the Kenyan Asian crisis of 1968, when Britain faced a large influx of Kenyan Asians expelled from their country. For by then, he had moved; and it was Jim Callaghan, not a liberal, who had to introduce the bill to stop them coming. Jenkins had the luxury of turning his nose up at it from the sidelines.

According to John Campbell, 'no-one except Crosland himself thought that Wilson had made anything but the obvious choice' when he appointed Jenkins to replace Jim Callaghan as Chancellor following sterling's devaluation in November 1967.[4] This is not literally true, since Callaghan

himself had told Crosland that he had assuredly got the job for which, as
an economist and President of the Board of Trade, Crosland felt himself
supremely qualified. However, Jenkins had strong claims as a professional
politician, if not as a professional economist. He had an authority in the
House, recently demonstrated in his demolition of a vote of censure over
the Blake escape. And, assisted by John Harris (who rates with Bernard
Ingham and Alastair Campbell in the triarchy of top post-war spin-doctors),
he enjoyed a superlative press. 'Roy's the Boy' proclaimed the *Economist*,
where Harris had once worked, on his appointment. With the government
rocked by devaluation, his political assets were clearly more important to
Wilson than Crosland's economic assets.

In any case, since devaluation was done, the central necessity of a
succeeding Chancellor was to do little and do it well. Devaluation created
an opportunity for Britain to get out of its chronic balance of payments
problems. The first snag was that it would only be able to do so if room
was made for increased net exports, which meant raising taxes, cutting
public spending or both. The second was that devaluation followed the
pattern known as the 'J-curve'. This meant that revenue per unit of export
was reduced at first by the devaluation, with the gap only made up later as
the volume of exports rose. That meant not only that it would take time
to work, but also that things would likely get worse before they got better.
What was required therefore was an exceedingly orthodox Chancellor with
an exceedingly strong nerve. Jenkins, rather than Crosland, fitted the bill.

Harris recalls crossing the bridge that connects the old Home Office
building to the Treasury as being like going into France in 1940. The
department was demoralised; and the government destabilised. Moreover,
and surprising as it may seem in an era where exchange rates are no
longer fixed and the balance of payments no longer seems to matter, it
appeared as if economic Armageddon was never far away. Certainly, a
second forced devaluation after a first devaluation that had been too
long and daftly resisted would have been a political catastrophe from
which even Harold Wilson could scarce have hoped to recover. In other
words, the burden on the Chancellor was onerous, while his capacity to
command events was distinctly limited. 'Two years hard slog' was the
most he could promise the House of Commons.

It was a hard slog for Jenkins too. It took five successive deflationary
packages before he had done enough. The £700m of public spending cuts
made in January 1968 took eight cabinet meetings and 32 hours of discussion
to get through, though Jenkins rather blames Wilson for stretching it out.
Jenkins was arguably too slow to get to grips with consumer spending.
Though not by this time a great socialist, he was fully aware of the need to
placate his own party; and ended up imposing big extra taxes on the rich

(for example, by a capital levy in 1968) when intellectually he was convinced of the case for cutting them. Whereas the public record is of budgets and taxes and cuts, the private record, in his autobiography, is of a man forced to live on the edge: of long nights and tense mornings when it seemed Britain's reserves might not hold.

Though he had been a radical Home Secretary, he was not a radical Chancellor. He invented no important new taxes; made no attempt to get to grips with reform of the tax system; contributed relatively little to the evolution of public expenditure control; and opened the door of Treasury secrecy only a slither. His main foray outside his ministerial field was to try to seize credit for reform of the trade unions, after they had failed to agree to further incomes restraint. When it went pear-shaped, however, Jenkins was not to be seen. His period as Chancellor was not a triumph of the intellect. It was a triumph of temperament, the more remarkable in a man more prone to mood and self-doubt than was apparent to outsiders.

How near did it bring him to the leadership of the Labour Party? If you believed the contemporary press, very near: savagely and near-universally anti-Wilson, it saw Jenkins as the most plausible (and comfortingly right-wing) alternative. What tended to ensue were great waves of speculation and intrigue which never came to anything. Thus in 1968 as industrial relations reform started to go wrong, and the party languished in the polls, the press was joined by considerable discontent, both in the PLP and in cabinet. It was the troubled summer days of 1968 of which Jenkins writes:

> [They were] in a small way, the equivalent of the same season of 1953 for Rab Butler. Having faltered for want of single-minded ruthlessness when there was no alternative to himself, he then settled down to a career punctuated by increasingly wide misses of the premiership. People who effectively seize the prime ministership – Lloyd George, Macmillan, Mrs Thatcher – do not let such moments slip.[5]

This view manages to be at once self-deprecating and a touch boastful. For the assumption is that he could have seized the crown. But this is by no means certain. For one thing, he was not the only member of Cabinet who wanted Wilson's job: Jim Callaghan for one, once off the rack at the Treasury, was a strong contender. Callaghan and Jenkins could never have combined to get rid of Wilson. If the time was not then ripe for Callaghan to push, he at least had every incentive to make sure that Jenkins was denied. For another, and this was a constant problem of the Jenkins camp, he tended to overrate his support. Labour's leader was then chosen exclusively by Labour MPs. It is true that his acolytes among the parliamentary party – David Marquand, Brian Walden, David Owen – were fervent. But they were never near to a majority in the PLP. And, with their air of ineffable intellectual superiority, their right-wing views and their Eurofanaticism, they were not even an asset. Anyone then aspiring to become leader of the Labour Party needed the support of the old and then primarily trade-union based centre, a group that was determinedly non-ideological but which paid homage to the party's shibboleths, and which also understood the value of party unity. To the centre, Jenkins could seem an aloof and divisive figure, and his allies merely reinforced the impression. Had Wilson gone in 1968, as happened when he did go in 1976, Callaghan, flaws and all, was the likely successor.

1968 was probably Jenkins' best chance of leading the Labour Party (though not necessarily of the premiership). The reason was simple. In the 1960s, Europe had not yet become quite the divisive issue in British politics that it was later to become. This was because, essentially, joining the Common Market was not a possibility, because of the French veto. But all that changed with Labour's (in the end surprising) loss of the 1970 election. For the Tories under Heath were able to take Britain into Europe. And in those days it was the Labour party that was split on the issue. For many in the Party, and by no means only for left-wingers, the Common Market was a capitalist plot. Though Wilson clung to a detailed critique of the terms of entry as his basis for opposing it, many of his supporters felt the same for more fundamental reasons. Europeans versus anti-Europeans indeed for a while dominated the not-altogether-identical rift between right and left as the issue around which Labour nearly fell apart.

In retrospect, the domestic policies of the Heath government seem mild. But they did not seem mild at the time: the Labour Party for example flirted heavily with defying a new Tory law which imposed increases in rents for council housing of just 50p a week. It was felt that the party should be united against the government's inegalitarianism and its trade union reforms. Even those in the party who did not feel strongly about Europe therefore felt strongly about the Jenkinsites' refusal to toe the party line.

In 1970, this was still in the future. Jenkins was comfortably elected Deputy Leader of the Party. However, he was faced only with semi-serious rivals in Michael Foot and Fred Peart, Callaghan having opted instead for the party treasurership.

He might have been electable in 1970, but things rapidly deteriorated from his point of view. Relations in the PLP were damaged very badly when, marshalled by the Jenkinsites, 69 Labour Europeans voted for entry with a further 20 (including Crosland) abstaining. Though this did not immediately destroy his position, it began to undermine it: despite the advantages of incumbency, he held the job against a further challenge by Foot only by 14 votes in 1972. He showed some sensitivity to the problem by holding his nose and voting against the Bill to take Britain in at second reading, which was both an unpleasant and futile compromise for him. For any chance of an early healing of the wounds disappeared through the months of the Bill's passage, where the Labour Europeans ensured that Heath always had a majority.

When Wilson climbed aboard a left-wing bandwagon to solve the issue by promising a referendum on Europe that proved the last straw for Jenkins. He resigned the deputy leadership of the party in 1972 in protest. That was proved by events to be a poor judgement at a difficult time for Jenkins. It was the device of the referendum that enabled the next Labour government both to keep Britain in Europe and keep the Labour Party intact. From then on, and realistically, Jenkins was never likely to be acceptable to the Labour Party as its leader. 'I had lost', he rightly says in his autobiography 'the inertial loyalist vote, that quite significant body of MPs which set more store by the party than by any question of issue or ideology.'[6]

If he was to become premier, it would have had to be by some other means than the Labour Party. As no such means were yet available – no-one then in the Party seriously contemplated splitting it – his position was not a happy one. Indeed, he continued to sit in discomfort on various fences. He did not, for example, go to Lincoln to back Dick Taverne, when he resigned his seat to fight a by-election in protest against Labour's drift to the left; nor did he personally vote for the Tory European Bill in the Commons. This all led to a period in which Jenkins was half-in and half-out: in his autobiography he admits he showed 'too much willingness to wound accompanied by fear to strike'. Resignation had left him with responsibility without position: the prerogative of the impotent down the ages.

He did return to a position of sorts, standing for and being elected to the shadow cabinet in 1973. 1974, 'according to my strategy was the year in which the temporising Labour Party leadership was due to receive its just reward in the shape of a lost general election', he records with more honesty than loyalty in his autobiography, but the electorate threw him into gloom by deciding otherwise. Jenkins was urged by his friends to stand out for the Chancellorship, which shows how out of touch they had become with his rather weaker position. He could, however, perfectly well have decided to sit the government out. Instead, he accepted the Home Secretaryship.

To eat at the same restaurant on two successive evenings is to invite disappointment; and this rather was how Jenkins' second stint at the Home Office was regarded. It had its achievements, for example, the Sex Discrimination Act; one at least memorable piece of courage when he successfully faced down IRA hunger strikers, including two pretty girls; and one illiberal, though perfectly justified, measure, the Prevention of Terrorism Act. But Jenkins seemed to be running on autopilot.

Much more notable was his performance on Europe. He embraced the referendum over which he had once resigned with enthusiasm, enjoying co-operating with politicians from other parties and jousting with the left of his own. The two-to-one vote that followed therefore seemed less a triumph for Wilson and Callaghan, who had invented the strategy, and more one for Jenkins, who had opposed it. The experience was important in loosening party bonds, and paved the way for 'breaking the mould' with the formation of the Social Democratic Party in the 1980s.

With Europe, for the time being, no longer dividing the party, it might have seemed that Jenkins was again up in the leadership stakes. When Harold Wilson did what he had privately said he would do without anyone much believing him, and resigned as leader in March 1976, the Jenkinsites probably thought they were in with a final chance to get their man in. The result therefore must have come as a disappointment. Though the candidate of the press, Jenkins polled only 56 votes compared with Foot's 90 and Callaghan's 84. True, Jenkins was well clear of Benn (37), Healey (30) and, satisfyingly, Crosland (17), but a candidate of one extreme or the other had to be in front or near after one ballot if he was to emerge victorious at the end. Withdrawing, Jenkins recalled the words of the defeated Adlai Stevenson: 'It hurts too much to laugh and I'm too old to cry.'

He claims not to have been further hurt by the sequel: that it was Crosland, not he, whom the eventual winner, Callaghan, made Foreign Secretary. He seems already to have – certainly afterwards he thought he had – been leaning to leaving British politics, having been offered the next presidency of the European Commission by Wilson; and he may have been – certainly afterwards he thought he was – sure that this was a more powerful job than British Foreign Secretary. In retrospect, it is strange that Callaghan's decision seemed even surprising. Crosland had powerful qualifications to be his Foreign Secretary. Crosland knew little about the subject, whereas the prime minister did, and could hope to control the big decisions. Crosland was also by now semi-agnostic on Europe, which meant he was ideal finally to bind the party and the government's wounds. Callaghan needed a powerful Eurofanatic as foreign secretary like a hole in the head.

However it may seem in prospect, in retrospect it does not seem that Jenkins ended up with the plum. The job of President of the Commission is an exceptionally hard one. The President lacks the ability to hire or fire his fellow commissioners. His power is contested by ministers, who have the legitimacy of national electoral mandates. Issues can be at once minor and obdurate. The Brussels bureaucracy, Eurofanatic both in its ideals and its interests, has high expectations of the president, but little tolerance. Perhaps only Jacques Delors, of recent presidents, has overcome these difficulties.

In the job, Jenkins had to endure some unpleasant new experiences. A bad press was one: he was criticised especially on the continent from the moment he refused to deliver his inaugural declaration in French as well as English. Another was the unwillingness of others to take him and his position at the value he put on it. In a long-drawn out episode, which hovers on the edge of farce, Jenkins pleaded, whined and manoeuvred to be granted full status at the World Economic Summit in London in 1977. (He was eventually allowed in for some bits but not for others, including dinners. That hurt.) Though Jenkins' European Diaries, reporting the experience, bear witness to much hard work, he was not believed by all his colleagues to show the necessary attention to detail.

Yet he had real successes too. The British budget crisis precipitated by Margaret Thatcher would not have been settled without his patience, in a cause for which he had little sympathy. He put monetary union, one issue big enough to engage a big mind, on the agenda whence it never disappeared. Only by his own high standards can he be accounted less than a success.

Breaking the mould

Again, only by his own high standards could his next adventure, the launch of the Social Democratic Party, be so accounted. The SDP did not, it is true, form a government. Nor did it smash the two-party duarchy in British politics: in the 1997 general election, the SDP's offspring, the Liberal Democrats, polled 16.8 per cent of the vote, not that much higher than its 13.8 per cent score before the SDP was even thought of in 1979. (The Lib Dems did however have 46 MPs elected, compared with 11 in 1979.) Its historians, Tony King and Ivor Crewe, even deny that it was a prime cause of the Labour Party's long journey back from the lunacies of 1982 to New Labour in 1997. Electoral realities would have achieved that anyway.

Nevertheless, it was a near miss – sufficiently near for a plausible case to be made that Jenkins came closer to becoming prime minister as leader of the SDP than he ever did as a leader of the Labour Party. The near miss falls into two bits. The first follows the triumphant series of by-elections of the early SDP days in 1981: Jenkins' own narrow defeat at Warrington, worth in its moral outcome several victories, Croydon North West, Crosby; a 44 per cent share of the vote in the by-elections and a national opinion poll showing that sometimes touched 50 per cent. It is true that things wobbled somewhat in early 1982, as a result of some ill-judged macho bargaining between the Social Democrats and their Liberal allies. However, what really set the SDP back was neither of these things but the Falklands War. The deep pre-war unpopularity of Mrs Thatcher's Tories is often forgotten, and, if there had been no war, might have led Tories as well as Labour voters to defect to the SDP.

The second bit was the 1983 election itself. As Labour imploded, the SDP nearly took second place in the popular vote, falling just short with

26 per cent compared with Labour's 28 per cent. Had the campaign lasted only a little longer, Labour might have found itself Britain's third party electorally. This might not have led to the collapse of the party. Labour had the huge advantage over the SDP of having a class vote, which was therefore a concentrated vote, which meant, under Britain's misbegotten electoral system, that it reaped rich rewards in seats for a scanty harvest of votes. Equally, however, its moral authority might have been dented beyond repair by a humiliating third. Certainly, leading Labour politicians thought they had escaped ruin by a hair's breadth. Had it happened, too, Britain's first-past-the-post electoral system would have been utterly discredited. One way or another, a Labour collapse might have meant a late-1980s premiership for Jenkins.

As things turned out, ill luck and all, the SDP was not in itself ultimately successful. What no fair-minded judge can doubt is that for Jenkins personally, it was something more important: a triumph of nerve and judgement which few politicians could have come near to matching. This was apparent from his first floating of the party in his Dimbleby lecture of 1980, with its famous analogy of the experimental aeroplane which could crash or soar. (He did not dwell there on the implications of these alternative fates for its pilot.) His courage in fighting Warrington, an apparently unsuitable seat in which for weeks he made no noticeable headway, was great. In Hillhead, for those who were there, he levitated a seemingly impossible victory by an effort of pure will. Throughout the period of the SDP's birth and youth, his judgement was sound: in particular, he resisted the exclusive prospectus for the party laid out by his rival for its leadership, David Owen. (It is a salutary warning to those who favour one-member, one-vote for the election of party leaders that Dr Owen actually persuaded 44 per cent of the members of the new SDP that he would make a better leader than Mr Jenkins.)

Jenkins devotes some space in his autobiography to refuting the allegations of Dr Owen and his acolytes: notably that Jenkins was a closet Liberal, always intent on merger with the SDP's Liberal allies. Jenkins points out that he always saw the need for a new party if the centre was to get a decisive boost. However he was not so foolish as to proclaim eternal independence. 'The Missouri,' he points out in one of the striking wrought metaphors that permeate his writing, 'is not a pointless river because, after a fertilising and dramatic course, it eventually unites with the Mississippi.' Jenkins' later years as leader were of course devoted to bringing about that merger, for which he was rewarded, first, by years of odium from the Owenites and secondly, by being effectively dumped as leader during the 1987 general election campaign. This became a bitter period, which, since it had no long-term significance, can be passed over as swiftly as possible.

Roy Jenkins, by 1983, was already 63. Only by a miracle could he become prime minister after that election: that is to say, if no party won an overall majority at some subsequent election and he emerged as a coalition caretaker. He nevertheless enjoyed the honours and rewards of a great man's later years: for example, the Liberal Democrat leadership in the Lords (where, naturally, he took the title 'of Hillhead') and the Chancellorship of the University of Oxford.

He also managed two other achievements. One was that, though never himself prime minister, he became close to a prime minister: Tony Blair, whom he at least seemed to convince that unity of the liberal and social democratic streams in British politics was essential if a century of largely Tory hegemony was to be replaced by one of hegemony of the left-of-centre. The second, which went with the first, was that, though never to be prime minister, he had a chance to influence the means by which all future prime ministers would be chosen. That means was the chairmanship of the Independent Commission on the Voting System, set up by Mr Blair following his 1997 victory to come up with the best alternative to Britain's first-past-the-post electoral system, to put before the British people in a referendum.

As a member of the five-strong commission, this author bears personal witness to Jenkins' performance, of which, in a career as a political adviser and observer, he has never seen the equal. His stamina, humour, patience and drive would have been extraordinary in anyone; in a man of 78, they were beyond belief. When the Commission toured Britain seeking views, Jenkins was always there: knowing better than the secretariat without consulting a timetable at what hour the train left; able to produce, for each provincial city entered a commentary on its architecture and history that most people would achieve only after a lifetime of study; lunching to the maximum of the railways' capacity, but then remaining alert chairing long meetings, forgetting no-one's name and no-one's point (however cracked). He attended every single Commission meeting, driving it on to meet its timetable of reporting inside a year. His knowledge not only of British political history but of that of the rest of Europe was encyclopaedic and brought a perspective to the Commission's work that no other chairman could conceivably have achieved.

He did one even more difficult thing. During the Commission's early work, he conceived of an elegant solution to its dilemmas based as one might expect on nineteenth-century British political history. He wanted one electoral system, the single transferable vote, for Britain's cities and another, the alternative vote in single member seats, for the country. This had intellectual attractions and intellectual drawbacks. It was however fatally flawed in that, whatever else might be said about it, it was biased against Labour in the cities, and biased against Labour in the countryside, which meant that it would have been absolutely impossible for the Labour government to embrace it. Once he was persuaded of this, Jenkins dropped it with regret but not hesitation.

Eventually, Jenkins found a compromise, 'AV plus'. AV plus preserved single-member constituencies. It made the result in them more democratic by ensuring that the winner had more than 50% of the vote. It also provided for a small number of additional members to give greater representation to parties which got fewer seats than their share of the constituency votes would merit. Lord Alexander, the Conservative on the Commission, rejected the 'AV' bit in a little note of dissent which was not, however, widely noticed. For the report itself, every word personally written by Jenkins in the Italian countryside, was generally acclaimed as a masterpiece. Perhaps the sentence which best explains this enthusiasm was that describing the defects of the Single Transferable Vote: 'Where the choice offered resembles a caricature of an over-zealous American breakfast waiter going on posing an indefinite number of unwanted options, it becomes both an exasperation and an incitement to the giving of random answers.' Jenkins' was a state paper that was a thing of beauty.

Unfortunately, that was not sufficient immediately to achieve what Jenkins hoped most to achieve: a solution, which, though not purist, by virtue of that avoided the fate of past schemes of electoral reform of mouldering, gathering dust, on history's shelves. His sharpest initial disappointment was the failure of any Conservatives to back it, despite the fact that the existing system disadvantages them against Labour. His later disappointment was that the government sat on the fence. The obstacle was that the number of constituency seats would reduce if Jenkins was adopted, and no Labour MP could be sure that it was not their seat that would go. Naturally, therefore, they were attracted by plausible though bogus arguments for the status quo.

By the year 2000, Jenkins was reported to be pessimistic as to the prospects of his scheme's success. There are those who are working hard to prove him wrong.

The conventional means of assessing the success or failure of any politician are, first, by the rank they achieved, and, secondly, by the policy legacy they left. By the first of these criteria, Jenkins got as close as you can get to the very top without making it. By the second, the scorecard is mixed. Britain is still in Europe but the relationship is not yet settled. In any case, Wilson and Callaghan with their ducking and weaving may have done more to secure that outcome than Jenkins. His very devotion was counterproductive, doing for Europe in the Labour Party in the 1970s and early 1980s what Ken Clarke was to do for Europe in the Tory Party in the 1980s and early 1990s, isolating and damaging the cause. On the other hand, his liberal record speaks for itself; he saw the country through serious though not overwhelming economic problems from 1967 to 1970; was a more successful President of the Commission than is generally recognised; and started a major party from scratch. This is not nothing.

But perhaps the criteria are wrong. After all, what looks like success from the perspective of one year, five years, ten years, may look like failure from the perspective of 25, 50, 100 or a millennium. What matters may less be what politicians do than what they are. Do they give the people a sense that they are being led by people of intelligence and moral integrity? What is their contribution not so much to the content of political life as to its tone? And are they good men?

In all these regards, the virtues of Roy Jenkins stand out.

Further reading

Jenkins' own *A Life at the Centre* (Macmillan, 1991) is long at 657 pages but not too long. His equally long *European Diary 1977–81* (London, 1989) contains rewarding nuggets and longueurs. *Gladstone* (Macmillan, 1995) is reckoned his best biography; it is so long as one is more interested in personality than in the substance of issues. *Asquith* (Collins, 1964) beats *Sir Charles Dilke: A Victorian Tragedy* (London, 1958) partly because the author's reticence about sex matters less in the case of the former than the latter. To sample his work as a miniaturist, try *The Chancellors* (Macmillan, 1998).

John Campbell's *Roy Jenkins* (Weidenfeld and Nicolson, 1983) though it stops before the election, is a fan's book, but not uncritical. Neither can be said of David Owen's *Time to Declare* (Michael Joseph, 1991), which is 165 pages longer than Jenkins' own autobiography and feels ten times as long. Ivor Crewe and Anthony King's *SDP: The Birth, Life and Death of the Social Democratic Party* (Oxford University Press, 1995) is much better value for effort. Then there are the well-canvassed autobiographies and biographies of Wilson, Callaghan, Crossman, Castle, Crosland, Benn etc etc ad infinitum; and of course, for relations with Crosland, Susan Crosland's singular masterpiece *Tony Crosland* (Jonathan Cape, 1982).

Notes

1. Roy Jenkins, *A Life at the Centre* (London, 1991), p 7.
2. Janet Morgan (ed.), *The Backbench Diaries of Richard Crossman* (London, 1981): entry for 15 February 1963, pp 978–9.
3. John Campbell, *Roy Jenkins. A Biography* (London, 1983), p 89.
4. Ibid, p 104.
5. Jenkins, *A Life at the Centre*, p 260.
6. Jenkins, *A Life at the Centre*, p 350.

7

Tony Crosland

Raymond Plant

(Charles Anthony Raven) Tony Crosland, b.1918–d.1977. Labour MP for South Gloucestershire 1950–55; Grimsby 1959–77. Minister of State, Economic Affairs 1964–65; Secretary of State for Education and Science 1965–67; President of the Board of Trade 1967–69; Secretary of State for Local Government and Regional Planning 1969–70. Secretary of State for the Environment 1974–76; Foreign Secretary 1976–77. His numerous publications included The Future of Socialism *(1956),* The Conservative Enemy *(1962) and* Socialism Now *(1974).*

Charles Anthony Raven Crosland, from the late 1960s universally known as 'Tony', was born into a comfortably-off family of Plymouth Brethren in Highgate in 1918. His father, Joseph, was a senior civil servant in the War Office who died when Crosland was 17. His mother, Jessie, taught French literature at Westfield College and became an authority on medieval French literature. After attending Highgate School and studying Politics, Philosophy and Economics at Trinity College, Oxford – a course which was interrupted by war service in the airborne branch of the Royal Welsh Fusiliers – he became the leading social democratic thinker of the second half of the twentieth century and a holder of high office in the Wilson and Callaghan Governments. He died suddenly of a stroke at the height of his powers in February 1977, having become Foreign Secretary a year earlier, when James Callaghan became Prime Minister. Few political thinkers of Crosland's stature have been able to influence politics as directly as Crosland, not just by his writings but also as a minister. So, for example, as Education Secretary he was able to preside over a more vigorous development of comprehensive education, a course of action which he had argued for in his masterpiece *The Future of Socialism*, first published in 1956.

This chapter will concentrate mainly upon Crosland as a political thinker rather than as a minister in Labour Governments. There are already studies of his ministerial career[1] and little can be added to these within the confines of a single chapter. Equally, however, his social and political thought is still relevant: partly in the context of his place in the history of social democracy and democratic socialism and partly because the emergence of New Labour since 1994 has brought into relief the relationship between Croslandite social democracy, which was firmly revisionist, and New Labour and Third Way ideas, which, it is sometimes claimed, fall into the same tradition.[2]

Nevertheless, it is important to give an account of Crosland's political career before embarking on an account and assessment of his position as a social democratic thinker. After gaining a first class degree on his return to Oxford after his war service, Crosland became the economics fellow of Trinity College, Oxford and during this period he wrote *Britain's Economic Problem*. He was, however, anxious to stand for Parliament and was elected for the South Gloucestershire seat in 1950. He retained the seat in 1951 but lost in the 1955 election having moved to what he mistakenly regarded as a more winnable seat at Southampton Test. During his period out of Parliament, before his election for Grimsby in 1959,[3] he acted as secretary of the Commission on the future of the Co-operative Movement and, more importantly, wrote his great book, *The Future of Socialism*.

During the 1950s the Labour Party was locked in disputes about ideology, policies and personalities. The two major protagonists in the debates in the early 1950s were Aneurin Bevan and Hugh Gaitskell. Bevan had the huge achievement of the establishment of the NHS to his credit but he resigned from the Government following Gaitskell's imposition of charges for teeth and spectacles in the 1951 budget – charges which, it was argued, were necessary to help fund rearmament costs incurred by the Korean war. Crosland found a good deal to admire in Bevan but during those long-running disputes gravitated towards Hugh Gaitskell and became something of a political, intellectual and emotional soul mate to him.[4] Certainly the publication of *The Future of Socialism* marked the intellectual high watermark of the revisionist/Gaitskellite position. Crosland was also very active in political support of Gaitskell, organising the Campaign for Democratic Socialism (with Bill Rogers)[5] in the aftermath of the Conference defeat in 1960 which Gaitskell sustained over unilateral nuclear disarmament. This campaign was successful and the sting was taken out of the defeat at the next party conference.

Following Gaitskell's untimely death in 1963, Crosland supported James Callaghan for the leadership. Harold Wilson, however, emerged as the victor and for a time Crosland's career as a politician failed to thrive. Following the election victory in 1964 he was nevertheless made Minister of State at the Department of Economic Affairs under George Brown, who was Secretary of State. In 1965 he became Secretary of State for Education – a post for which he was well suited since education was for him a central way of striving for a greater degree of social equality, an argument he set out in cogent detail in *The Future of Socialism*. This commitment led Crosland to issue the famous circular 10/65 which requested local education authorities to submit plans for the reorganisation of secondary education on comprehensive lines in their areas. He established a commission to look over the future of the public schools. He also announced the establishment of 30 polytechnics, which were to concentrate on vocational and industry related courses as part of a binary – separate but equal – system of higher education which he had adumbrated in a very provocative speech at Woolwich in 1965. Polytechnics were conceived as part of his strategy for equality – widening access to higher education. Critics argued that the binary system would in fact create as divisive a higher educational system as the secondary school system which Crosland's commitment to comprehensive education changed.

Crosland was made President of the Board of Trade in a reshuffle in August 1967. As an economist he was clearly fitted for the post and he saw it as a step towards the Chancellorship of the Exchequer – a post which he coveted. However, he was to be thwarted in the ambition by the appointment of his friend, but more recently rival, Roy Jenkins, following devaluation in November 1967. Callaghan as Chancellor had fought alongside Wilson to rule out devaluation during the previous three years of the Government. Crosland had, in fact, been a supporter of devaluation since the 1964 election and his influence as President of the Board of Trade appears to have been important in the taking of the final decision to devalue. Nevertheless, Crosland was not to succeed to the Chancellorship following Callaghan's resignation. Wilson clearly regarded the easiest arrangement to be to exchange posts between Callaghan and Jenkins. So Jenkins as Home Secretary was moved to the Treasury; Callaghan moved from the Chancellorship to the Home Secretaryship.

In 1970 the Government lost the election and Crosland became the Shadow Environment Minister. This was in the early days of the environmental movement and the issue was of vital importance for Crosland. As we shall see below, he regarded economic growth as a central feature of the strategy to achieve a more equal society. Many environmentalists were, however, arguing forcefully for restrictions on growth or even for zero growth.

In 1974 the Labour Party came back to power and he became Secretary of State for the Environment. During the previous two years, the issue of Europe had played a very divisive role in Labour Party politics. It was clear in 1970 that the Conservative Government under Edward Heath was keen to take Britain into the Common Market if favourable terms could be negotiated. Many on the revisionist, social democratic side of the Labour Party regarded the issue to be one of principle and on which they would vote in the affirmative. Crosland, however, was much more tentative. The important thing, he argued, was to defeat the Government. The Heath Government was still in its hard right 'Selsdon Man' mode and he argued that Labour had to be united if it was to defeat the Government and prevent it inflicting considerable social damage on British society. He argued that there was, at the time, no majority in the Labour Party for entry into the Common Market and that therefore a proposal to vote with the Government would split the Party. In fact, that is what happened. Sixty-nine Labour members led by Roy Jenkins voted with the Government; without their support, the proposal would have been lost. Crosland himself abstained, incurring accusations of cowardice. He was a pro-European but he did not regard it as the highest political priority at the time – a view for which he paid quite a heavy price in terms of the support of his fellow revisionists in the Labour Party.

Following the agreement by the Shadow Cabinet in April 1972 to propose that a future Labour Government should hold a referendum on membership of the Common Market, Roy Jenkins along with two others resigned from the Shadow Cabinet and in his case, the Deputy Leadership of the Party. Crosland stood for the post along with Ted Short and Michael Foot coming third and polling 61 votes. Ted Short was elected as Deputy Leader.

In 1976 Wilson resigned and Crosland stood for the leadership with Callaghan, Foot, Healey, Jenkins and Benn. Crosland came bottom of the poll with only 17 votes. It looked as though this was the nadir of his political career. However, the election of Callaghan whom he had supported for the leadership against Wilson and Brown in 1963 secured for him the Foreign Secretaryship. For a significant period of his tenure at the Foreign Office the dominant issue was the economic crisis and the need for an IMF loan and the terms under which such a loan might be granted. The Cabinet was divided on the issue and Crosland led one of the three dissenting groups. The main issue was the level of cuts in public expenditure required to secure the loan. Public expenditure, like growth, was essential in Crosland's view as a vehicle for greater social equality and as a social democrat/democratic socialist, he found it very difficult to support the drastic cuts proposed. He was in favour of a combination of limited cuts and an import deposit scheme. Other groups led by Benn wanted to turn down the IMF loan and move to a siege economy. Others still, such as Peter Shore, wanted selective import controls. In the end however, Crosland supported the Callaghan/Healey position largely for political reasons. He believed that the Government would fall if the Prime Minister and the Chancellor were defeated in Cabinet and the effect on sterling would be dire. He did, however, make it clear that the proposals 'were wrong economically and socially, destructive of what he had believed in all his life'.[6] Within three months he was dead.

We now need to consider Crosland's contribution to the political thought of the Labour Party and its modern salience.

In an early letter to a lifelong friend, Philip Williams, subsequently a Fellow of Nuffield College, Oxford and biographer of Hugh Gaitskell, Crosland claimed that his aim was to be a revisionist like Edward Bernstein. He certainly achieved his aim, since Bernstein and Crosland are central to the revisionist pantheon. What was it that the revisionists were supposed to be revising? The answer is Marxism and particularly the more materialist, mechanistic and determinist forms of Marxism which predated the discovery and elaboration of a more humanistic Marxism in the 1960s derived from Marx's early writings and in particular the *Economic and Philosophical Manuscripts of 1844*. Russian and German Marxists portrayed a rather different picture of Marxism from this later variety and it was the earlier form combined with Soviet political, social and economic praxis which had influenced a generation of leftist intellectuals in the 1930s when, with the post-1929 collapse and the rise of Fascism, it seemed that capitalism was in terminal decline and that Marxist socialism was the only alternative to Fascism. The Webbs, Harold Laski and John Strachey were amongst prominent intellectuals of the left who were seduced by Marxism in the 1930s. Crosland, despite being passionately interested, was not. Nevertheless, it was essential for a social democratic revisionist to have a view about the nature of Marxism since this seemed to be the most theoretically developed approach to socialism and provided the theoretical and scientific veneer of legitimacy to what was happening in the Soviet Union. So as revisionists both Crosland and Bernstein, the former's hero, sought to take the measure of Marxism and to develop a form of social democracy that would be relevant to the modern world without this being underwritten by what they took to be the pseudo-scientific approach of Marxism. Both Bernstein and Crosland defined social democracy in ethical terms – in terms of the achievement of certain basic values. This achievement was not, in Crosland's eyes, to be awaited as an inevitable outcome of an historical process but was to be a matter of political struggle and commitment. For Crosland, equality and social justice were the central values of social democracy/democratic socialism and it was the central task of a party of the left such as the Labour Party to struggle for greater social and economic equality and social justice. So we need to understand both his conception of equality and his view of the strategy for achieving greater equality in a democratic society. Before doing this however, it is important to see why Crosland rejects Marxism as providing the most authoritative version of socialist theory and practice.

Bernstein's critique in *Evolutionary Socialism* concentrated on the predictive failures of Marx's theories, which he believed had undermined the plausibility of the materialist theory of history and thus the scientific claims of Marxism. These predictions had failed in respect of Marx's claims that in the long run capitalism would lead to the immiseration of the proletariat and the polarisation of society into two classes: the capitalist and the proletarians – those who do and those who do not own the means of production. Crosland endorsed Bernstein's views on those matters but also had additional reasons for rejecting Marxism as a guide for the left in 1956: immiseration had not occurred nor had class polarisation. There were other reasons too in Crosland's view for rejecting the Marxist analysis.

Crosland argued in the early part of *The Future of Socialism*[7] that capitalism in the post-war world was fundamentally different from the economic system which Marx had confronted. This was so for a number of reasons which I shall just identify, rather than discuss in detail. Capitalism had changed first of all because ownership of the means of production had been dispersed and continues to be so – we do not confront a number of individual owners of capital who form an homogeneous class with common economic and political interests, as Marx had assumed. Indeed, the 1945 Labour Government had taken into public ownership those means of production which bore most directly on the infrastructure of the economy – coal, steel, railways, etc – a settlement which Crosland welcomed and showed no signs of wanting to change. Because of the dispersal of ownership and the common ownership of central industries, the question of *management* was now much more important than *ownership* – how to ensure that the management of private industry with a dispersed ownership could become more socially responsible and incorporate some sense of the public interest. This was much more important in this context than further acts of nationalisation.

Secondly, greater democratisation in British society had put severe constraints on the power of private ownership in the modern economy. Not only did dispersed ownership mean that there was no capitalist class with a common interest, but the growth of democracy (again a change from Marx's time) was a major countervailing power to the interests of private owners. This was backed up with the view that trades unions now had a central role in politics and economics and again acted as a strong countervailing role in society to that of private owners.

Thirdly, Keynesian economic techniques meant that government was able to manage the general macroeconomic climate within which firms operated and the idea that capitalists (even assuming that we were still in a situation of non-dispersed ownership) could pursue an economic agenda which did not take account of government managed macroeconomic conditions was false. Keynesian economic management implied, to a degree, the relative autonomy of politics, in that it could no longer be seen as an arena of class interest; governments, using Keynesian techniques, could pursue macroeconomic policies that would serve its view of the public interest, and which would in turn be shaped by its political values.

Finally, the growth of the welfare state and welfare rights after the reforms of the 1945 Labour Government, meant that in terms of health, education and welfare, citizens were no longer subject to the vagaries of the market but had a stake in society mediated not only by non-capitalist institutions but also based on the principle of recognising need, a profoundly anti-capitalist notion.

All of these meant that for Crosland, we were no longer living in the kind of capitalism which Marx had confronted. This allowed socialism to be seen in value terms because capitalism had been reshaped by the economic and political forces outlined above, and Marx's critique of the politics of social democracy looked threadbare in the light of this. Political action in the pursuit of values could reshape society. Politics was not just an *epi phenomenon* of economic interests. Nevertheless, Crosland did want to be seen as a revisionist, updating the idea of what a just society might mean and how it might be achieved. At the time that he was writing, and particularly later in the 1960s, the main challenge to the coherence of the social democratic project seemed to come from a revitalised form of humanistic Marxism identified with the New Left rather than a reassertion of classical liberalism (which Crosland, no doubt, would have regarded as having been consigned to the lumber room of history). This is not because political opponents on the right would have been happy to be described as social democrats, but they were certainly not at that time in possession of an alternative paradigm of politics and economics. Indeed, those vestiges of updated classical liberalism – for example the writings of Hayek and Friedman and the assiduous pamphlet-writing going on at the Institute of Economic Affairs – just seemed eccentric. So in mid-century it did look as though the social democrats had perhaps the most coherent political and economic paradigm. It was not really effectively challenged on the left, whether 'Old' or 'New', from a Marxist perspective, for the reasons Crosland gave and the potential for revitalised neo-liberalism looked minimal. Yet it is precisely the challenge of rampant economic liberalism that social democracy of the Croslandite sort has had to face since his death.

One of the central consequences of Crosland's writing was a tendency for social democrats to draw a much clearer distinction between ends and means[8] in social democratic and socialist thought. Because Marxist thinkers held that the possession of economic power was determinative of political capacity, it followed for them that common ownership, state ownership, nationalisation of the means of production, were essential and necessary features of a socialist society. They were therefore to be seen as constitutive of the socialist project. For Crosland, however, the goal was greater social equality and social justice. It followed from this that nationalisation was to be assessed empirically as a means – whether or not it would be likely to advance the cause of greater social equality. As he argues in *The Future of Socialism*:

> It… means that the ownership of the means of production… is no longer the *essential* determinant of the distribution of income: private ownership is compatible with a high degree of equality, while state ownership, as the Russian experience has demonstrated, may be used to support a high degree of inequality.[9]

This distinction between ends and means became a central feature of revisionist debates in the late 1950s and indeed has re-emerged in debates about New Labour's rewriting of Clause IV.

In his last book, *Socialism Now*, Crosland described his own view of equality as being more or less the same as that developed with great philosophical force by John Rawls in *A Theory of Justice*. It seems clear from unpublished correspondence with Professor I.D.M. Little concerning the proofs of *Socialism Now* that Crosland had read Rawls's book and he took from Rawls the phrase 'democratic equality' to describe the nature of his own commitment, as set out nearly 20 years previously, in *The Future of Socialism*. Crosland's view of equality, like Rawls's democratic equality, lies on a spectrum between equality of opportunity and equality of outcome. While Crosland recognises and welcomes the gains which greater equality of opportunity has secured, he makes it clear that he does not think that it is a sufficiently rich conception of equality for a recognisably social democratic commitment. It is not, in his own words, 'enough'.

It is not enough for two main reasons, both of which he shares with Rawls. First of all, equality of opportunity does not pay sufficient attention to starting points and unequal endowments. Family background and genetic legacy make an enormous difference to starting-points and are morally arbitrary, in that those who benefit from a regime of equal opportunity will be those with fortunate backgrounds and genetic endowments, but an individual bears little or no responsibility for these. Thus a regime of equal opportunity alone may be unjust in its outcomes, since it will offer greater rewards to people who bear little personal responsibility for their success. In Crosland's view, there is certainly a case for income inequality and those positions which carry differential rewards should be subject to the fairest competition under equality of opportunity, but two conditions are important. The first is that differential rewards should not be seen as a matter of personal desert for the reason given above – namely that those who are successful in the competition can bear only small personal responsibility for their position at the starting gate (which is influenced by family, environmental and genetic factors that successful individuals cannot claim credit for). This undermines the idea that what income inequality there should be is to be justified by desert. It is rather to be justified by the rent of ability criterion – that higher rewards will motivate and mobilise people with talent to use their talents to the benefit of the community as a whole. In this sense, Crosland's view of equality of opportunity is close to Rawls's 'difference' principle. The second point, which is closer to social policy and bears on Crosland's commitment to comprehensive education, is that we have to be concerned with starting points and use education to compensate, so far as possible, for negative features in family and environmental background, so that the starting point in the competition for differentially high rewards is fairer.

On this point, he argues as follows in *The Future of Socialism* as part of his critique of equality of opportunity and meritocracy:

> Why should this one trait [intelligence] or even a group of traits, alone determine success or failure, riches or poverty, a high or low prestige? Why should marks be given for saintliness, generosity, compassion, humour, beauty, assiduity, continence or artistic ability? These questions denote no anti intellectual bias... It is the injustice of isolating as a basis for extreme inequality, certain selected ones out of the multiple strands that go to make up the human personality.[10]

He recognises of course that it is economic efficiency which selects intelligence as the important personality trait but he rejects the view that the selection of an elite of ability has to imply the degree of inequality which he sees in British society.

In addition, equality of opportunity concentrates upon and rewards only a small number of human attributes – those which are of most economic value. In Crosland's view society depends upon a very wide range of human qualities most of which would be neglected in a meritocratic/equality of opportunity society. From these points, it should he obvious that Crosland is also a critic of strict equality of outcome. Everyone benefits from a system in which talent is mobilised for the public good, and if talent will only be mobilised by differences in income, then it is rational to do that. The point however, to reiterate it again, is that such rewards are not based upon the principle of deserts but on the principle of rent of ability.

So Crosland has a commitment to democratic equality. The important political question is how far is its pursuit a viable political project. This issue poses particular problems for an egalitarian, in that it may well be that, by and large, people's preferences are not of an egalitarian kind (or not sufficiently so to support a direct egalitarian strategy). To put the point crudely, how, in a democratic society, does an egalitarian get people to vote for the degree of taxation necessary to pay for those forms of public provision which will compensate for the effects of poverty, poor schooling and limited health provision and which, taken together, would compensate for inequality of starting-point? One approach would be to argue that one needs to convince the better-off to pay more tax by changing their values. That is to say, an egalitarian strategy can only be pursued by creating egalitarian citizens – what might be called a bottom-up strategy. The alternative is to look for a more indirect strategy, which might create a more egalitarian outcome without having to create shared egalitarian values. Crosland opts for the second course. Before going on to say something about this, it is perhaps worth alluding to an important distinction between 'moral' and 'mechanical' reformers in politics, a distinction that the historian Peter Clarke propounded in his seminal work *Liberals and Social Democrats*. Moral reformers are essentially bottom-up reformers. Values can only be effective in politics when they are widely shared, and the task of the moral reformer is to take the long view and try to transform the values by which people live in the direction that he/she wants to see. The mechanical reformer is a top-down reformer, who believes that there might be political, social and economic strategies available which would produce the desired results, without necessarily having to transform the underlying moral culture of citizens. As I shall try to show below, in Clarke's sense, Crosland is a mechanical reformer. The cost of mechanical reform though can be very high and, I would argue, the Croslandite position has borne this cost. If one attempts to pursue a political strategy that does not draw deeply on values held by the population at large, it may well collapse very quickly once it is challenged by a belief system which is more confident about its salience to the values of the society in which the reform is sought. It is really quite amazing that a political settlement so influenced by social democracy could have collapsed as quickly and as comprehensively as it did after 1979, and one of the explanations of this may well be that it was a form of mechanical or indirect politics. In so far as a Croslandite strategy assumed that one could produce a social democratic society shaped by egalitarian outcomes of his preferred sort, without creating a more social democratic and egalitarian culture, this rapid demise may well be partly explained by the fact that it was a mechanical rather than a moral reform which actually was anchored in only a rather shallow way in the culture of society, and one whose general weakness was exposed by a neo-liberalism confident and direct about its moral force.

The role of public expenditure on health, education, social security and welfare was central to Crosland's egalitarian strategy. This was partly due to his conception of equality, which meant that the state had a role in compensating for unmerited and undeserved social disadvantage, though he eschewed expounding an explicit strategy for redistributing income. This was, I think, for a number of reasons: direct redistribution would actually have limited effects, in the sense that the amount to be redistributed, given the levels of taxation which might be acceptable, would make only a limited difference to the worst-off and that it would not tackle family-cultural disadvantage, which could only be addressed through state-provided services (particularly in education). In addition, while public provision would differentially help the worst-off, it was nevertheless something in which all might share and would make the more egalitarian effects of public expenditure more acceptable than direct redistribution. Finally, and this takes us back to the issue of mechanical reform, direct redistribution through the tax system, which would require an explicit appeal to citizens to make substantial numbers of themselves worse off, would raise the question of the general salience of egalitarian values. High levels of public expenditure to finance high quality public provision in which all could share and most would, was therefore central to Crosland's egalitarianism. This was, in his view, to be financed by economic growth. Economic growth allows indirect levelling up rather than levelling down – a point which he is perhaps most explicit about in his Fabian pamphlet *Social Democracy In Europe*. Here he argues that

growth will produce a fiscal dividend for government to invest in public
services which will have an egalitarian effect (at least in terms of social if
not income equality) and will allow the absolute position of the better-
off to be sustained while incrementally improving the relative position
of the worst-off. Economic growth and its fiscal dividend for public
provision were therefore critical for Crosland's indirect or mechanical
strategy. It meant that the absolute position of the better-off would not
have to be challenged directly through redistributive taxation but would
allow an incremental advance in social equality by improving the relative
position of the worst-off. Thus greater social equality could be produced
by Keynesian economic techniques to produce incremental growth that
would avoid a direct challenge to substantial numbers of citizens who
may not share egalitarian values but who would also benefit from
increased public provision.

Despite surface similarities his conception of democratic equality was
quite different from a New Right or economic liberal perspective. The
economic liberal is not interested in relative positions or the gap between
rich and poor, which were vital for Crosland. For the New Right what
matters to the poor is whether they are better off this year than last – ie
their absolute position not their position relative to the better-off. The
New Right strategy is in fact exactly the opposite of Crosland's. They
believe that the trickle-down effect of the economic market will improve
the absolute position of the worst-off while improving the relative
position of the better-off. For Crosland as a democratic egalitarian,
economic growth and its fiscal dividends invested in public services would
improve the relative position of the worst-off while maintaining the
standard of living of the better-off.

In some ways this is the current unresolved dilemma in modern forms
of social democracy. Contemporary social democratic revisionism seems
to suggest that the relative position of rich and poor cannot and perhaps
should not be a direct aim of policy in a global economy. What matters
is improving the absolute position of the poor, but not as the neo-liberal
would suggest just by the trickle-down effect but also by means of income
guarantees, the minimum wage and improving levels of skill. On this
view the main problem of the Croslandite approach is the relevance of
its emphasis on relative positions in a global competitive economy – a
situation Crosland did not face.

The other problematic aspect of the Croslandite approach has been
focused upon the claimed egalitarian effects of investment in public
services as a central part of the strategy for equality. Here there are two
difficulties which have come much more into focus since Crosland's
death. The first is the use made of public services and the ability of the

middle classes to secure differential advantages for the operation of these services. This is for example the central theme of Julian Le Grand's *Strategy for Equality*, which focuses on these differential effects. Secondly, there is the extent to which the social democratic state as part of a strategy for equality has developed many centralised bureaucracies which are not sufficiently sensitive to the needs of the consumers of services and are not sufficiently flexible to respond to changing needs and circumstances. There are hints in Crosland's writings that he did recognise some of these things but they are never really developed or responded to as an important challenge to his own views.

Some of the issues at stake in understanding the relationship between Crosland's version of revisionism and New Labour as a form of contemporary revisionism remain to be worked out as New Labour develops. For those of a Croslandite persuasion, the more recent evolution of New Labour has been perhaps more reassuring than its earlier forms, both in opposition from 1994 and during the first Blair government. There is now an emphasis upon the importance of public services, if not as an instrument of creating greater social equality, at least in terms of enhancing the quality of life. No doubt the fundamental reform in the management and delivery of public services was probably not part of Crosland's agenda but equally, so long as this initiative stops short of the privatisation and marketisation of the public sector, there is nothing anti-Croslandite about it. Equally, the vast new investment in public services which has so far been financed by economic growth and buoyant tax revenues resulting from that can also be seen as being equally within the revisionist position. Had the Blair Government been less social democratic and more economically liberal as many of its critics claim, then it would have wanted to put more money than it has into tax cuts and resources for private consumption. It has not done this for strong social democratic reasons. Equally, it might be said that there have been hints from the government that taxation might well rise later in the parliament to sustain investment in public services rather than cutting back on that investment if existing revenue streams could not pay for this. Again, this fits with the general thrust of Croslandite social democracy.

Of course, in many respects the infrastructure of social democracy has changed. Crosland was able to pursue his vision for social democracy in a Keynesian context and in an economic context less exposed to the consequences of global competition. New Labour has had to develop a set of instruments to deliver its vision. In so far as the vision may differ from the Croslandite one, perhaps the crucial issue remains equality. As I have argued, Crosland had a complex and subtle view of equality which goes beyond equality of opportunity while falling short of equality of outcome. It did, however, as I have suggested, lay stress upon the relative position of the worst-off. It may well be the case that many of the government's policies in relation to the minimum wage, Working Families Tax Credit and various income guarantees will indirectly improve the relative position of the worst-off. It is, however, quite doubtful that the relative position will be improved without higher direct taxes on higher levels of income. The absolute position of the poor may improve; the relative position may not. This is where the greatest potential cleavage between Croslandite revisionism and New Labour may come.

Tony Crosland still remains a major figure in Labour politics in the last century. Many politicians during his lifetime made more direct impact in speeches and policymaking; nevertheless, *The Future of Socialism* is likely still to be read when many of these other figures have been forgotten.

Further reading

Crosland was the author of four substantial books. His masterwork and certainly the most influential was *The Future of Socialism*, published in 1956. *Britain's Economic Problem* was published in 1953; *The Conservative Enemy* (a collection of essays, many of which were published elsewhere) in 1962; and *Socialism Now*, edited by his friend Dick Leonard containing essays and speeches, published in 1974.

Susan Crosland is the author of a penetrating and moving biography, *Tony Crosland*, published in 1982. Kevin Jefferys, *Anthony Crosland: A New Biography*, is the most thorough study of Crosland's career as a thinker and a minister, and was published in 1999. After Crosland's death, two volumes of essays were published: one in 1981, *The Socialist Agenda: Crosland's Legacy*, edited by Dick Leonard and David Lipsey; and *Crosland and New Labour*, edited by Michael Jacobs and published in 1998. Geoffrey Foote's *The Labour Party's Political Thought: A History*, 1997, and Nick Ellison, *Egalitarian Thought and Labour Politics: Retreating Visions*, 1994, provide focused academic studies on aspects of Crosland's thought and the role of revisionism more generally within the Labour party.

Notes

1. See Kevin Jefferys' excellent biography, *Anthony Crosland* (London, 1999).
2. On this issue see D. Leonard and M. Jacobs (eds), *Crosland and New Labour* (London, 1998).
3. Crosland had a close shave in his first election in Grimsby, scraping home by 101 votes against 'Wink' Pearson. The present author remembers as a school boy in Grimsby's docklands marching with a group of others singing:

> Old Pearson sells fish
> At three ha'pence a dish
> Don't buy it, don't buy it
> It stinks when you fry it

Not very elevated sentiments, but it did show an interesting degree of involvement of working-class youngsters in elections at that time.

4. For further elaboration on this see Jefferys, op. cit., Chapter 9, 'Mr Gaitskell's Ganymede'.
5. Subsequently Labour MP for Stockton on Tees. A founder member of the SDP, see his autobiography, *Fourth Amongst Equals* (London, 1999).
6. Tony Benn, *Diary*, 2 December 1976, p 674.
7. See Chapter 2.
8. C.A.R. Crosland, *The Future of Socialism*, abridged edition, (London, 1963), p 64.
9. Ibid, p 51.
10. Ibid, p 168. For the connection with Rawls, see R. Plant, 'Democratic Socialism and Equality', in D. Lipsey and Dick Leonard (eds), *The Socialist Agenda: Crosland's Legacy* (London, 1981).

8

Denis Healey

Edward Pearce

Denis Healey, later Baron Healey of Riddlesden, b.1917. Secretary of the Labour Party's International Department 1945–52. MP for South East Leeds 1952–55; MP for Leeds East 1955–92. Secretary of State for Defence 1964– 70. Chancellor of the Exchequer 1974–79. Deputy Leader of the Labour Party 1980–83. Life peer 1992.

Denis Healey was praised at the end of his time at Defence by Air Chief Marshal Elworthy for having transformed the NATO stand from trip-wire to limited strategy. It was, he said, a case of Healey's intellect and MacNamara's muscle. He would be described by Admiral Hill-Norton as 'beyond question the ablest Secretary of State for Defence since the war'.[1] Both men, who each served as Chief of the Defence Staff, had worked closely with him. Edmund Dell, his deputy for two years at the Treasury, a man with Cordelia's inclination to flattery, wrote of Healey's handling of the financial crisis of the last four months of 1976, that with his back to the wall, he showed the qualities of a lion.

Roy Hattersley, a cabinet and shadow cabinet colleague across 11 years and, before that, his deputy at the Ministry of Defence, speaks of 'the bliss of working for somebody who had the subject absolutely at their fingertips, who knew what he wanted and pursued his own concept of defence policy with a degree of critical rigour which I have never seen from anyone else'.[2]

But Healey would be denied his party's leadership in favour of Michael

Foot, a man shuffling, mannered, inexpert, prejudiced, fluently incoherent and intellectually shabby, genteel and uniquely unfitted to lead anything. The answer may lie in the index to Dell's brilliant if imperious account of that economic crisis, *A Hard Pounding*. 'Healey, Denis' it reads, then, among a dozen citations, 'saves government and ejected from NEC'! So he did, so he was. In that year Healey saw the country painfully through the second great British economic crisis of the century and the visitation of the IMF, pushing himself to a point of personal exhaustion. And in the middle of it he was dropped at conference from the party's governing body.

To risk a paradox, Healey might be called 'a brilliant workhorse'. He was fond of something said in a Party cell meeting in his Oxford Communist days. 'Who under socialism,' asked an earnest comrade, 'will do the dirty jobs?' To which someone replied 'Denis Healey'. Work, long and laborious, not dirty but unpopular provokes the commonest expression in the latter pages of his unpublished diary. 'Dead tired', sometimes varied by 'appallingly tired', and 'Out on my feet' are the refrain.

Healey was a man for flinging himself into whatever task or dispute awaited. Having been a Communist in the idealistic, absolutist spirit of so many decent and gifted young people in the 1930s (and enduring a quantity of foolish-paranoid muttering subsequently), he became the most dedicated anti-Communist after the war. This was not the result of a mercurial or erratic temperament, though he could be the most vivid and hilarious company. Ministerially he would trek through problems in pursuit of an answer, win furiously unpopular cuts, make sense of chaotic defences, sweat through supposed (and false) totals of debts. They were great burdens and he carried them, slogging his way through. The young man's sympathy for Communism had included a speech at Labour Conference in 1945, which applauded the socialist revolutions taking place in Eastern Europe. The post he took up at the turn of that year, International Officer of the Labour Party, took him from 1946 to 1949 where very few people thinking well or ill of sovietised regimes in the East *could* go – to Hungary, Romania, Poland and Czechoslovakia. He was shifted by the experience from a high plane of theoretical hope into the world where people like Zdenek Fierlinger sold the Czechoslovak Socialist Party into Soviet control, where the leader of the majority (and non-Communist) party in that country was whisked off the street and not seen again.[3] The douche of reality was applied full in the face instead of being slowly learned from printed sources. Healey became not just against communism in the way that Roy Jenkins or Tony Crosland were against it, but an expert and devoted enemy.

He was something else. At Transport House he was the servant of

Ernest Bevin before anything else. It was Healey who when Bevin was under fire from the Left – 'What are we to do about Mr Bevin?' asked Kingsley Martin in a *New Statesman* editorial concerned at his lack of balance between camps – wrote the cool but fierce, and very lucid, pamphlet *Cards on the Table*. It gave all sorts of offence but put an unanswerable case. And as naïve pro-Soviet sympathies retreated inside the Labour Party, after the Prague *putsch* of March 1948 had validated Bevin's stark early judgement, expounded by Healey, it stood as a record of getting things right. Healey was never easily awed and coming from active service was even less so. But for him Bevin was the great man, someone he cared for, admired and followed, as he did no one else.

The subject coloured his relationship to Hugh Gaitskell. He was nearer in outlook on foreign affairs to Gaitskell than either Crosland or Jenkins, though both were nearer to Gaitskell, the man. This is another paradox. Gaitskellism, so far from being desiccated or calculating, was an intense affair, full of fierce, electric friendships, devoted and slightly Arthurian. But the closest friends were not technically expert – apart from Patrick Gordon Walker's Foreign Affairs expertise – in the fields affecting Gaitskell's impassioned anti-Soviet beliefs. But Healey, who was, stood several paces back from the inner circle.

After his election at the Leeds by-election of 1952, Healey brought to politics both a direct personal knowledge of Eastern Europe, to parallel the 1934 acquaintance with counter-revolutionary Austria which had charged Gaitskell politically, and a growing, intensely pursued, understanding of defence, *matériel* and strategic. But he only had one hero, Ernest Bevin. He is best seen as a trusted consultant to Gaitskell, someone in coincidental agreement with the Gaitskellite general view of the world situation, who fought his corner when the left of the party disputed it, but who was not quite of the blood royal. He was wholly a Labour Party man, not a Gaitskellite first. The differences of 1981, between leaving Labour to form a new party and staying to save it, were minutely present very early.

He had been a soldier, present at the Calabrian and the Anzio landing and had engaged as a transport officer during the Italian campaign in the practicalities of docking Liberty ships at Bari or Augusta and getting them and their contents up to places like Ancona. The soldier side of Healey is important psychologically and never left him. But married with his East European experiences, it turned him easily and naturally to detailed and expert study of defence, not paralleled by anyone in Labour politics except the cranky and corridor-creeping George Wigg. Healey, the Royal Engineer, had been sufficiently rated in the Army as a logistics specialist to have been invited to write the whole section on transport in the official history of the Italian campaign. And a good deal of work was done on this before the International job for Labour materialised. Otherwise he would have spent several years in an Austrian *schloss* with the rank of Lieutenant Colonel, writing history. The fantasy of a subsequent military career, General Sir Denis Healey making expert difficulties for future Defence Secretaries, has its charms.

His early line on defence could hardly have been harder, stemming as it did from the arenas of democratic Czech and Hungarian socialist parties in the process of suffering conquest. He is to be found in 1951 debating with John Freeman, a resigner with Bevan and Wilson in 1951, but an essentially moderate man, and talking very darkly – about how the Korean War was a pitch by Stalin, miscalculated, but part of a general aggrandising will to probe and break through, which must be resisted by clearly adverted readiness for full scale resistance and retaliation.[4]

This was said in rebuttal of Freeman who thought involvement in the Korean War right but also successful and unlikely to be risked again by the Soviets elsewhere. Since Stalin died in March 1953, we can hardly judge who was right. But Healey's thinking at this stage was highly alerted and more American than British. Even his passing reference to General MacArthur was not unfriendly.

Since the real division in the Labour Party concerned defence and specifically, nuclear defence against the Soviet Union, Healey was set on a pre-ordained political course as an indispensable technician with the hardest line credentials. That (and his great ability and capacity for work) raised him to the side of the leaders by express promotion. In those days there was no proliferation in parliament of second and third line posts entitling bagmen to call themselves frontbenchers, but Healey was both in full leadership confidence and speaking *from* the front bench very early indeed. And after Gaitskell's accession in 1955, he was a close counsellor preferred to many in the Shadow Cabinet. During the Suez debates he speaks of himself as 'a mere backbencher', modesty of an implausible and half-humorous kind, though he did not formally enter the Shadow Cabinet until 1959, a seven year wait, itself extraordinarily little in those days, especially in the democratic (and grudging) Labour Party. Healey was a technocrat before the term was coined.

But his very first speech in the Commons was a demonstration of his status. It was the time of that footnote or unbuilt cathedral, the EDC (European Defence Community). This had been devised, with Eisenhower's blessing, as a way of persuading fractious France to tolerate German rearmament at a time when the idea of letting the Germans into NATO with their own generals commanding was thought too tricky for the hellishly divided and baroque French politics of the day.

Healey made his maiden speech in May 1952, showing the quality Hattersley described of 'having the subject absolutely at his fingertips'. He had made his mind up, consonant with his concern to resist the Soviet Union, in emphatic favour of bringing Germany into the ring – he talked of 12 German divisions. But as a mechanism, he said, the EDC was not going to work, chiefly because the French, for whom it had been designed, with national commands moved sideways, were less pleased to have their troops run by somebody else's generals than the Germans. (In its highly wrought impossibility, the EDC was an ancestor of the multilateral manning notion of the early sixties which Healey, the Minister, helped knock on the head.) Thus, he said, there was only one thing to do, bite the bullet and bring Germany into NATO as a full dress partner under her own commanders. He also paid the Germans the compliment of calling them a great nation, not something easily said seven years after Luneberg Heath, something impossible to Margaret Thatcher to this day.

It was a fine logical speech, getting to a thought-out point without flannel. But what was most notable was the style of address. Speaking for the government that afternoon was Anthony Eden at almost the high point of his career, a star, a first-class diplomat, everybody's idea of a Foreign Secretary and someone between whom and Labour people there was good feeling. Healey said that, as he made his uncompromising proposals, he had noticed the Foreign Secretary purse his lips – as well he might. The French would be very stroppy, but he had every faith in Eden's ability to manage matters. It was affable effrontery, a civil conversation between equals in which the new member assured a Foreign Secretary in that office for the third time in 16 years, that he enjoyed the maiden speaker's full confidence.

And of course, Healey was right. The French Assembly, close to collective nervous breakdown, would throw the EDC out, and Germany would in due course come into NATO. Though what neither Healey nor anyone foresaw was how little of a military nation, how laggard, pacific and ill-disposed even to the forms of war, Germany, West or united, would agreeably be – less Von Moltke than young Werther.

On sitting down, he was complimented by no less a person than the soldier, diplomat and writer, Fitzroy MacLean, at that time a Conservative MP, who remarked that it was interesting to hear direct someone he had grown used to getting at second hand. Healey, the Transport *apparatchik*, had been a busy speechwriter for Bevin, his inept successor Herbert Morrison and others. Actually, Conservative MPs had done more than hear him vicariously, they had spent a day in 1951 denouncing him anonymously across ten fences. Healey, who would always have mixed

(and fluctuating) views about Europe, had written a pamphlet in response
to the Schuman Plan, that ur-root of the European Union. Called
'European Unity', its sub-title might have been 'Better Not'. The
pamphlet caught Healey in one of his downswings on the subject – he
was always *amo et dubito* – it expressed some particularist socialist
arguments – we could never share in the economy of quasi-capitalist
states – plus doubts that the thing would work. His views were close to
those of the Foreign Office, then as much a heckler of Europe as it would
later become a pom-pom girl, where Sir Roger Makins responded to M.
Schuman and M. Monnet with the immortal comment: 'The French
have got themselves into a hole and we shall have to get them out of it.'

But the Healey pamphlet without by-line, not read by Attlee or the
NEC and made much rougher by the virulently German-hating Hugh
Dalton, hit the market in a phase of Conservative enthusiasm for Europe.
They had just been at Strasbourg, Winston Churchill was going through
one of *his* phases so they had a day out denouncing this socialist
isolationism. John Maclay, David Eccles and Eden himself, also in brief
respite from permanent doubts, all had fun, Eden making a playful, good-
humoured speech, pleasant to read, at the expense of such excess.

But Healey the pamphlet writer had a reputation made before
parliament was contemplated, serious research, non-froth stuff: two
papers on Europe, two on Soviet power. He would follow *Cards on the
Table* with *The Curtain Falls,* a dark affair, drawing in Czech, Hungarian
and Polish contributions and belonging in the company of the Koestler/
Kravchenko literature of ardent disillusionment.

Healey is insistent that for him parliament was almost a chance thing.
He had sought no other seat for the elections for 1950 or 1951, had
faced logistical problems with a chair in prospect at Aberystwyth and
bureaucratic ones over the foreign editorship of the *Daily Herald.* While
it is difficult to think of anyone who enjoyed politics so much as Healey
and who would turn down both challenging and succulently remunerated
posts, NATO, the IMF and GEC, at the other end of his career, he was
different from the normal healthily ambitious politician. No one can
live without trimming, it is standard healthy politics, but Healey had
little aptitude for that and less still for the vaporous noise-making of the
pure party politician. His honesty, and he was a profoundly honest man,
was intellectual. The claim made in his memoirs that 'I want to do not
to be' should be seen as simple truth.

But he was also a fighter and the Labour Party of the 1950s afforded
more chances of fighting than doing and he thoroughly enjoyed them.
But he first made something like a national name, and first showed the
rough unacademic side of his nature, in the great Suez conflict of 1956.

Hugh Gaitskell had handled the first day's debate, 2 August, both too circumspectly and too vividly, using overblown language about President Nasser, which contradicted his strong commitments to legal proceeding. It was Healey, and interestingly Douglas Jay, who edged him into a firmer stand, spelling out what would become Labour doctrine in a joint letter to *The Times*. And when the explosion came in October, with Gaitskell outraged by Eden's distressed duplicity, Healey leapt in and asked the key questions, caught Eden misleading the House and memorably enquired of the Speaker 'could [he] please tell me what is the Parliamentary expression which comes closest to expressing the meaning of the word "liar"?' It brought out a combination of intellectual grasp and furious commitment, the politics of commitment, spilt 1930s and something which would always be there in him across unilateralism, defence and most certainly through the great struggles over IMF and after. Healey was two sorts of speaker. Lucid cerebration came easily enough, but so did words used sardonically, wittily and also angrily, words above the droning substitutable parliamentary norm. 'Who is the Mephistopheles behind this shabby Faust?', 'Out of their tiny Chinese minds' and 'Can I get it into your heads Comrades, that Mr Khrushchev is not the George Lansbury type?'

It hasn't been said yet, but should be now, that a key aspect of Healey is his intense literacy. At 16, he wrote a 4,000-word exposition of the artistic theories of Heinrich Woelfflin and another on those of F.R. Leavis. His reading at Bradford Grammar, which he listed, was vast and international. The diaries are full through a lifetime with 'bought books' and 'bought records'. This is the famous Healey hinterland. Other politicians have had it, Gladstone, Asquith, Churchill, Butler, indeed Michael Foot, but it grows rarer. The high-IQ philistinism of Harold Wilson, the re-reading of Frederick Forsyth adventures by Margaret Thatcher and the near blank of Mr Blair being more the style.

But the instinct, which took Healey into any half-decent art gallery in any city he visited for 24 hours, was matched by a passion for travel, for converse with other minds, for the discussion of ideas. David Lodge has compared the modern academic conference with the medieval pilgrimage, part specific purpose, but also broadening of minds and new encounters with people. From Koenigswinter to Bilderberg by way of scores of seminars on defence, foreign affairs and related matters, Healey was, if not assured of heaven, a passionate pilgrim. Given narrower interests among colleagues, the visits attracted comment, often resentful. But through them he had better contacts – in Germany, the United States, Italy, even in later, thawing days, in the Soviet Union, than any British politician of his generation or the next.

It was typical that when the Russians, at the most hopeful period of the late-1950s, began to drop hints about demilitarisation in central Europe allowing latitude to the Polish Foreign Minister, Adam Rapacki, to float such a plan, that Healey was quickly onto it, drafting a variant called the Gaitskell Plan which, until hostile events took over, ran as serious thinking on the diplomatic scene.

There was an irony in Healey's surprising caution over integration in Europe, since he knew more about European countries and personally knew more of their politicians, Brandt, Schmidt, Nenni, Saragat and a multitude more, had read their literature and embodied a perfect opposite of King George V's sullen 'I hate abroad.' The doubts came from several angles, disbelief in federal structures as such, distrust of the old upper classes of at any rate southern Europe and the possibility of honest municipal government south of the olive line. But they had nothing in common with the huddled, union jack keening of people like Peter Shore or the Tory Eurosceptics. And he turned passionately on the German-baiting which crept into the great CND debate at Scarborough in 1960. In a wonderful five-minute speech, as memorable in its way as Gaitskell's 'Fight, fight and fight again' triumph of the same afternoon, he pointed to Fritz Erler, fraternal delegate of the SDP and long-term prisoner of the Nazis, saying that he would respect, but not accept, criticism of Germany from someone who had endured as much.

But the Campaign for Nuclear Disarmament struggle was a central event for Healey. The crisis was really rooted in the collapse of credibility of Britain's independent deterrent. Casual accounts of this crisis ignore how irrational Hugh Gaitskell became early in 1960, talking wildly of retreating to the backbenches with a hundred or even ten loyal supporters. Gaitskell filled Patrick Gordon Walker, his immediate adviser, with despair at what he called a self-destructive urge. It was left to George Brown to get Labour off a dreadful hook by disowning in parliament independent ownership of a deterrent, doing this during Gaitskell's absence abroad, presenting his leader with a *fait accompli*. But this was the year of CND's breakthrough and what now became the issue was Britain's engagement in an alliance holding nuclear weapons.

Healey had a double function; he spoke with force, supporting Gaitskell, now defending the defensible at the conference. But partly because of his excellent American contacts, he had seen coming a deal like the one to be reached at Nassau. He understood that this, the Polaris deal, had to be endorsed by Labour, both for credible defence purposes and electoral reasons. Now a member of the NEC, he subsequently juggled with words in a candidly Machiavellian fashion as Labour set about drafting a defence policy with which to face the next conference and the settling of its position. He is to be found outfoxing Barbara Castle with a nice disposition of auxiliary verbs, 'should' for 'must' providing a handy ambiguity for accepting delivery systems when the time came.

It was a defence of Labour in government from Labour in opposition, a problem running through the party's life. The Labour left came and went historically, hitting high points in 1952, 1960 and 1980 with painful lead-ups to those peaks. All three occurred in opposition, two of them just after a fall from office. But even before entering Parliament in 1952, the year of the dreadful Morecambe conference and the left-wing surge onto the NEC, Healey had been the left's reliable enemy. He it was who, back in the 1940s, wrote the document circulated to local parties rebuking the statement advocating the so-called Third Force position (not to be confused with Third Way), one neutral between Stalin and Truman. This paper, drawn up probably by Richard Crossman and signed by the young James Callaghan, was known as the Spelthorne Memorandum and Healey took it apart. He had also suggested expulsion for signers of the Nenni telegram supporting in an election the then pro-Communist faction of the Italian Socialist Party. It produced a mass flight of dabbling signatories.

So when issues like nuclear disarmament came up, Healey was to be heavily in the action. There was nothing extreme or paranoid about his position. He had seen Stalinism close up and would take neither non-sense nor risks. When he could have taken career-friendly refuge as a technician, he was happy to be seen as the least flinching of Labour leaders. And Labour was supremely a party of factions. To read the diaries of Crossman, Castle and Benn and the writings of Jenkins and Rodgers is to recognise that for the most ardent, faction membership came above residual feelings for the party. But ultimately, Healey, the candid putter of his view and happy fighter, would put his last best efforts into saving the party as a whole.

But for a period during Healey's first period in office, the conflicts were out of sight, if only hibernating and ready to rise like the Kraken. But having saved the Polaris option – though he had early mistaken anxieties about costs – he was able in office as Secretary for Defence coolly to endorse the order with a small reduction. One does not readily link the name Denis Healey with diplomacy, but his draughtsmanship in opposition had given the Wilson government a smooth run into orthodox NATO defence, able to say that it was involved with a NATO deterrent rather than owning a British one, a delicate adaptation of Macmillan's cleverness in obtaining Polaris from Kennedy at Nassau.

This would not be his pre-occupation at the office. That came from the continuation of something developing across party lines since military weaknesses and destructive rivalries had been exposed in 1956 by Suez. Through three Ministers, the lowering Sandys – 'Poor Duncan, so *cassant*,' wrote Macmillan; 'I think he must have German blood' – the emollient Harold Watkinson and the tart and fed-up with America Thorneycroft, Harold Macmillan had set about military reform. We went primarily nuclear and got rid of a conscript army under Sandys, then commenced a dismantling of the historic and immobilist military command.

By Healey's time, the Ministry itself was well programmed for unification and he put through the last effects. But he resisted, surely rightly, the objective of the Chief of Defence Staff, Lord Mountbatten, who favoured, Canadian style, a single, one-uniform service with a single military and civil command (and a huge amount of power for Lord Mountbatten). The former Major Healey was willing to change anything but not for the sake of streamlined aggrandisement, and though he made great demands on the Chiefs of Staff and had many struggles with them, he was not *cassant*, understood military morale and protected its self-respect. Mountbatten, who had hoped for prolongation in power, was gently given his quietus by Healey who, through such men as Hull, Elworthy and the still rising Michael Carver, consolidated shape while obliging the military to give and give over economy.

This was the chief thing. Labour had committed itself to defence cuts in much the way Conservative oppositions commit themselves to cuts in public spending, on the grounds that they will cut waste, a waste never to be dangerously defined or thought about. But these were financially specific cuts – £2 billion. And Healey had thought a great deal. He picked his way through projects, planes ordered and part-developed, losing this, keeping that. He was at the same time very good at knowing what the Chiefs and their services would loyally take. An instance is PEG, the Performance Evaluation Group, the employment of rising but relatively junior officers to probe the actual utility of the various favoured planes, tanks and ships of the several services and to report to him back across lines of the service closed shop. It had early brilliant results through the exertions of the young Neil Cameron, though colleagues set out to destroy Cameron's subsequent career, which Healey had to protect. But he saw the escaping gas and wound PEG up as something good only for a limited period.

He had also to look at overseas commitments, at the whole concept of Britain being East of Suez. He was working under a Prime Minister, Harold Wilson, who engaged in soft left-wing talk while retaining soft imperial sentiments. Wilson at heart wanted to be seen cutting defence while keeping ships and troops in and about the Indian and Arab seas. With great skill, Healey made his cuts, causing inevitable grief – most of it over the ending of further building of aircraft carriers – but providing a service able first of all to sustain (and win), in defence of Malaysia, the confrontation with Indonesia over Sarawak and Sabeh, an undertaking which had to be explained to an America at first inclined to see Indonesia as what it calls 'the good guys.' The second function which Healey had apparently won by the end of 1968 was a reduced, but real involvement with the Americans, not in their gratuitous warmaking, still less in the Vietnam war which he privately told Robert MacNamara was doomed, but as general back-up.

This, we have to remind ourselves, was the time of Mao's Cultural Revolution, of Singapore as a poor vulnerable city shaken by riots, of general fear, false or otherwise, of great parts of Asia coming under Chinese or other Communist control. Healey withdrew from Aden and South Arabia, cutting losses to local but non-contagious revolution. But broadly, he sought to prevent response to the Nationalist/Far Left ferment being an all-American affair.

But in all of his exertions, Healey was dogged by the failure of the economy. Failure to devalue in 1964 or 1966, the two post-election opportunities, failure to cut credibly enough in the July Measures of 1966 or the first crisis of 1967, led later that year to devaluation and something widely forgotten, a continuing run against the pound even *after* devaluation. This led to the two bitter Cabinet meetings of January 1968 when the new Chancellor, Roy Jenkins who, as he relates in his memoirs, had had a bad fright from the crisis, cut housing and education expenditure and insisted also upon further severe cuts in defence.

There was more to this than met the apolitical eye. Jenkins, devoted to Europe, shared few of Healey's American sympathies and none of Wilson's sentimental Kiplingry. He regarded East of Suez as a place where painters might be cut. And as a fellow 1930s Balliol man and rival, he saw no real harm in an elbow planted in the eye of Healey.

The cuts thus ultimately made, went further than Healey intended. But he saw no utility in resignation. As he told Admiral Hill-Norton, who hotly suggested that course, 'Who else in my party could do what I'm doing?'. 'And of course he was right,' says the admiral today.

In fact what Healey had done across six years, the succeeding Conservative government, blessed with a sensible minister in Lord Carrington, hardly altered. The military consensus was that despite impossible economic circumstances, Healey had made the transition from too much to less, leaving the forces effective within the limits imposed on him. To quote Hill-Norton again, Healey's doctrine was that there should be no commitment beyond the means available. If government gave him less, the forces would be adjusted to that less. But at the level they were committed, those forces would be very good. And by general consent, the British military represent one of the things in this country which work.

Healey had gone through a stretch of bad relations with Wilson in 1967–68. 'Harold would speak of nothing but the wickedness of Denis Healey,' delightedly wrote Richard Crossman, a silly clever politician – ready to surrender West Berlin – who loathed Healey and was despised back. It rose from Healey's exposure in Cabinet of Wilson's bad faith in doubling back on and untruthfully denying his support for arms sales to South Africa, something worth £100 million to a strapped economy. It was demonstrable and, reading out a letter, Healey demonstrated it. The row almost certainly diverted Wilson against his prejudices into assent to the plans of Jenkins.

It was an instance of an excessive candour and warmth of feeling which would be quoted against Healey and given as a reason for his not becoming leader. But these were human failings. Healey *is* a warm man, one who can be moved to tears as when reciting, for Michael Cockerell's 1989 documentary about him, verses about British soldiers killed in Italy, who can blow up in anger, as with a couple of impolitic but salutary public strip-tearings of left-wingers, but a bearer of no grudges, planner of no revenges, maker of no calculations on how to get the better job. Brilliant workhorse, warm-heartedly cerebral, Healey is a paradox. He was also the only man who, on Labour's return to office in 1974, could have coped with an economic crisis which would be compared with that of 1931.

The tragedy of the 1970s, years of inflation, deficit and currency crisis which inspired the shrill American cry, 'Goodbye Great Britain', is that blind men followed the blind. There was little Treasury criticism of Edward Heath as, blunderingly, he turned from a half-cock attempt at non-intervention to panic reflation with money thrust upon local government and all other channels of demand stimulation, a dance of death for Keynesian economics. Inheriting this, Healey also inherited wrong figures, wildly optimistic ones, billions out, so that his first budget, meant to be cautiously neutral, was actually yet more inflationary.

Beyond that, Healey served a cabinet which did not begin to understand the problems involved, a party already on the shallow register of constituency activism, drifting left, and ugly, stupid left at that. As every number on all the dials went wrong, he had two allies, his own self-confidence and the trade union leadership. Of the first, Frank Cooper his Private Secretary at Defence where he later became Permanent Under-Secretary, has a story. A few months into Healey's Chancellorship, Cooper met Edna Healey in Whitehall. How was Denis? 'Oh you know Denis. It takes him a full six months before he knows more about a department than the people who have been working in it most of their lives.' That was said (and retailed) affectionately. But without such cheerful assurance, one doubts if Healey could have come through that particular dark wood.

Healey having delivered, on calamitously wrong data, a budget pushing things further in the inflationary expansionist direction, made a series of cuts and used interest rates heavily. But his greatest success lay in tackling the inevitable inflation by way of an incomes policy. To adapt Enoch Powell on political careers, all incomes policies end in failure. But what Healey did, aided by Michael Foot and two successive prime ministers, was to create one which lasted for more than three years, one which brought inflation down from 27 per cent to 10 per cent and which turned a dumb slogan into a vital and effective policy. The term, Social Contract, nothing to do with Rousseau here, had been revived by Tony Benn and adapted in modified form by a Labour Party not expecting to be elected, another example of the binary law by which parties in government are hoist on the many petards of opposition talk. Much of the original social contract, starting after Labour's uncovenanted election in March 1974, was economic and social poison, non-wage benefits which were supposed to restrain pay increases and did not, plus privileges enthusiastically given by Michael Foot as Secretary of State for Labour, including an extension of the closed shop, attempts to impose the disastrous dock labour schemes which had ruined Liverpool and London upon thriving non-scheme ports and a finally frustrated pitch at driving this nonsense inland to cold store depots and waterway ports. It was all consonant with Foot's transferred class solidarity and his little, under-remarked, despotic streak. And none of this had any restraining effect upon wage inflation whatsoever.

But when crisis came, the social contract which emerged was Healey's model. It turned upon trust and private discussion with key trade unionists, Lionel Murray, Jack Jones, Hugh Scanlon, Alf Allen and others, the so called 'Neddy Six', senior trade union leaders who were also members of the NEDC. The rapport was real. It turned upon the perception by people like Hugh Scanlon, who now talked of having seen the abyss, and Jack Jones, the strength of whose word was a given, was vital, together with very close social/political contacts, the dinner every two months where issues were talked through, confidences given, matters explained. The outcome was a series of voluntary restraints which stuck and worked, bringing inflation impressively down.

It was Healey's trouble to have to deal not only with a real crisis of the economy, which by early 1976 he had almost done, but with one of sentiment and again mensuration. Leo Pliatzky, a gifted Treasury civil servant, would at about this time, expose one set of wrong figures which miscounted public expenditure, making its share a horrendous 60 per cent of GDP when the real figure was around 40 per cent. But in respect of the PSBR no such immediate exposure took place. And the currency markets looked at figures showing two billions above the correct figure.

The effect upon sterling was to make it brittle. Across the period when the economy was sick and/or recovering, the pound stayed above $2. But it was watched nervously until in early March 1976 an attempt was made by the Bank, about which they have never come either clean or coherent, to sell a batch of sterling. We don't know and won't be told if this was an attempt to shade the pound down to a more competitive level to improve the balance of payments or an equally foolish bid to cream off a profit. The markets saw a weakness underlined by its own bankers. They feared either a substantial larger devaluation which would burn holders of sterling and especially those countries like Nigeria and Kuwait, custodians of the sterling balances or a weak currency which would weaken further anyway. The message to get out was clear. And agonisingly across the early months of 1976, the pound fell and fell again.

The hungry men of the gilt edged market, knowing that more would have to be paid for taking British paper, went on a discreet strike never denounced as unpatriotic in the *Daily Mail*. They refused to buy gilts and the government faced the catastrophe that it might be unable to finance its own debt. Healey understood, and Callaghan did not, that a two per cent jump in interest rates was the only available step. He was brought to the very brink of resignation by the refusal of prime-ministerial support, when Callaghan changed his mind and sent in his private secretary to indicate support. A 15 per cent minimum lending rate is no joy, is terrible headlines, is every kind of trouble for a government party, but it worked, as in the quite different circumstances of 1992 Norman Lamont's similar efforts did not. Lamont on that occasion was trying to avoid a devaluation which should have been embraced; Healey was trying to sell gilt edged and the taps flowed.

This was a period of edge between Prime Minister and his political advisers, the Chancellor, the Cabinet – also fourth and fifth parties, the Treasury! Most of the Cabinet wanted soft exits from their problems, the amiable Harold Lever providing them in his humorous and good-tempered advocacy of borrowing. 'Harold never liked us to spend our own money if we could possibly spend somebody else's,' said Healey without bitterness. Callaghan was primarily a politician, though one of great skill. (Healey would speak of his seeking in Cabinet to suffer 'Pyrrhic defeats', putting up something to lose so as to get, what he wanted, a lesser proposition to which he would lead the Cabinet in triumphant retreat.) Up to a point this made him effective, but Callaghan having been Foreign Secretary and enjoyed the sojourn, put too much trust in his ability, in Lyndon Johnson mode, to pick up the phone and bend ears in chancelleries. As for the Treasury, one shouldn't speak of it as a collective noun. Healey was confronted on one occasion by senior civil servants saying 'We are sorry Chancellor, but we cannot offer you a united Treasury view'.

Given such failures and irrelevancies in the run-up to and throughout the IMF crisis of 1976, Healey was forced to adjudicate between competing Treasury advice, endure his Prime Minister's failure of faith in him and those futile excursions into rattling unconnected levers in Bonn and Washington, and then with Callaghan finally reconciled, to share with him the persuading of a fearful cabinet into measures of unpopular retrenchment. Throughout it he had also to endure the ignorant abuse of a right-wing press screaming for blood, outraged at the moderation of the final settlement and offering headlines like 'The Chicken Chancellor', while a little earlier commentators in the *Guardian*, picking up Callaghan's half-thoughts, had murmured that Healey should and probably would, go.

No one within reach of the emotions of the time should write history as a succession of cold facts. Healey had the reserves of stamina, courage and intellectual command to come through this four-month crisis, September–December. But he speaks of them in his memoirs as the worst four months of his life and would describe one dark moment as a twelve-hour period close to total demoralisation. He would not be quite alone, supported by his wife, one substantial colleague, Edmund Dell, certain civil servants and the remoter good will of trade unionists like Murray and Jones, who trusted him and understood that things they did not like might have to be done. Healey came through and the economy made a fine recovery. It was leadership, but hardly a career path.

The decline in the currency which the bank had precipitated led by way of the anxiety on funding to a final heavy drop as Healey was about to leave for a conference in Manila. Healey, commencing those twelve hours, turned back, something for which Callaghan would later blame him, feeling that he should not be out of reach at such a time. And after a change of mind by the Prime Minister, he was asked to go to Party conference at Blackpool. Under the party's crazily bureaucratic rules he was allowed only a floor speech of five minutes, but it was a memorable fighting affair spoken through violent abuse from the left and ending in his winning an ovation.

He had then to fall back on a loan on terms for the IMF. It was not a friendly affair, American government and banker-led as it was. The actual occasion of the visitation, wrong figures on the PSBR and a falling currency had probably been seen right by the hike in interest rates. But they came for all that and could not be wished away.

The debate which followed between Healey and Crosland showed them both right. In some ways what would now be done would be a placebo cure for a spurious disease. But it was also the outcome of long-term mistakes: Heath's grotesque and mindless reflation, the growth in excessive trade union power which the first 12 months of Labour's social contract had accentuated, plus those wrong-the-other-way-round numbers of 1974 and the budget they had brought from Healey. But while Crosland rightly argued basic economic soundness, he also proposed hermetic measures of protection close to a siege economy, which would have been nonsensical and looked like a tantrum as policy. He also spoke contemptuously of 'ignorant market traders'. Well so they were, but they sold pounds and until their ignorance could be enlightened, deceived or deflected, they went on selling them and had to be propitiated.

Healey proceeded to arms-length negotiation with the IMF, while Callaghan muttered against them and him and tried his hand on the phone to Bonn or, through a travelling Lever, in Washington.

In the end, cuts very much smaller than demanded were finally agreed after a process of grinding and exhausting negotiation and refusing to negotiate and at a two-day Cabinet, settled upon. The economy, actually healthy, was now free to demonstrate the fact and the results of Healey's earlier work sprang up in outstanding economic numbers.

In terms of courage, in terms of getting things essentially right, Healey was the one assured success of that Labour government. But he would not become leader. He had to accept some responsibility for the party's defeat when a rigid five per cent wage norm created the explosion of low-pay protest we call the Winter of Discontent. But five per cent was James Callaghan's obsession. He would tell Alf Allen of USDAW in the Cabinet room 'I mean to go nap on inflation'. The psychology was absolutely wrong. At the end of a remarkably successful voluntary pay policy it was necessary to *reculer pour mieux sauter*. Callaghan proposed, Healey loyally accepted. And loyally accepting was one of Healey's great faults. The soldier quality which let him slog on in adversity also made him the Colonel who accepts what the General says. Healey followed Callaghan in the same regimental spirit over his refusal to call an election in the autumn of 1978, a decision which obviated the Prime Minister's previous record for shrewdness. Healey was in two minds about the election when briefly consulted, but a month later Callaghan simply announced his decision first to Healey then the cabinet: masterful, decisive and wrong.

Failure to fight back at Callaghan's decision to linger as Leader of the Opposition, something influenced by a desire to get constitutional changes through and which, in the circumstances of the Bennite left-wing surge, hung Callaghan up with disastrous ones. When he finally went, the left had hopes for a 'Stop Healey' candidate and Healey's plain-spokenness, or downright rudeness, to them ensured this. But he was also afflicted by the mistake of saying too little. Aware that he was controversial, he declined to write a piece for the *Guardian* as his opponents Foot and Silkin did. In a contest where five or six votes tilt in the first ballot would resolve things, at least one expected supporter, Phillip Whitehead, turned primly against him on that count, while at least three of the departing contingent about to join the SDP, Neville Sandelson, Tom Ellis and Jeffrey Thomas, voted in a spirit of 'worse means better', seeking to damage Labour with a weak left-wing leader. But, at bottom, the rejection of Healey was a reflection of a frightened middle of the party buying off trouble by seeking not to provoke the left. As I have remarked elsewhere, Healey was defeated not by the rats but by the mice.

But whatever his mistakes and theirs, one more thing has to be remembered about Denis Healey. He had splendid jobs to go to. He owed the Labour Party of that time less than it owed him. Instead of turning away, he took up the miserable job of deputy leader – attendance at interminable, bitter meetings of an NEC exactly balanced and so dependent on the whims of a leader, Michael Foot, most charitably described as 'inadequate'. Denis Healey once said that the best job he ever had was as International Officer and the worst was as deputy leader.

But when Tony Benn, riding the surf of the left-wing tide, stood against him for that post, Healey fought back with everything he had, fought the campaign missing over the leadership – and by a small fraction won. I was standing close to Edna Healey when the result was relayed in the press room at conference and heard her say: 'Denis has won. Nothing else matters.' This was the literal truth. This was the Bennite high-water mark. The flight which had to be expected of great numbers of Labour MPs never took place. Labour were far down a deep slope but they would fall no further.

It is a good moment to sum up Healey. He has to be credited for unquestioned ability, intelligence, courage and obduracy under fire, as well as for the wit and originality which made him such an enjoyable politician – as remote from the current matinee plastic as could be. But one should remember also the dispassionate service, the unselfishness, the quality at the highest level, of the good party man. Denis Healey did not give up to party what was meant for mankind. But he did serve his party with less regard for self-interested advancement than anyone in sight. He enjoyed power but in a creditable way, not the giving of orders or the glamour, but the engagement, the problem-solving, the sheer tingle of politics. He didn't betray, didn't conspire, didn't look after number one. As unsaint-like as they come, profane, noisy, combative, offending tender plants on all sides, but taking no offence, he actually gave an example of disinterested service. And having not won final glory Healey shrugged his shoulders and went back to his hinterland, the books, paintings, photography and music which made the politician only a part of him. Any failure was rather creditable.

Further reading

Healey's autobiography, *The Time of My Life* (London, 1989), is essential. Among Healey's colleagues, there is much revealing material in the diaries of Tony Benn, Barbara Castle and Richard Crossman, as well as in Joel Barnett's *Inside the Treasury* (London, 1982). On the background to Healey's work at defence, see Sir William Jackson and Lord Bramall, *The Chiefs* (London, 1992) and Dominick Graham and Shelford Bidwell, *Tug of War* (London, 1986). The economic crises of the 1970s are assessed in Edmund Dell, *A Hard Pounding* (Oxford, 1991), Kenneth O. Morgan, *Callaghan: A Life* (Oxford, 1997) and Kathleen Burk and Sir Alec Cairncross, *'Goodbye Great Britain': The 1976 IMF Crisis* (New Haven, 1992). The author's biography, *Denis Healey: A Life in Our Times*, was published by Little, Brown in 2002.

Notes

1. Conversation with Lord Hill-Norton.
2. Conversation with Lord Hattersley.
3. Bela Kovacs, leader of the Smallholders Party of Hungary, did survive this experience and was seen again on release from secret imprisonment in 1956.
4. The debate was later reproduced as a Fabian pamphlet.

9

George Brown

Kevin Jefferys

George Brown, later Lord George-Brown, b.1914–d.1985. Labour MP for Belper 1945–70. Parliamentary Private Secretary to the Minister of Labour 1945–47; to the Chancellor of the Exchequer 1947. Joint Parliamentary Secretary, Ministry of Agriculture 1947–51; Minister of Works 1951. Under Harold Wilson served as First Secretary of State and Secretary of State for Economic Affairs 1964–66; and Foreign Secretary 1966–68. Deputy Leader of the Labour Party 1960–70.

History has not been kind to George Brown. Few historians or commentators have been prepared to endorse the claim made by *The Times* in 1976: 'Lord George-Brown drunk is a better man than the Prime Minister sober.'[1] Even this seemingly favourable judgement was no more than a backhanded compliment. *The Times* had hitherto been no friend of Brown while he served as a senior minister. Although it was happy to depict him as a man of principle when he resigned from the Labour party – in contrast to his long-term adversary Harold Wilson, who announced his surprise resignation as Prime Minister only weeks later – *The Times* was unable to resist drawing attention to the heavy drinking for which Brown was renowned. Indeed George Brown is most often remembered as a flawed personality. In addition to hard drinking, he was well known at Westminster and beyond for his violent outbursts of temper, his accident-prone public appearances and his inferiority complex about the 'middle-class intellectuals' who dominated Labour politics. The only full-length biography so far published takes as its title the euphemism favoured by *Private Eye* in summing up Brown's neurotic, overwrought character: *Tired and Emotional*.[2] And yet, as this chapter will show, George Brown was also a figure of considerable dynamism and ability. He rose from the humblest of beginnings to become an influential force in Labour politics, the party's deputy leader for a decade and a minister who was able to leave more of a mark on the public imagination than many of his contemporaries.

Brown was born in Lambeth, London on 2 September 1914, the eldest of four children. His father, also called George Brown, was a chauffeur to officers in the Army Service Corps and later a van driver; his mother was Rosina or Rose Harriet Brown (née Mason). Brown's commitment to left-wing politics was shaped initially by the poverty of his working-class background. Soon after his birth, the family moved to Southwark, where they occupied two rooms in a barrack-like series of ugly flats, sharing washing facilities with other residents on a communal landing. When his father was sacked by his employers for bringing fellow van workers out during the 1926 General Strike, George was required to go to the local workhouse to collect the family ration of food, consisting of bread and treacle. This was an experience, he later recalled, which left him with a burning desire to change society so that such a 'shaming process' would be unnecessary.[3]

Brown was educated at Gray Street Elementary School and passed an entrance exam to attend West Square Central School in Southwark. Central schools offered a broader course of study than the elementary schools that most children from poor backgrounds attended between the wars. Brown left however before taking formal exams in order to help contribute to the family income; the strains on this income had been increased with the arrival of two sisters and a younger brother, Ronald, who was also later to become a Labour MP. As a teenager Brown developed an interest in politics, campaigning for George Isaacs, the Labour candidate in Southwark at the 1929 general election. He was much influenced by a local Anglican vicar, the Reverend John Sankey, who combined High Church religious practice with a deep commitment to social justice. He also became active in the Labour League of Youth, which introduced him to the world of factional divisions among rank-and-file activists. At the time the decision not to carry on studying in an effort to get into higher education did not much concern Brown, though it was later to come to the fore in his deep resentment of the 'intellectuals' who dominated the senior ranks of the Labour party.

For several years Brown's growing interest in politics was subordinated to the needs of earning a living. This he did initially as a clerk with a firm of merchants in the City of London and then by working in the fur department of John Lewis's Oxford Street store, where he was responsible for beating fur skins with a cane as a moth preventative. When he was 17 he was promoted to become a junior salesman, and for the next few years he made a good living from commission, having more money, 'relatively speaking', than he was to earn until he became a Cabinet minister. By this time, with father and son both steadily employed, the family had moved to a new council estate in Streatham, for the first time experiencing the luxury of an internal bathroom which did not have to be shared with others. In April 1937, at the age of 22, Brown married Sophie Levine, the second of three daughters of Solomon and Kate Levine, a Jewish couple living in the East End, who were prime movers in the founding of the Mile End Labour party. Brown and his wife moved first to a semi-detached house in Barnet, North London, but he found his employment at John Lewis difficult to reconcile with increasing interest in trade union and political activity. He spent two years as a union ledger clerk attempting to support his family, which grew with the arrival of two daughters, and he was eventually appointed as a full-time official with the Transport & General Workers' Union (TGWU). At this time the TGWU was firmly under the control of Ernest Bevin, and Brown, like his leader, became concerned with political as well as industrial issues.

Before long Brown had become secretary of the St Albans Labour party and he tried without success to get elected to his local council. His chances of a career in politics were much improved though after he came to prominence at Labour's 1939 annual conference, held in early summer at Southport. With great nerve and skill, Brown made a considerable impression when he was called to speak by the conference chairman, George Dallas, another influential figure with a TGWU background. Brown won loud applause when he expressed his annoyance at spending 'nine blasted months' discussing the fate of Stafford Cripps and the call for a Popular Front to unite progressive forces against fascism. The speech was so effective that further debate was curtailed and conference quickly moved to vote in confirmation of the expulsion from the party of Cripps. Brown had made a name for himself, though one consequence was that Cripps refused to speak to him thereafter, even when they later served in the same government.

Two further factors worked to Brown's personal advantage in the war years. One was that as a union official he was exempted from military service. Unlike many young hopefuls who were serving in the armed forces abroad when the time came for seeking parliamentary seats, Brown remained on the home front dealing with production hold-ups and disputes in the aircraft and armaments factories of north London. This

experience also confirmed his politically moderate views as he fought
against what he saw as the obstructionism of Communists in the
workplace. The second factor in Brown's favour was his friendship with
George Dallas, who for many years had been Labour's candidate for the
parliamentary constituency of Belper in Derbyshire. Dallas decided that
he would be too old to stand at any post-war election, and instead he
threw his weight behind Brown's bid for the nomination. Belper was
one of the many seats that Labour captured as part of its 1945 landslide
victory, enabling Brown to become an MP at the age of 30.

After only three days at Westminster, the young MP was asked to
become Parliamentary Private Secretary (PPS) to the Minister of Labour,
George Isaacs, for whom Brown had campaigned many years earlier in
Southwark. He was given responsibility for working on displaced persons
in Britain after the war, and in the spring of 1947 he was invited to
become PPS to the Chancellor of the Exchequer, Hugh Dalton, who
told him the move would strengthen his prospects of promotion to
ministerial rank whenever a government reshuffle took place. While
working at the Treasury, Brown became embroiled in a plot to remove
Attlee as Prime Minister; the intention was that he would be replaced by
Ernest Bevin, the Foreign Secretary. As soon as Bevin got wind of events
he summoned Brown, accusing him of acting as 'office boy for that
bastard Dalton'.[4] The young MP was also brought before Attlee, who
instead of giving him the sack – as Brown expected – offered him the
post of Parliamentary Secretary at Ministry of Agriculture. The Prime
Minister no doubt calculated that this excitable newcomer would be
better off fully occupied and out of Dalton's orbit. Attlee's instincts were
proved correct as Brown knuckled down to the demands of ministerial
life, playing his part in steering through new legislation on agriculture.
Instead of sitting, as he recalled, 'night after night with next to nothing
to do', he gained invaluable experience in learning about parliamentary
procedure and the framing of legislation.[5] His climb up the rungs of the
ministerial ladder was under way.

In April 1951 Brown took up the position of Minister of Works in
the reshuffle that followed the resignation of Aneurin Bevan over health
service charges. This was another considerable step forward: he had
achieved full ministerial rank (though still outside the Cabinet) at the
age of only 37. But for the Labour administration in general the outlook
was bleak. Attlee's majority had been greatly reduced at the general
election in 1950 and with little prospect of major new policy initiatives,
Brown decided to concentrate his energies on a personal crusade to secure
the opening of the Tower of London on Sundays. This he achieved –
with the Tower first opening on a Sunday in July 1951 – by displaying

attributes that were to become characteristic of his later career, such as a refusal to bow to opposition from vested interests. Running a department proved to be a challenging but short-lived experience. In October 1951 Labour was defeated at the polls; Brown could little guess that he would celebrate his 50th birthday before he returned to the corridors of power.

During the 1951–64 period in opposition Brown steadily advanced to become a senior figure in the Labour hierarchy. After the loss of his ministerial salary he supplemented his income as an MP by secretly accepting a retainer from Cecil King, chairman of Mirror newspapers, a decision that caused resentment and controversy when it later became public knowledge. In the factional in-fighting of the early 1950s he was a firm supporter of his fellow London moderate Herbert Morrison. He was an outspoken critic of the Bevanite group, blaming them for Labour's loss of office and calling them a 'little band of splenetic furies'. By taking on his opponents at PLP meetings he earned venomous and lasting hatred among the Bevanites, one of whom dubbed him a 'pimp'. Bevan himself called Brown 'Arthur Deakin's lackey'.[6] This last reference underlined Brown's trade union credentials and his profile as an emerging spokesman of the Labour right. In 1955 he was elected to the Shadow Cabinet and allocated the portfolio of Shadow Minister of Supply. He was among the few who remained loyal to Morrison in the leadership contest that followed Attlee's retirement in 1955, but he was nevertheless able to flourish under the new leader, Hugh Gaitskell. After observing his diligent work on the problems of the aircraft industry, Gaitskell promoted him in 1957 to the post of Defence spokesman, where he had responsibility for developing Labour's policy on the controversial question of nuclear weapons.

Brown's prominence as a public figure, if not his reputation, had by this time been further enhanced following a famous dinner given by Labour's National Executive Committee (NEC) to the Soviet leaders Nikita Khrushchev and Marshal Bulganin in 1956. Labour speakers prompted an unscripted response from Khrushchev in which he attacked Britain's role in the war, causing Brown to interject that it was the Russians 'who signed the treaty with Ribbentrop'. Pandemonium ensued and the meeting ended in chaos with accusations flying all round. Accounts of the episode in the days that followed gave the Tory government of the day great pleasure, keen to play up Labour's incompetent handling of the meeting. Brown was heavily criticised by those in Labour ranks who felt that the Soviet system could no longer be condemned as pure totalitarianism; at the NEC several speakers described his behaviour as intolerable. But at the same time the incident appeared to increase Brown's popularity in the country, with sections of the press hailing him as a breath of fresh air and a forthright 'character'.

Brown's rise through the party ranks was also helped by a reasonable working relationship with Gaitskell, although they differed over some areas of policy and Gaitskell was never entirely exempt from Brown's distrust of his 'intellectual' social superiors. In contrast, there was deep and mutual dislike between Brown and his main rival for the mantle of 'coming man' in the Labour party, Harold Wilson. Brown was jealous of the younger man's superior academic pedigree and more rapid rise to Cabinet rank in the 1945 government, but after 1955 Brown had the advantage that Gaitskell's distrust of Wilson matched his own. When Wilson challenged for the party leadership in 1960, Brown secured the vacant deputy leadership by defeating Jim Callaghan and Wilson's running-mate, Fred Lee. In November 1962 Wilson challenged Brown himself for the deputy's post. Brown's anxieties about the outcome were exacerbated by his differences with Gaitskell at this time over Europe, but in the event he won by the comfortable margin of 133 to 103 votes. Unfortunately for Brown, he was not able to repeat this victory when another, more important contest was held only a couple of months later, following the sudden death of Gaitskell in January 1963.

This fresh ballot was of a different order from the earlier contest. Labour MPs were now being asked to judge the best party leader and potential Prime Minister. Brown relied on an assorted bunch of backbenchers led by Desmond Donnelly, who urged colleagues to vote to 'keep the spirit of Gaitskell alive'. Brown knew that Wilson would attract most votes on the left of the PLP, but his chances of success were seriously impaired when Jim Callaghan decided to stand. This split the anti-Wilson vote as numerous Gaitskellites decided that Callaghan was preferable to Brown. Some like Tony Crosland bravely confronted George to his face, telling him that his problem was volatility, coupled with heavy drinking. Others were never to be forgiven for this act of 'betrayal'. The most vicious campaigning was between the supporters of Brown and Callaghan, and personal relations between the two were soured thereafter. On 7 February the result of the first ballot came as a severe blow: Wilson 115 votes, Brown 88 and Callaghan 41. This put Wilson in pole position. Callaghan was eliminated and only a few of his supporters needed to back Wilson to confirm the latter's victory. This they did in a second ballot (won by 144 votes to 103), which Brown insisted upon in spite of pressure to concede defeat in the interests of party unity.

Angry and bitter, believing he had been let down by his friends, Brown flew off to Scotland and went to ground for a few days. Press commentators made much of this disappearing act, implying there were serious doubts over his political future. He eventually returned to continue as deputy leader, but as Wilson rapidly made his mark on the party and the country, Brown found it difficult to recover from the body blow of being passed over for the leadership. His heavy drinking came to the full attention of the nation's television viewers when he was invited to comment on the death of the American President, J.F. Kennedy, in November 1963. Brown gave a performance described by one writer as 'deeply, excruciatingly, embarrassing, a compound of maudlin sentimentality, name-dropping and aggression'.[7] His references to 'Jack' as a great friend (they had only met on three occasions) were accompanied by a slurring of his voice and windmill movements of his arms. There was a rumpus in the PLP, a flood of letters of complaint and much comment in the newspapers about how the incident confirmed Brown's lack of fitness for national leadership. One woman said she had always thought of Brown as a 'small man'; now she believed he was simply a 'small drunken man'.[8]

With Labour looking set to return to power, he could however look forward to playing a key role in an incoming Wilson administration. As chairman of the Home Policy Committee of the NEC, he was in a pivotal position to influence discussions with civil servants and leading economists about the need for structural change in government to facilitate higher growth. As Britain increasingly struggled to keep pace with international competitors, it was felt that the creation of a new ministry – the Department of Economic Affairs (DEA) – would galvanise industry and provide long-term proposals to end Britain's economic underachievement. 'Modernisation' was in vogue, and Labour was much impressed by the success of French models of economic planning. Brown's involvement was finally agreed in a taxi-ride with Wilson, who hoped to create 'creative tension' between his two senior colleagues, Brown and Callaghan, the Shadow Chancellor. Hence in the wake of Labour's narrow victory at the general election in October 1964, Brown was appointed as Secretary of State for Economic Affairs, as well as First Secretary (in effect deputy Prime Minister). His early weeks back in office were spent physically establishing a new ministry in Whitehall. Bill Rodgers, appointed as a junior minister in the department, spent a frustrating half-hour in Great George Street simply trying to find his new place of work.[9] After the disappointments of recent years, these were heady days for Brown. It was he who energised the new DEA by 'shouting, cajoling, arguing, driving, sulking, cheering, scolding, drinking, and hardly ever sleeping'. As Bill Rodgers put it: 'Life in the DEA was more, not less colourful than the newspapers came to describe it'.[10]

The main aims of the DEA were to maintain and strengthen voluntary restraint on prices and incomes, and to produce a national plan to encourage expansion, with particular concentration on supply side measures. Negotiations were never easy. In spite of his background, Brown found it difficult dealing with the new generation of trade union leaders. But after several months of hard talks with representatives of both sides of industry, he was in a position to unveil the centrepiece of his strategy in September 1965, a white paper running to some 500 pages. The National Plan projected an annual growth rate of 3–4 per cent and was hailed as a significant breakthrough – a bold measure that gave substance to Labour's modernising rhetoric. But within months the Plan was dead in the water. In the 'July crisis' of 1966 the Cabinet backed the Chancellor's view that a massive deflationary package was essential to stabilise sterling, which was under attack on the currency markets. Like other ministers, Brown had become convinced that ambitious targets for growth could not be achieved without devaluation. Wilson and Callaghan persuaded the majority of the Cabinet that this was a dangerous leap in the dark, threatening to undermine American support for the pound. Brown in his frustration threatened resignation – a threat that resulted in a highly embarrassing climb down. Rumours of his departure reached the nation's television screens. A hundred Labour MPs hastily collected a petition urging him to stay and he eventually made a midnight appearance before the TV cameras in Downing Street saying that the resignation was off. The scale of his humiliation was difficult to disguise. Brown thereafter had to accept collective responsibility for spending cuts that made a mockery of the DEA's plan for sustained growth.

In his memoirs Brown looked back on the experiment of the DEA as a 'revolution that failed'. He believed that the department had qualified successes, such as the machinery it established for the development of regional policy. But its central failure he attributed to a betrayal by some of those pledged to support it. This was a coded attack on the Prime Minister for failing to resolve differences between the DEA and the Treasury, which fought hard to maintain its overriding responsibility for economic policy. The Treasury resented the emergence of a rival department and with its greater resources eventually won the day in its insistence on traditional cost-cutting measures at a time of crisis. In this light, Brown believed that the DEA was doomed from the start. It was a mistake, one colleague told him, to set up the ministry behind the Treasury in Great George Street as it was likely to end up as the 'backside of the Treasury'; in the view of Brown, this was exactly what happened.[11] The most detailed assessment of the DEA concludes that a range of factors contributed to the demise of a ministry that was wound up altogether in 1969. Not only was there much ambiguity in the division of responsibilities between the Treasury and the DEA, but there was also a fundamental contradiction between the government's commitment to sterling and its desire for economic expansion.[12]

What was certain was that Brown realised there was little point in staying after July 1966. He remained long enough to pilot through new prices and incomes legislation. But he willingly accepted an offer to move when Wilson decided in August that a reshuffle was required to give an appearance of a fresh start after the traumas of the summer. Brown's pleasure was enhanced by the offer to take up one of the most senior positions in the government, that of Foreign Secretary. For the Prime Minister this appointment had several advantages: it assuaged backbench support for Brown, as reflected in the petition collected on his behalf; it confined his two warring colleagues – Brown and Callaghan – to separate spheres of influence; and it checked the ambitions of Callaghan, who had annoyed Wilson by telling journalists of his own wish to leave the Treasury for the Foreign Office. Bill Rodgers noted in his diary that it was uncertain how long Brown would survive in his new post. Success in foreign policy, he wrote, could be even more difficult to achieve than in domestic politics: 'You can't bully, bribe, charm and outwit the world's leaders and give them a drink at the end'.[13]

Brown was to be a forceful Foreign Secretary, though in his 19 months in the post he was unable to emulate the achievements of his trade union hero Ernest Bevin, who had served with distinction in the 1945 government. Relations between Brown and his officials were never easy, in part because – unlike Bevin – he never came to terms with the social gulf that separated him from his overwhelmingly public-school, Oxbridge-educated civil servants. Tensions were made worse by some of Brown's unorthodox behaviour: his defiance of tradition by interfering in the appointment of diplomats; his tendency to shout down senior officials with whom he disagreed in the presence of their juniors; and his willingness to humiliate British ambassadors in public. He once attacked an ambassador's wife as being too old to represent Britain abroad. Departmental arguments were, nevertheless, more about style than the substance of policy. Although constrained by initiatives taken before he arrived, for example in the case of Rhodesia, Brown pursued what his officials regarded as sensible and consistent policies. Perhaps his most important and lasting contribution came in the Middle Eastern conflict, where he was credited with formulating 'Resolution 242', a United Nations Security Council initiative which sought to find a peaceful way forward acceptable to both Arabs and Jews.

But in three areas of policy central to British interests Brown's tenure of the Foreign Office was marked by frustration. As a keen advocate of closer ties with Europe, he strenuously tried to push forward the case for

Britain joining the Common Market. He undertook a lengthy tour of European capitals early in 1967 and had some success in winning over sceptics within his own party, including the Prime Minister. But his efforts were to no avail. In November 1967 General De Gaulle issued his second veto on British membership of the Community, leaving Brown to insist – more in hope than anticipation – that the British bid remained on the table. A second area of great difficulty was the Vietnam War, which attracted widespread public opposition in Britain. As an ardent pro-American Brown found the conduct of the war intensely humiliating, as well as being a source of further disagreement with Wilson. The same was true of a third area of policy – the proposal to end an embargo on arms sales to South Africa. In the aftermath of devaluation, Wilson suspected that the Foreign Secretary and others were using this issue in a direct attempt to oust him from the leadership. The bitterness of the exchanges that ensued persuaded Brown that his working relationship with the Prime Minister had broken down irrevocably. It thus provided the backcloth for his resignation from the government and his rapid decline as a senior figure in Labour politics.

Brown's temperament was such that he frequently spoke of resignation; one estimate claims that he threatened to go 17 times before finally quitting, though many of these threats were never put into writing. On one occasion an excited civil servant was said to have rushed into the Prime Minister's office clutching a resignation letter from Brown. Without looking up Wilson told him to put it 'in the file with the rest of them, there's a good chap'.[14] Matters finally came to a head in March 1968 when, with a fresh economic crisis brewing, the British government received a request from the American president to temporarily close the London gold market – an action that required a meeting of the Queen's Privy Council. The Prime Minister hastily complied by calling together the required number of ministers for a late evening meeting, stating later that efforts to contact Brown had proved unsuccessful.

When the Foreign Secretary learnt that others had been called along in his absence he flew into a rage, inviting over half the members of the Cabinet to join him in the House of Commons, where there were many complaints about No. 10's lack of consultation. Angry telephone exchanges followed in which Brown told Wilson his behaviour was intolerable; the Prime Minister in turn accused Brown of being drunk and of having no right to convene a 'cabal', an irregular meeting of ministers. When the leading protagonists gathered at Downing Street in the early hours of the morning arguments continued over what efforts had been made to contact the Foreign Secretary. After much shouting Brown left, slamming the door and returning to the Commons, where he was reported as saying he'd 'had enough – I've resigned'. He spent all of the next day at his London flat reflecting on events and wondering if, as in the past, Wilson might ask him to reconsider. But no message from Downing Street arrived, and on the evening of 15 March the resignation became official. There was no going back.

Newspaper reaction was mostly unsympathetic. Some commentators, with help from the Prime Minister's press advisers, claimed that Brown had made a fool of himself, resigning out of 'pique' or because of some form of 'gratuitous personal crisis'. In his resignation letter Brown said he had gone because of 'the way in which this Government is run and the manner in which we reach our decisions'. Wilson brushed this aside, thanked Brown for his contribution as a minister and rested content that he had got rid of a troublesome colleague without raising any major issues in the process. Some Cabinet colleagues agreed however, at least in private, that important principles were at stake. Richard Crossman wrote in his diary that the episode was being portrayed as one of petty opposition, yet 'there's a great deal in it'. If he himself were to resign, he continued, it would be precisely over the question of Wilson's presidential style: his failure to build up an inner group to devise government strategy, working through cronyism and clique rather than through genuine collective means.[15] This grave charge was not taken up in Brown's resignation speech in the Commons on 18 March, which proved to be an anti-climax. In careful language Brown pledged loyalty to the government – so removing any threat that he might lead dissident opinion among Labour MPs – and failed to bring out his concern about Wilson's leadership style. He later maintained that the tone of his resignation speech was designed not to spare the Prime Minister's feelings, but rather to minimise the effects of his departure on the party's electoral fortunes. His only regret was that he had not gone earlier, notably at the time of the refusal to devalue in July 1966.[16]

After his resignation, Brown continued to serve as Labour's Deputy Leader and as chairman of the Home Policy Committee on the NEC. In the latter capacity he helped to influence the appointment of Harry Nicholas as the party's new General Secretary instead of Wilson's preferred choice, Arthur Greenwood. This ensured that his relationship with the Prime Minister remained one of mutual suspicion; it 'never rose much beyond what might be called a civilised level'.[17] Although there was much press speculation, no firm offers to rejoin the government were made. Brown instead filled his time with writing for newspapers, preparing his memoirs and engaging in business interests to make up for the loss of his ministerial salary, taking on in particular the role of part-time Industrial Relations Adviser at Courtaulds. After the disappointments of office, he fought to energise the party in the 1970 election campaign, addressing over 100 meetings in a fortnight and winning plaudits for his skilful handling of hecklers. But part of the reason for his nationwide tour was that he knew the writing was on the wall in his Belper constituency, where there had been an influx of new voters on private housing estates. His majority of nearly 4,300 was easily overturned as the Tories under Edward Heath swept back to power, leaving Brown out of parliament and underlining the speed with which his career at the top level in politics had come to an end.

In his later years Brown kept in touch with political developments as a member of the House of Lords. He changed his name by deed poll to become Lord George-Brown of Jevington, in Sussex, and his disenchantment with Labour 'extremism' became increasingly obvious in the articles he wrote for papers such as the *News of the World*. In March 1976 he eventually resigned from the party over the issue of the legalisation of the 'closed shop' in trade unions. Returning to the House of Lords from television studios after making his announcement, and under the influence of drink, he stumbled and fell outside parliament. He was pictured the following day being helped to his feet by reporters. The *Daily Mail* spoke of his 'tragic exit from the party he had delighted, horrified and mesmerised for nearly half a century'.[18] Senior Labour figures were scathing in their reaction – especially in the light of the contrast between Brown 'drunk' and Wilson 'sober' made by *The Times* – saying they thought he was no longer a member of the party anyway given his attitudes and voting record in the Lords. From this time onwards Brown largely disappeared from public view. The only subsequent occasion he made the headlines in his lifetime came when he announced his affiliation in 1983 to the SDP, though as President of a forerunner organisation the Social Democratic Alliance (and as a cross-bencher in the Lords) it was widely assumed that his sympathies had moved in this direction.

He died from cirrhosis of the liver at the Duchy Hospital in Truro, Cornwall on 2 June 1985. A memorial service was held a few weeks later at St Margaret's, Westminster. Much of the newspaper interest generated by the memorial service, particularly among the tabloids, centred on the presence not only of his wife, Lady George-Brown, but also his former secretary, Maggie Haimes, with whom the 70–year-old peer was living at the time of his death. Brown's marriage had become increasingly unhappy over the years, particularly after his resignation from high office, and after 40 years together he walked out on his wife at Christmas in 1982 and went to live with his young secretary, first in Sussex and then in Cornwall. This relationship was also often strained, but it was Miss Haimes who bore the brunt of looking after Brown as his health deteriorated in his final years. In spite of this, he never divorced his wife and she was the sole beneficiary of his will. Nothing was left to Maggie Haimes, who later accepted an out-of-court settlement with the family lawyers.

In spite of the attention paid to his complicated personal life, the memorial service shortly after Brown's death was also able to pay tribute to the mark he left on public consciousness. Although he served for less than four years as a senior minister, he would be remembered for his consistent espousal of the pro-European cause, which he successfully combined with a deep and lasting admiration for the USA and for the maintenance of the 'special relationship'. He also deserved credit as the architect of the National Plan, which although it was never carried through represented a serious attempt – at least in his eyes and those of his supporters – to forward a vision that combined economic efficiency with social justice. He was of course, as his colleague Richard Crossman had noted at the time of his resignation as Foreign Secretary, a Jekyll and Hyde character who could be by turns charming and enormously rude. This split personality may have cost him the party leadership, but it also gave him an appeal with voters which many colleagues envied. He was, Crossman concluded, 'tough and crude and yet brilliant and imaginative', in many ways the most gifted member of the Cabinet in the 1960s.[19]

Further reading

Lord George-Brown's autobiography, *In My Way*, was published by Gollancz in 1971. The only biography at present is by Peter Paterson, *Tired and Emotional: The Life of Lord George-Brown* (London, 1993). There are brief overviews in Brown's obituary in *The Times*, 4 June 1985 and in *The Dictionary of National Biography 1981–85* (the latter entry written by his colleague, also a Labour Foreign Secretary, Michael Stewart). There is much information on Brown in the diaries written by Cabinet colleagues in the 1960s, notably Richard Crossman, *The Diaries of a Cabinet Minister*, Volume 1: 'Minister of Housing 1964–66' (London, 1975) and Volume 2: 'Lord President of the Council and Leader of the House of Commons 1966–68' (London, 1976); Tony Benn, *Out of the Wilderness: Diaries 1963–67* (London, 1987); and Barbara Castle, *The Castle Diaries 1964–76* (London, 1990 edn). On the role of the DEA, see Christopher Clifford, 'The Rise and Fall of the Department of Economic Affairs 1964–69: British Government and Indicative Planning', *Contemporary British History*, 11, 2 (1997), pp 94–116. Clifford's article is followed in the same journal (pp 117–42) by an edited transcript of a witness seminar on the DEA held in London in 1996, attended by politicians and officials who played a key part in the history of the department.

Notes

1. *The Times*, 4 March 1976.
2. Paterson, *Tired and Emotional: The Life of Lord George-Brown* (London, 1993).
3. George Brown, *In My Way* (London, 1972 paperback edition), p 20.
4. Ibid, p 45. See also B. Pimlott, *Hugh Dalton* (London, 1985), pp 505–8.
5. Brown, *In My Way*, p 48.
6. Ibid, p 54. See also K. Jefferys, *Retreat from New Jerusalem* (London, 1997), pp 22–4.
7. Paterson, *Tired and Emotional*, p 150.
8. Ibid, p 151.
9. Bill Rodgers, *Fourth among Equals* (London, 2000), p 78.
10. Paterson, *Tired and Emotional*, p 165; Rodgers, *Fourth among Equals*, p 81.
11. Brown, *In My Way*, pp 87–9, 108–10.
12. C. Clifford, 'The Rise and Fall of the Department of Economic Affairs', *Contemporary British History* 11, 2 (1997), pp 108–10.
13. Cited in Rodgers, *Fourth among Equals*, p 96.
14. *Guardian*, 3 March 1976.
15. Richard Crossman, *The Diaries of a Cabinet Minister*, Volume 2: 'Lord President of the Council and Leader of the House of Commons 1966–68' (London, 1976), 17 March 1968, p 714.
16. Brown, *In My Way*, pp 195–6.
17. Ibid, p 190.
18. *Daily Mail*, 3 March 1976.
19. *Crossman Diary*, 17 March 1968, pp 714–5.

10

Barbara Castle

Tim Bale

Barbara Castle, later Baroness Castle of Blackburn, b.1911–d.2002. Labour MP for Blackburn 1945–50, 1955–79; Blackburn East 1950–55. Minister of Overseas Development 1964–65; Minister of Transport 1965–68; Secretary of State for Employment and Productivity 1968–70. Secretary of State for Social Services 1974–76. MEP for Greater Manchester North 1979–84; Greater Manchester West 1984–89. Leader, European Parliament British Labour Group 1979–85. Life peer 1990.

Although Barbara Castle came closer than any other woman to the Labour leadership, there was initially little to distinguish her, on paper at least, from the tiny minority of women who represented the Party before the sudden leap in their numbers in 1997.[1] She came from a politically-conscious, middle-class family. She had a post-secondary education (at Oxford). She had local government experience (as a borough councillor in north London). She worked in a job where communication skills were crucial (she was a journalist). She wasn't held back by dependants (she remained childless).

But she was also exceptional, possessing as she did:

> that kind of star quality given only to a tiny handful of entertainers in any generation – and almost to no politician – that of making the crowd lean forward in their seats when she steps onto the stage. Another attribute of the star is that she must throw herself entirely

on the mercy of the audience. Nothing must be held back. The tears, smiles, hopes, fears, loves, hates, must all be shared with the fans… We can see that she is courageous, opportunistic, intelligent, self-deceiving, emotional, calculating, principled and ambitious. But we never know in each breathless instalment which quality or combination of qualities is going to win.[2]

Not surprisingly, then, the ups and downs of Barbara Castle's political career, as detailed by journalists, biographers and by her own diaries and memoirs, lend themselves readily to dramatic interpretation. But they are more than just the tales of a fondly-regarded old trouper. Spanning almost all of Labour's first century, they reveal a woman who, because of what she was, what she took on and what she might have become, unquestionably deserves her place on any list of the Party's all time greats.

Beginner to the stage

Barbara Castle's early life equipped but also handicapped her for the future: her vices were the defects of her virtues, and both were inculcated in childhood. Her father, Frank Betts, was 'a one-man challenge to orthodoxy' who managed to combine his job as a provincial tax inspector with radical politics and a burning desire to see his children, male or female, fulfil their full potential.[3] Castle took from him her passion for argument, her concern for accuracy and her determination to see things through to the very end. The flip sides of her inheritance were her unapologetic egocentricity, a lack of empathy that sometimes bordered on solipsistic, a tendency to lose the wood for the trees, and an inability to know when to stop or let go.[4] Politically speaking, her father and other early mentors schooled her in the romantic socialism of the middle-class ILP – a creed which had little sympathy for what it regarded as the blinkered gradualism of the organised industrial wing of the Labour movement. Its utopia was planned collectivism, its militant antifascism ensuring that the downsides of existing state socialism were underplayed or ignored – even by those who, like Castle, actually visited the Soviet Union.[5]

Castle's first big break came at the 1943 Party Conference when, as an ordinary CLP delegate, she mounted the rostrum to defend the crucial importance of the Beveridge Report to Labour's rank and file. In so doing, she pitted herself against Arthur Deakin, the bombastic, right-wing fixer who took over from Bevin as general secretary of the TGWU. Labour supporters, she cried, were fed up of being told to keep quiet until after the war, of being offered 'Jam yesterday, and jam tomorrow, but never jam today'! Her soundbite put 32-year-old Miss Barbara Betts on the front page of the *Mirror*, the most popular paper in the land. By the time she was selected to fight as one of the Labour candidates for the double member seat of Blackburn, a Lancashire mill-town, she had met and married the man who made the decision to put her on the front page that day, journalist Ted Castle.[6] For a woman, getting selected – especially for a seat that wasn't hopeless – was generally harder than getting elected.[7] And so it proved. Castle was borne to Westminster on the tide of Labour's landslide victory of 1945, one of the Party's record-breaking total of 21 female MPs.

Even if she was routinely picked out by fellow journalists as one of the most 'glamorous' of the new intake, Castle faced a great deal of competition for advancement. But she was lucky. Her anti-fascist activities of the 1930s and her association with *Tribune* gave her a connection with Stafford Cripps, prime mover in the popular fronts before the war, financial backer of the paper and now President of the Board of Trade. He appointed her his PPS. But although picked as a high-flyer by several leading lights in the PLP including Hugh Dalton, that was where she stayed. Possibly this was because, unlike, say, Jim Callaghan, whose flirtation with dissent was brief, she continued to express vocal opposition to what she saw as the Government's dangerous drift to the right, especially on foreign policy. But at least she wasn't sacked for it. Thus it was that when Cripps moved on, she became PPS to rising star, Harold Wilson. So began a political relationship which was to sustain but also constrain her for the next 30 years.

Character development

Castle's closeness to Wilson did not mean she lived in his shadow. Indeed, she spent the 1950s developing a profile so high that it often eclipsed his own, especially on the left. In spite of the irritation her outspokenness provoked among some trade union leaders, she was sufficiently well thought of to be elected to the Women's Section of the NEC for the first time in 1950. When Wilson joined Bevan in leaving the Government over Gaitskell's insistence on imposing NHS charges to pay for rearmament in 1951, she resigned too, ending any chance of trade union support a second time around. Instead, she ran for the constituency section – the first woman to do so. Sensationally (no other word will do) she came second only to Bevan, outpolling not only Wilson, who was only a runner-up, but also Cabinet Ministers like Morrison and her unlikely hiking-partner, Hugh Dalton. It was the start of a love affair without parallel in the Party. The rank and file elected her (the only woman member in the section till 1967) to one of the three top places every year until 1972 and, though she was always haunted by the fear that she would be voted off it, she served without a break until 1979. Almost overnight, then, Castle had established a power base within the

Party that worried not only the right but also those on the left with leadership ambitions of their own – including the man whose radical yet flexible brand of socialism she always revered, Aneurin Bevan himself.[8]

Castle may have been charismatic, and her radicalism may have suited the spirit of the times, but popularity and prominence did not simply fall into her lap. She worked at it, assiduously. Sure that sometime down the line the leadership was a serious possibility and not just a long-held dream, Castle kept herself in the public eye: accidentally by way of numerous libel cases,[9] and on purpose through her tabloid journalism, her lecturing and her television appearances. As a woman, she may not always have been taken as seriously as she should have been (though it was less of a problem than might be imagined). Even back then journalists and editors were always on the lookout for ways in which political coverage could be made entertaining. Adding a 'fiery redhead' to a mix which already depended heavily on personalisation and conflict was an easy way to do it. No doubt journalists in Fleet Street and elsewhere breathed as big a sigh of relief as Castle when, at the Tory landslide of 1955, she squeaked back into parliament with less than 500 votes to spare.

Already, however, it was clear that Castle would find it difficult to translate her high profile into high office. In part, this was because she was a woman and a left-winger in a movement that was male dominated and politically cautious. But it was also because she tended to make her most positive impression on those who hardly knew her – party rank-and-filers, ordinary people she came across on visits and in her dedicated constituency work – or on those who got to know her incredibly well – Dick Crossman being the most obvious political example. But with those whom she really needed to impress to have any serious chance of the leadership – the potential 'selectorate' of fellow MPs and eventually ministerial colleagues – she was often hopeless. Unlike Wilson or Callaghan, she had no inclination to network, to work the tea-room.[10] And even when she did spare the time, she was solipsistic, patronising and often plain contemptuous.[11] Paradoxically, but fatally, when she thought she was among equals, she often seemed to treat them like fools. And she didn't suffer fools gladly.

Admittedly, Castle was operating in what might have proved a hostile environment however hard she may have been prepared to try. If parliament was 'like a boys' school which has decided to take a few girls', it most certainly did not treat them as equals.[12] All too often, 'Lady members' were patronised, valued more for their glamour and/or homespun housewifeliness than their opinions on the great issues of the day. Castle's response to such treatment was predictably assertive. Like many of her female colleagues, she made sure that she was as conscientious and well informed as any of her male counterparts, sometimes to the point of overwork and overkill.[13] Unlike most female members, however, she tended to steer clear of so-called 'women's issues' (the care and protection of children, domestic violence and divorce, widows' welfare, housing conditions and consumer affairs),[14] choosing instead to engage the men on their own territory.[15] This did not mean she avoided such issues completely. In 1950, for instance, Castle successfully piloted a ten-minute rule bill on the protection of prostitutes through the Commons and onto the statute book. In 1961, though, she had a less happy experience when, to the evident hilarity of male members, she introduced a bill aimed at abolishing the turnstiles which made it so difficult for women with disabilities or who were pregnant to use public toilets. Possibly, the ridicule she endured made her feel justified in sticking to the so-called 'real issues'. If so, it was perhaps a little unfortunate. As the biographer of another woman MP who adopted a similar stance, Jennie Lee, points out, 'the price of that was to accept men's definition of what was important and what was not'.[16]

Whether her avoidance of 'women's issues' made much difference, however, to the often strained sisterhood between Castle and other female MPs, particularly on the Labour side, is doubtful. Even to Jennie Lee, Castle was 'more competitor than friend', while Labour's ideological civil war of the 1950s, which 'played havoc with women's networking', ensured that she had few allies among the likes of high-profile MPs like Alice Bacon, Jean Mann, Edith Summerskill or Bessie Braddock.[17] Sheer human jealousy may also have played a part. The average woman MP could expect more extensive – if not necessarily helpful – media coverage than her male counterpart. But Castle left them all in the shade. In part, this was because she looked so good.[18] Her arrival in the Commons, according to one lobby correspondent remained 'the sartorial moment of every parliamentary day'. It was not an effect achieved by accident or despite herself. Castle's concern with her appearance was a long-standing personality trait.[19] Yet it was something she shared with many women MPs, who had to balance the risks of trivialisation against their desire to shake off the 'cartoon image of the tweed suited women... camouflaging... femininity in order to compete with men'.[20] Every woman in the Commons faced the Catch-22 neatly captured by a contemporary journalist: 'If she plays it tough, she is accused of being unfeminine; if she behaves like a woman she cannot be trusted with a man's job.'[21] Looking attractive at the same time as putting both the fear of God and the boot into her opponents was an obvious way for Castle to overcome, or at least elide, the dilemma.[22]

In Castle's case, those opponents were often on the Labour as well as the Conservative side of the House. But her membership of the Bevanite awkward squad did not leave her completely out in the cold. In the days before rule changes that obliged MPs to vote for some women, Castle was not elected by her fellow backbenchers to the Shadow Cabinet. Yet Gaitskell, now Labour leader, appointed her shadow Minister of Works in 1959. Arguably, he had little choice: even if he hadn't needed to achieve some semblance of balance between right and left, he would have been hard pressed to ignore someone so obviously able in parliamentary debate. Castle had been building a reputation for combining emotional force with equally devastating forensic skill – a talent which shortly before her appointment had helped her to recover from a very damaging spat with the press (and the Labour leadership) over British brutality in Cyprus.[23] She sealed that reputation when in March 1959 she turned the tables on her critics by exposing in parliament an attempt to cover up unlawful killings of Kenyan independence advocates in the Hola detention camp, effectively demolishing the reputation of the Conservative Colonial Secretary, Alan Lennox Boyd, in the process.

But Castle's role as a shadow spokesperson for Gaitskell did not last long. He sacked her in 1960 for her very public opposition to his attack on Clause IV and his repudiation of Conference on nuclear weapons. Yet two years later he was intimating privately that Castle (whose sceptical views on Europe were something they had in common) would join Dick Crossman in his Cabinet should he become PM.[24] Such a scenario was looking increasingly likely. The Conservatives were beginning to implode and to provide Labour with a number of issues on which it could unite instead of divide.[25] Meanwhile, three years' worth of leadership contests seemed to have drawn some (though not all) of Labour's own poison. Unfortunately for Castle, they also sorted out the order of preference for the Party's left-wingers. Wilson, whose own rising parliamentary reputation could do nothing to overcome his being forced to stand before he was really ready, had been roundly defeated by Gaitskell in 1960. In 1961 Castle challenged Gaitskell's deputy, George Brown, but was beaten by 56 votes to 169. This may not have dampened her hopes in the long term, but the following year's contest, in which Wilson got within 30 votes of Brown made it clear that she would have to wait her turn behind him.

Big time

Wilson of course had less time to wait than he could have guessed. He was elected leader upon Gaitskell's death, and wasted little time in telling Castle that she would join him in his first Cabinet. The Shadow Cabinet, however, was another matter: since he felt unable – so soon after defeating the right for the leadership – 'to impose people unacceptable to [its] other members'.[26] Such spinelessness gave Castle considerable cause for concern,[27] but she accepted his invitation to be Labour's spokeswoman on overseas development, a post for which her active involvement in colonial issues seemed to fit her nicely.[28] And it was to the new Ministry for Overseas Development (ODM) that she was posted by Wilson when he formed his Government in October 1964, only the fourth woman ever to obtain Cabinet rank in Britain.[29] While she hankered after a more heavyweight job and cheerfully talked to the press about the possibility of a woman Prime Minister, 'she had the ability, and the egotism, to treat whatever she was doing as the most important thing because she was doing it'.[30] This led almost from the start to a feeling amongst her colleagues (already irked by her tendency to take on the role of the Cabinet's socialist and anti-racist conscience) that she lacked a proper sense of her own relative unimportance and of the claims of her ministry on Government time and resources – a feeling heightened by her attempt to draw toward ODM those parts of other departments whose work touched on hers.[31]

While not denying Castle's empire-building tendencies, they have to be seen in the context of her sincere belief that the Government should reorganise itself on more rational, managerial lines. Even as a lowly PPS, she had learned a lot from Cripps (including unfortunately his tendency to overwork)[32] and revealed a natural flair for administration. At the same time, she was always on the look out for improvements, exemplified perhaps by her insistence on bringing in outside expertise, especially economic expertise, into her ministry. This irritated the more antediluvian among her civil servants (her strained relationship with Sir Thomas Padmore at Transport is legendary). But for many she was a breath of fresh air. Indeed Castle's reputation among those who worked for her far exceeded the estimation of many of her political colleagues. Despite her claim that 'a good Minister... must eat a civil servant before breakfast every day', most of her staff and many of her junior ministers, saw her as conscientious but considerate, someone who could master the detail without losing the thread, single but rarely narrow-minded, firm but not altogether inflexible.[33]

No-one else of course could ever have as high an opinion of Barbara Castle's ministerial performance as Barbara Castle herself. Indeed, she was quite convinced by the time she left ODM that nobody could possibly fill her shoes.[34] But given the fact that her stay was so short and involved starting things almost from scratch with limited resources, she had cause to be proud of her achievements. In August 1965, she published (and personally wrote much of) a White Paper, *Overseas Development: The Work of a New Ministry*, which went some way to balance the alleged racism of the Government's newly-announced immigration restrictions. She made something of a breakthrough on the use of interest-free loans to developing countries. She also saw to it that the department came through relatively unscathed when in July 1965 the Government embarked on the first of what was to become a depressing and predictable annual round of public expenditure squeezes.

Equally depressing and no less predictable was the way so many of her Cabinet colleagues attributed her success solely to her so-called 'womanly wiles', be they those of the pouting tease or the nagging wife. Her supposed plaything-cum-henpecked husband, Harold Wilson, told her – perhaps to make her laugh, perhaps to subtly undermine her – that 'one of the more irreverent members of the Cabinet had said of me as I left the room, "Look at her. She only has to waggle that bottom of hers and she gets all her own way."'[35] When she wasn't doing that she was apparently 'achieving her many successes by boring the cabinet to death; they very often went along with things just to shut her up'.[36] According to one colleague, speaking it would appear for them all, 'she used to screech at Harold during Cabinet meetings mercilessly... She went on like a mechanical drill until your nerves couldn't stand it any more'.[37] Such techniques, of course, are hardly confined to women.[38] They are often just labelled as such by men who resent losing out to them but who no doubt have their own repertoire of equally reprehensible tricks, the legitimacy of which is rarely questioned because they are more familiar. True, Castle was not above 'tears and tantrums' if she thought they would get her what she wanted.[39] But if they did, whose fault was that? In any case, by stoking up festering resentment, they may well have done her more harm than good in the long run.

But not all that resentment can be put down to plain jealousy, casual sexism or the frustrations of chivalry. Castle's technique in Cabinet did leave something to be desired – both at the interpersonal and the administrative level. One can imagine the not necessarily macho exasperation of colleagues who, having been treated to a Castle monologue, watched as the consummate egotist then 'busied herself when others babbled on, writing notes for her diary in shorthand, drawing up shopping lists... composing departmental minutes, topping and tailing White Papers, writing speeches, doing any urgent departmental work, or just doodling'.[40] More technically, the irritation she provoked was often the consequence of her tendency to ignore the need to build up bilateral support prior to Cabinet. This reinforced her natural tendency to present proposals in a manner which suggested they were incapable of improvement and self-evidently urgent priorities – a habit that she did nothing to break and which helped get her into serious trouble in years to come.[41]

Meanwhile, however, Castle had done enough to persuade Wilson that she deserved a bigger job. In December 1965 she was promoted to Transport, with a brief to make good on Labour's ambitious but rather vague manifesto promise of an integrated policy. Her tenure began with a press conference that reflected Castle's rising reputation – especially with the media, hungry as always for an entertainment angle on politics. As ever, she rose to the occasion:

> Transport was heavy lifting, a man's job, roads and railways. How would men react to this 'woman who cannot even drive' [her phrase]? Barbara... did what worked so well for her in the past with predominantly male and potentially hostile crowds: she applied her femininity with a trowel. She hammed it up for the gallery, swathed in red and gold, draped with a garland of coyness, playing the role Quintin Hogg [later Lord Hailsham] ascribed to her: 'the Pussy Galore of a Goldfinger Government'.[42]

Yet beneath the style there was real substance – or at the very least a willingness to get her hands dirty. Speaking at the Hull by-election, which was instrumental in persuading Wilson to go to the country (and win a landslide majority) in the spring of 1966, she promised eager locals the Humber bridge. She, with Wilson, also managed to use her good offices to bring about a last-minute 'beer and sandwiches' solution to a threatened national rail strike. Her next task was to see through some controversial innovations inherited from her predecessor. By the time she left the ministry, those innovations were well on the way to becoming universally accepted aspects of modern life – which may say more about their inherent good sense than Castle's skilful stewardship. But there is no doubt that the quick collapse of much of the initial hostility toward the breathalyser, sensible speed limits and the compulsory fitting (if not yet wearing) of seatbelts, only increased the new Minister's profile and popularity.

Castle's dogged pursuit of an integrated transport policy proved rather more problematic. Vested interests – be they road hauliers, railway workers or BR management – proved a constant source of political irritation and inertia.[43] Her Transport Bill was the longest bill since the war. It attempted to coordinate train and bus schedules, set out a new infrastructure for freight, balance the social and the business aspects of railways, and plan and build roads sufficient to cope with the possibility (not obvious at the time, incidentally) that car ownership would come to the masses and not just the middle classes. It passed, despite determined opposition. But many of its provisions were overtaken by time and social and technical change, or deliberately undone by later Conservative administrations, to the extent that an integrated transport policy is today no less of an oxymoronic holy grail than it was in the 1960s.

This notwithstanding, it was at Transport that Castle cemented her reputation as a strong departmental minister. This came – as she herself sometimes reflected – at the cost of her capacity to think collectively about the Government's wider problems. Certainly, she proved herself no more able than others to think outside the square when in early 1968 the Cabinet was bounced by the Treasury, the media and the markets into a public expenditure package which failed to re-establish the Government's credibility either internationally or with its own supporters. Instead, she fell prey to a tendency (by no means unique or unfamiliar to her) toward 'departmentalism' and 'ministerialitis' – preoccupation with one's own patch and how to defend it, often accompanied by the conviction that anyone else, especially one's own backbenchers, is so ill-informed as to be incapable of any meaningful contribution beyond unthinking support or irresponsible sniping.[44] On the other hand, such events also confirmed her in the view that only a few privileged ministers really knew what was going on, especially when it came to the economy and foreign policy. Castle was at the height of her popularity even as the administration of which she was a part was breaking records for unpopularity; later in the year, for instance, she moved back up to number one in the NEC elections. But though the press declared that she carried all before her,[45] she was sure that she remained, like all but two or three of her Cabinet colleagues, 'on the fringes of ignorance and uncertainty'.[46]

Villain of the piece

The events of late 1967 and early 1968, then, left Castle more convinced – and more frustrated – than ever that the really big business of government was conducted beyond and behind the Cabinet. That was where she wanted to be, and she deserved to get there. She was popular and effective. She provided a semblance of left-wing balance in a cabinet composed largely of the centre-right. She'd supported Wilson during his darkest hours, most recently in bitter in-fighting over arms sales to South Africa and party indiscipline.[47] She was therefore in a strong enough position to turn down his offer of a new job as Leader of the House: after all, she argued, economics, not parliament and publicity, was where real power lay. Instead, she accepted his second offer – First Secretary of State at the Department of Employment and Productivity (DEP), taking in the Ministry of Labour and some of the responsibilities of Wilson's failed experiment, the Department of Economic Affairs. Given her ambitions and her analysis of the needs of the nation, it was a logical decision. It was also the worst mistake she ever made.

By 1968, the press, the public and the Prime Minister had convinced themselves that Britain had a particular 'trade union problem'.[48] The Tories were promising to get tough. The markets and the IMF, to whom the Government was now in hock, wanted an indication that the increased export earnings resulting from devaluation would not be swallowed up by compensatory wage increases. Some kind of statutory incomes policy would have been best. But if Wilson could no longer prevail on his parliamentary support or the unions themselves to accept one, then he must prove his good faith in some other fashion. What better way to demonstrate 'the smack of firm government' than to tackle the unofficial strikes that, according to the media/market consensus, cost the country not just millions but its good name as well? The potential pay-off for the Prime Minister was huge: he would help restore the economy and his own rock-bottom reputation; he would deny the Tories at least one stick with which to beat his party; and he would finally prove that centrist social democracy was capable of running the country in the national interest.[49] And he knew just the woman who could help him: 'little Barbara' (as he liked to call her) would charm her way to success with the unions, the media and eventually the voters.

Castle herself, though pleased to have finally arrived, was rather less sanguine about what she regarded as a potentially tragic brush with political destiny:

> Well, I am in the thick of it now, for better or worse – probably worse. I am under no illusions that I may be committing political suicide. I have at last moved from the periphery of the whirlwind into its very heart... My fan mail has been growing, and I am about to change all that for the very focal point of unpopularity. And yet I know I couldn't do anything else. If I go down in disaster as well I may, at least I shall have been an adult before I die.[50]

She was, then, labouring under no illusions. Unless of course one counts the biggest illusion of all. Namely, that Wilson was right to send anyone on such a fool's errand, least of all a loyal lieutenant whose convictions and character made it inevitable that she would treat the whole enterprise as a personal crusade.

To Castle, as Wilson well knew, the 'trade union problem' was philosophical bordering on theological – an underlying tension in Labour politics that had to be addressed. The majority of influential trade unionists saw Labour's job as to help them extract the maximum possible share of capital's surplus. This it was to do by increasing tax-funded state provision and maximising their bargaining power by maintaining full employment and the freedom from legal liability that the Party was set up to defend in the first place.[51] Many Labour politicians agreed.

Others, Castle among them, believed that this was a recipe for chaos and eventual collapse: disputes wasted resources and fuelled inflation, leading to a sluggish, internationally uncompetitive economy which would prove incapable of delivering the standard of living and state services to which all citizens had a right. Britain's transition to welfare capitalism had to involve a move away from pluralism toward corporatism, with entrenched tripartite structures that would allow properly organised employers and workers to reconcile their interests in national agreements that could be made to stick.

After falling into disarray by the end of the 1945–51 Government, these ideas had regained momentum by the time Labour made it into office in 1964, trumpeting the benefits of planning. But little had happened, not least because the fight to save the pound made it difficult to think of much else and impossible to establish the climate of good will needed to facilitate change. In Castle's view, devaluation provided the Government with an opportunity – indeed made it imperative – to impress and impose the logic of corporatism upon the Party and the country. The trade union problem, which had been preoccupying her for some time and which played into her Bevanite and pre-Bevanite bias against bullying trade union barons, was the best place to break out of the standard pluralist boom-bust cycle.[52] Wilson agreed. But he was also aware, as were others, like Roy Jenkins, who were initially sympathetic, that there existed a potential trade-off between such a policy and the preservation of both Party unity and his own position. If it came to a choice, it was more than obvious which way he would jump.

Whether or not Castle could ever have won with the hand Wilson dealt her, no-one could possibly argue that she played it well. The policy process that turned the continuation of voluntarism in industrial relations recommended by the Government's own Donovan Report into the statutorily backed framework suggested by Castle's White Paper, *In Place of Strife*, was extraordinarily elitist and ad hoc. As if this weren't bad enough, Castle's handling of the proposals proved to be an object lesson in how not to win friends and influence people. She ignored private warnings that her ideas simply would not fly with trade unionists. Then she revealed them to the TUC before the Cabinet, so that by the time the latter got to comment, they had already leaked to the press. These leaks, which were hardly unpredictable, were then used as justification for almost immediate publication of their proposals as a White Paper with the supposed support of Cabinet. Having bounced colleagues once, Wilson and Castle then tried to bounce them again. As trade union opposition mounted and Labour's own NEC (including, most notoriously, Jim Callaghan) publicly voted against their proposals, Castle and Wilson argued that the Government's credibility now depended on dropping plans for consultation and legislation in the autumn and going for a short, sharp Industrial Relations Bill. They also raised the stakes by allowing Jenkins to commit the Government to such legislation in his April budget speech.

Cabinet colleagues were not only angry; they were also scared. Feedback from a deeply demoralised party in parliament and the country, and from trade unionists top to bottom, was that this was an unnecessary attack on traditional industrial freedoms which risked splitting the movement and losing votes. It wouldn't be allowed to pass, even if that meant Wilson – breaking new records for unpopularity anyway – losing his job. Anyway, backing down could hardly cost the Government the election because, as far as most politicians and pundits were concerned, it was already lost. Even for those who supported industrial change, better it should be forced on the country by the Tories than by a Labour Party attacking its own core support. On 17 June 1969, what little support there remained in Cabinet for legislation rather than a voluntary commitment on behalf of the TUC evaporated. Unwilling to resign, yet seething with resentment at this reassertion of collective Cabinet government over (prime) ministerial fiat, Wilson and Castle were left with little more than damage limitation. The most the TUC would offer was a 'solemn and binding' undertaking to encourage intervention in disputes. The straw was clutched at. But it didn't need a gloating media to tell people that it was a defeat and a bad one. Wilson recovered quickly, helped by the fact that even his most reluctant supporters realised that he was going to be leading them into an election which, as the economy at last began to turn around, suddenly began to look winnable. Castle – his lightning rod – had no such luck.

Most explanations of Castle's defeat argue that at the time the unions were simply too strong – and too incestuous – a sectional interest to take on, especially after the Government had squandered so much good will on pay and public spending restraint. Castle herself had some sympathy with this line of argument but believed that she still could have won the day had she and Wilson not been stabbed in the back by their Cabinet colleagues. Typically, her analysis underplayed the parliamentary dimension, the fact that (for reasons which had as much to do with personal style and political contingency as structural or ideological factors) she failed, as so often, where it really counted – with the PLP. After over a year of unprecedentedly bad opinion polls and catastrophic local election and by-election results, Labour MPs were either angry or apathetic. In both moods they were looking for someone, something, anything to blame. Castle allowed herself to become their

scapegoat because, although she understood such 'transference', she had
no real respect for or understanding of those doing the transferring.
Instead of taking the sort of careful soundings that would have led the
average Minister to think again, Castle simply sprung her proposals on
the PLP just two hours before the publication of the White Paper, and
then proceeded to completely discount their overwhelmingly negative
reaction. Indeed, she had become so much the 'adult' minister that such
discounting had by now become a habit: discontent was merely the
childish whining of those 'grown soft on a diet of soft options because
[they] never had to choose', less an indicator that there was something
wrong than a sign that she was doing the right thing – for both the
country and the Party, even if the latter were too stupid to see it.[53]

Harold Wilson believed almost as strongly in re-educating his Party
in the political and economic realities of government. But he was astute
enough to know that politics is as much like comedy as drama: the first
rule is timing; the second is picking the right material; the third is
knowing your audience; the fourth knowing that without them you are
nothing. He also knew that Castle, especially when it came to the unions
and the PLP, did not. But he not only failed to save her from herself; he
actually made things worse. He neither prevented Callaghan breaching
collective responsibility nor punished him for so doing. He replaced
Castle's ally John Silkin, whose liberal regime might have stood at least
an outside chance of allowing the Government, as it had done so before,
to haemorrhage votes in the name of 'conscience' and yet still pass its
proposals. He indulged in all-boys-together private negotiations with
the very same trade unionists who were conducting a no-holds-barred,
and characteristically misogynistic, campaign against her.[54] And when
Castle was beginning to come round to the idea of compromise he made
the latter impossible by repudiating – in her name but without consulting
her – a TUC fudge that seemed to have satisfied even the right-wing
press. He couldn't have done much worse if he was hobbling a rival, let
alone helping a friend.

None of this negates the fact that Castle could have helped herself –
she should, for example, have resigned as soon as the PM failed to sack
his errant Home Secretary, thus leaving on a point of principle and
throwing into stark relief the weakness of the former and the latter's lack
of loyalty. But, in continuing to blame Jim Callaghan, she avoided a
more painful truth, namely the essential asymmetry and profoundly
damaging consequences of her relationship with Harold Wilson. In
retrospect, Barbara Castle blew what little chance she had of achieving
trade union reform for the same two reasons that she blew what little
chance she, as a left-winger and a woman, had of leading the Labour

Party. She had no feeling for the PLP, and she allowed herself to be captured and undermined by a man she couldn't bear to think of as anything other than on her side.

Castle was back within months infuriating trade unionists and Labour MPs alike with prices and incomes legislation. But the fact that it passed – albeit grudgingly – probably owed less to her courage than to a widespread feeling that she had been put in her place and it would be counterproductive to the Party's unexpected opinion poll recovery to defeat her a second time. Rather more positively, Castle was also able to get passed the Equal Pay Act – a cause for which she had long been a supporter, though not it must be said (perhaps because it was one of those 'women's issues') a particularly vocal or aggressive advocate. Despite the long-term impact of such legislation, it could do little to shake the impression that Castle was anything other than a lame duck.[55] Though her insistence on remaining at Employment was undoubtedly convenient in that she continued to soak up all the blame, Wilson considered her refusal to move foolish. He explained it away in terms which again reflect a tendency even among those male politicians supposedly sympathetic to her to frame her behaviour in profoundly (and in this case cruelly) sexist terms: 'Poor Barbara,' he commented to a civil servant. 'She hangs around like someone with a still-born child. She can't believe it's dead.'[56]

Brief interval

Labour's unexpected loss of office in 1970 finally put paid to any chance Castle may have had to make up for *In Place of Strife* and put herself back in contention for a crack at the leadership. One consequence of Labour's poor showing was the defeat of George Brown, which left a vacancy for Deputy Leader. Castle, like a doomed co-dependent trying one last time to break free from a relationship that has long-since become pathological, declared to friends that she would stand whether Wilson liked it or not.[57] He didn't, and predictably he was able to talk her out of it. Perhaps she was wise. In the elections to the Shadow Cabinet, dependent once again on the PLP rather than the Party in the country, she gained only 98 votes – just enough to be elected but paltry in comparison to her supposed nemesis, Jim Callaghan, who came top with 80 more than her.[58] But giving in to Wilson's logic meant she was tied as closely as ever to him. And his desire that she should not make a fool of herself only extended as far as the leadership question, in which he had a personal interest; it did not stop him from allowing her to shadow DEP. As a result, instead of putting as much distance as she could between herself and the union question, she spent the first parliamentary session in opposition leading Labour's attack on a Conservative Industrial

Relations Bill that, however hard she tried to argue to the contrary, was not so very far removed from *In Place of Strife*. By all accounts, the whole episode was excruciating. Castle – already under stress because of her husband's ill-health and going-nowhere career – may have convinced herself that she was rebuilding her reputation and sticking to her principles. Others, though, looked on in embarrassment as she relitigated the past and even hinted at an infuriating 'I told you so' to the unions. Tony Benn confided to his diary that, for all her vigour and activity, 'Barbara really has no future'.[59] Even among those who admired her most, few would have argued with him.

Castle's opposition to the Heath Government's plans to bring Britain into the EEC was obviously of longer standing, rooted as it was in Castle's belief in the value of Commonwealth trade to both British consumers and developing world producers.[60] As such it proved more productive in winning back some of the good will she had lost in 1969 from both the NEC and the left of the PLP. On the other hand, of course, it did nothing to endear her to the pro-European, often centre-right, part of the PLP, almost 90 of whom either abstained or voted with the Conservatives in October 1971 to ensure British entry. It was not altogether surprising, then, when later in the year Castle lost out in the elections to the Shadow Cabinet. Not that she lost her place: Wilson appointed her as Labour's spokesperson on Health and Social Security, simultaneously throwing her a lifeline and providing yet more ammunition for those who'd spent a political lifetime sneering that she was nothing without him. It also did her little good with the PLP. Having beaten Eric Heffer in a straight fight to replace the resigning Roy Jenkins as an elected Shadow Cabinet Member in the spring of 1972, she was promptly thrown off it later in the year. This time she turned down Wilson's offer to continue as an appointed member and left the front bench.

Last act

Labour did not really expect to win in February 1974. Given the multiple economic crises affecting the country, it might have been better – as in 1992 perhaps – to have lost. Whether, in that event, Barbara Castle would ever have served in government again seems doubtful. She was nearing her 64th birthday and had recovered little of the reputation she had so suddenly lost in 1969. But though she had decided that her next ministerial job would be her last, she was unsure whether it would be the last before retirement or, somewhat incredibly, 'a bigger bid'.[61] That the latter was a fantasy was surely evident by her demotion back to the far-flung corner of the Cabinet table, notwithstanding the importance of her Health and Social Security portfolio to the Party's manifesto and the 'social contract' it had drawn up with the trade unions.[62]

Just as she had in Wilson's first Government, Castle – now assisted by a young political adviser called Jack Straw as well as a host of social policy academics – combined solid work with a headlong rush into controversy. While her legendary ability to fight off Treasury inroads into whichever budget she was currently in charge of remained an important aspect of her success, her biggest public achievement was surely her pension reform at the DHSS.[63] This introduced both an inflation-proofed flat-rate state pension and a state-run, earnings-related pension (SERPS) for those not in an occupational scheme of their own. The second part of this two-tier plan treated women equally to men, and the two together were intended, by the end of the 1990s, to produce incomes sufficient to reduce the need for elderly people (many of whom were too proud) to apply for means-tested benefits. SERPS received widespread support, not just from the public but also from both sides of industry. Had the Thatcher Government not dismantled it in favour of private provision, the scheme would have been fully operational from 1998. How much better off today's retirees – some of them victims of the misselling scandals of the 1980s – would have been can only be guessed at.

In the health field, Castle's reasonable record of quiet achievement was completely overshadowed by political controversy.[64] Prompted in part by the public sector trade unions that represented understandably resentful, low-paid workers, the Labour manifesto had promised to remove private pay beds from NHS hospitals. While she sympathised strongly with this manifesto commitment, Castle had to take into account the reaction of the hospital consultants (many of them part-timers) whose sometimes extensive private practice relied on their continued existence. Early on in the piece, Castle decided that the way to square the circle was to get as many consultants as possible to move onto full-time NHS contracts, thereby limiting their demand for the continuation of private facilities in public hospitals. Since resources were limited, this attempt to move toward full-time working for the NHS had to rely less on carrots than on sticks: working part-time was to be made significantly less attractive and a phased withdrawal of pay beds was to begin. Unfortunately, just as it had been when she tried to overcome the trade unions, the political also became personal: after meeting with her haughty medical opponents, she had determined 'to go down fighting [rather] than meekly submit to that autocratic lot'.[65]

The consultants hit the roof, and began a work-to-rule, sparking months of intensive, and often highly acrimonious negotiations with Castle (and her junior minister, David Owen), complicated by a dispute with the junior doctors over a pay award which technically breached the

Government's own incomes policy. For all its 'unenviable record for assaults on the government of the day on matters great and small', the British Medical Association's attack on Castle was its most concerted since it had fought Bevan over the creation of the service.[66] And, no less than in her confrontation with another male bastion, the trade union movement, it was often conducted through the media in a woundingly personal (and often sexist) manner.[67] True to form, Wilson only made things worse. In an echo of his behaviour over *In Place of Strife*, he attempted to sideline Castle – this time via the sudden appointment, without consulting Castle, of his favourite establishment fixer, Arnold Goodman, who had initially approached Wilson in his capacity as paid adviser to the private hospitals. He made things worse when, again without consulting Castle, he agreed to a chaps-only meeting with the consultants behind her back. Incredibly, rather than resign, which presumably would have meant preserving her dignity at the cost of the Government's capitulation to the BMA, she rushed to No. 10 and literally gatecrashed its meeting with Wilson in order to prevent him giving away too much.[68] Arguably she succeeded, though only in part. But the success was to be short-lived and could not obscure the fact that once again her supposedly special relationship with Wilson had offered her no protection yet prevented her from acting in her own best interests.

The familiar scenario repeated itself one last time. Castle had already decided that she would not contest the next election. Even she knew now that she would never lead the Party, and she had long since lost her position as darling of the left – now a rather different kind of left – to Tony Benn.[69] By the spring of 1976 she had also decided she would give up her ministerial position once the (albeit toned-down) pay-beds legislation had been passed. She confided this to Wilson, who hinted that this would fit in well with his own plans to retire. In fact, he announced his resignation publicly in less than a fortnight, handing the succession to Jim Callaghan on a plate and practically guaranteeing a swift and involuntary end to Castle's Cabinet career. Callaghan duly beat off Healey and Foot, assumed the premiership, and, ignoring Michael Foot's plea – prompted by Castle herself – that he keep her on, Callaghan sacked her. He also had the gall, first, to play for sympathy as the reluctant butcher and, second, to use both her age (she was 65, he was 64) and the fact that Wilson – betraying a confidence – had told him of her intention to retire. If one is looking for someone to blame for Castle's demise, Callaghan – in 1969 and in 1976 – is all too easily cast as the bad guy. But that ignores two things. Firstly, Castle's career owes more to tragedy than melodrama, pride coming before a fall that in retrospect seems predestined given both her personality and the particular fates which were ranged against her. Secondly, if we must pin the blame for her demise on another individual, then Wilson fits the bill better than Callaghan.

Typically, however, Castle declined to go quietly. She carried on creating problems for Callaghan – and more immediately for his campaign manager and her successor at the DHSS, David Ennals. Getting herself onto the standing committee on the pay beds bill, Castle kept him up to the mark on the public-private divide in the NHS. Using her continued tenure on the NEC as a bully pulpit, she led an eventually successful rearguard action against the junking of her Child Benefits bill – legislation which, by ensuring that child benefit would be universal, paid for every child and directly to the mother, settled in her favour an argument that had been going on with Callaghan since the mid-1960s.[70] Yet Castle's more general offensive against the proto-monetarism, spending restrictions and moves towards means-testing of the Labour Government was not simply a vendetta. Nor was it, as some on the left argued, a hopelessly hypocritical and cynical bid for sympathy and support.[71] Although she herself had been frustrated, especially when in government by the left's knee-jerk reaction to government restraint,[72] she had always voiced doubts both openly to her colleagues and in private to her diary, about the wisdom of such policies. Unlike Callaghan, however, she had always taken Cabinet collective responsibility to mean precisely that. Given her treatment, she had little reason to hide her opinions, especially as she became convinced that, as in 1931, 1951 and 1970, the Government was going to trade its principles and its popularity for a Treasury-driven definition of the national interest – 'a scenario for another Tory victory just in time for them to reap the harvest of our bitter self-sacrifice'.[73]

Events were to prove her right. Castle was one of the first Labour politicians to take Margaret Thatcher seriously, presciently picking up on the resonance and power of her appeal to the citizen as consumer over the unions and government as producers.[74] Callaghan began, like Wilson, by patronising Thatcher and ended up losing an election to her. That election made little practical difference to Castle: she did not contest her seat. Perhaps that was a pity: despite a record number of women standing, Britain's first female prime minister was joined by fewer women MPs than had joined Barbara Castle when she had first entered the House 34 years previously.[75]

Curtain calls

True to form, Castle eschewed any ideas of a graceful descent into uncontroversial obscurity. In 1979, despite her having played a leading role in the campaign for a 'No' vote in the 1975 referendum on Britain's continued membership of the EEC, Castle contested and won a seat in the first ever direct elections for the European Parliament. Her decision was not as perverse as first it seems. Labour's first contingent of 17 directly elected MEPs, which she was to lead, contained many Eurosceptics. Some still believed in withdrawal. Others, like Castle, who were doubtful that such an option really existed any longer went to Strasbourg with the intention of heading off the slide to full-blown federalism which they saw as inherent in the Community's hopes for 'ever closer union.' Castle had also by that time become quite familiar with the EEC as a result of her husband Ted's sojourn in the Parliament as an appointed member. She may also have hoped that her new job would have given them more time together. Any such hopes, however, were dashed when, after a period of ill-health, he died in December 1979.

Castle's work as an MEP had the merit of providing her with a distraction from her grief, but in so doing was possibly marred by her characteristic tendency to immerse, not to say drown, herself in detail – in her case on the CAP. This was a recipe for frustration, both on her part and on the part of officials and colleagues. To the latter she appeared obsessive, as well as naïve: at a time when the Parliament had only consultative status, what possessed her to think that she could change anything? Despite what she might think, she was no-one now. And what gave her the right to treat them so patronisingly – when, that is, she wasn't ignoring them altogether? Worse, how dare she come out so publicly against what was now Party policy, namely complete withdrawal from the Community! A year after the second round of direct elections, which saw over 30 Labour MPs (a good 20 of whom were anti-Marketeers) in the European Parliament, Castle was voted out as group leader. She did not stand in 1989, preferring instead to turn her attention back to British politics.

Never one to do the expected, Castle then completed another U-turn by agreeing to her elevation to the Lords in 1990, justifying her decision on the grounds that, since the institution was there, it had to be used and that the quickest way to reform (or destroy) it was from within. Mostly, however, she used the Lords – and the media and various Party forums – as a platform for passing comment on Labour's direction and performance in opposition and in government. This was not always entirely welcome to the leadership. Neil Kinnock coped diplomatically with the largely private 'advice' from his self-appointed critic in the wings.[76] But Tony Blair had to put up with rather more public prodding from the stalls. In 1996, 'the immaculately turned out blast from the past'[77] came close to inflicting a conference defeat on pensions policy when she spearheaded a campaign to drag the leadership back from what she considered its descent into knee-jerk anti-statism. It was just like old times. Too much so in fact, when retired T & G baron, Jack Jones, now leader of Britain's nascent 'grey-power' movement, agreed to lend his support to the leadership's deal with some (though not all) of the trade unions.

Castle, however, did not give up and continued to whip up criticism of the Blair Government's policy, which finally came into operation in April 2001. The fact that the Government decided to up-rate the state pension only in line with inflation not earnings, and the fact that millions would be left out of the employer-operated 'stakeholder' schemes, would mean that many people would be left relying on the means-tested (and inadequate) minimum income guarantee, Castle argued. After local election defeats which were blamed in part on a public backlash against the derisory 75p increase in the basic pension, Conference came round to her way of thinking. In September 2000, Castle, this time joined by Jones and, most importantly, by union bosses like John Edmonds and Rodney Bickerstaffe, persuaded the delegates by a margin of three to two to demand that the Government reinstate the link between earnings and pensions. With pensioners constituting some 11 million electors and tending, unlike the young, to exercise that vote, the issue was unlikely to go away. Indeed the Conservative's pledge to an across the board increase of £10 seemed to indicate a return to the bidding war of the 1960s and 1970s rather than a breakthrough into some nebulous 'new welfare for a new century'.

Epilogue

As well-supported as they are, and as the product of a political career spent partly at the heart of government, Castle's views cannot be convincingly dismissed by party spin doctors as the ranting of a heretical has-been. Whatever her faults and limitations, and however damaging some of the confrontations she provoked in her long career, Castle always displayed a knack for getting to the heart of the matter. Far from bogging herself down in the unnecessary and the tangential, as her opponents often argued, she had the perspicacity and pertinacity to focus on underlying issues – which was why the confrontations were so intense. Her calls on the trade union movement to exercise the restraint and responsibility demanded of it by full employment and welfare capitalism fell on deaf ears. But in hindsight they were profoundly correct. Likewise, her campaign to separate private and public healthcare addressed the fundamental question of whether, in the interests of equity and efficiency, a self-interested but strategically important group of employees should command time and facilities that are essentially parasitical on the NHS's core business. It is obviously a question that still demands an answer, as the Blair Government's own attempt to encourage the consultants to forfeit their right to private practice clearly showed.[78]

Castle may have fought what in hindsight can sometimes seem like doomed campaigns. But the question is not so much whether they were worth fighting. It is more whether it was in her interests, or her party's interests, to fight them in the way that she did. 'In politics,' Castle often said, 'guts is all.' Except in so far as she allowed both misplaced personal loyalty and sheer enjoyment of 'the febrile, exacting and fulfilling world of power'[79] to prevent her from breaking free of a fatal dependence on Harold Wilson, Castle never lacked courage. But politics is about so much more. It is sometimes better conducted as a war of position rather than a war of manoeuvre – something which Barbara Castle never fully appreciated nor managed to do. This, and her inability to build the personal networks which might have overcome the deep-seated sexism and factionalism of the Labour movement, ensured that she never came close to becoming the party's first female leader. Given how few women made it into the upper reaches of the first Blair Government, and given how poorly some of them who did were treated, it is hard to imagine anyone coming much closer anytime soon.

Further reading

The obvious next port of call is the recent biography by Lisa Martineau, *Politics and Power: Barbara Castle* (London, 2000), a well-researched and entertaining book with a useful section on sources. *The Red Queen*, a BBC TV portrait of Castle by Michael Cockerell, first shown on 29 January 1995, is also useful. Castle's biography *Fighting All the Way* (London, 1993) is well worth a read, even if its refreshing self-disclosures are diluted by the usual dose of self-defence and self-justification. Likewise her *Diaries*, which are best read in the original, separate editions (London, 1980 and 1984), always remembering that they were written with publication in mind! The same goes, of course, for the diaries of Richard Crossman and Tony Benn. Castle crops up at least fleetingly in all the autobiographies and biographies of her colleagues, but most useful in this respect are Ben Pimlott, *Harold Wilson* (London, 1992) and Kenneth O. Morgan, *Callaghan: A Life* (Oxford, 1999), the latter because it provides the other side of the story as regards *In Place of Strife*. That episode, and others involving Castle, are also dealt with in Clive Ponting, *Breach of Promise: Labour in Power 1964–1970* (London, 1989), and in more general histories of the Party, like Eric Shaw's *The Labour Party since 1945* (Oxford, 1996) and Kevin Jefferys' work of the same name (London, 1993). Those interested in the party-union link should read Lewis Minkin, *The Contentious Alliance* (Edinburgh, 1991), while those wanting to read more about Castle at the DHSS should consult Charles Webster, *The Health Services since the War*, Volume II (London, 1996).

Notes

1. For historical commentary on the backgrounds of women MPs, see Melville Currell, *Political Women* (London, 1974), p 68.
2. David Watt, *Financial Times*, 19 April 1969, cited in Melanie Phillips, *The Divided House: Women at Westminster* (London, 1982), p 116. See also Castle, *Diaries*, 22 November 1974.
3. Barbara Castle, *Fighting all the Way*, p 2.
4. See Phillips, *The Divided House*, p 25.
5. See Martineau, *Politics and Power*, pp 59–62.
6. Castle's selection was not unprecedented: Blackburn had elected a woman Labour member between 1929 and 1931. See Pamela Barnes, *Women at Westminster* (London, 1967).
7. See Currell, *Political Women*, pp 25–8.
8. See Martineau, *Politics and Power*, pp 114–115, and Castle, *Fighting*, p 207.
9. See Martineau, *Politics and Power*, p 102.
10. See Castle, *Diaries*, 16 March 1968, and Castle, *Fighting*, p 335.
11. See Martineau, *Politics and Power*, p 131.
12. See Vallence, *Women in the House* (London, 1979), p 6.
13. Ibid, p 72.
14. See Vallence, *Women*, p 107.
15. Currell (*Political Women*, pp 87–8) found that most women MPs in her survey did feel pushed into making a particularly female contribution, though many saw themselves as doing this in addition to their work on more general issues.
16. Patricia Hollis, *Jennie Lee: A Life* (Oxford, 1997), p 149. On this as a dilemma for Labour women outside and inside parliament see Pat Thane, 'The women of the British Labour Party and Feminism, 1906–1945' in Harold L. Smith (ed.), *British Feminism in the Twentieth Century* (Amherst, 1990).
17. Ibid, p 152. See also Currell, *Political Women*, p 36, and Amy Black and Stephen Brooke, 'The Labour Party, Women, and the Problem of Gender, 1951–1966', *Journal of British Studies*, 36, 1997.
18. The same of course can be said of a number of male MPs, Labour's Tony Greenwood being the most obvious example. But, predictably, their appearance rarely, if ever, drew media comment – which is not to say that their looks did not work to their political advantage.
19. See Martineau, *Politics and Power*, p 70.
20. Currell, *Political Women*, p 178.
21. 'Women around the House', *Sunday Times*, 21 June 1964.
22. Whether it really did so is a moot point. As a fascinating discussion of the issue in wide-ranging historical terms notes, a powerful woman's femininity almost automatically leads to hints or outright claims that the basis of her influence is sexual – something which, as we shall see, Castle had to deal with as a Minister. See Susan Dixon, 'Conclusion – The Enduring Theme: Domineering Dowagers and Scheming Concubines', in Barbara Garlick et

al (eds), *Stereotypes of Women in Power: Historical Perspectives and Revisionist Views* (New York, 1992).

23. Castle almost made the same mistake in March 1963 when she helped precipitate the Profumo scandal. Fortunately, though she got her facts wrong, the impact of the true story was such that all was forgiven and forgotten. See Martineau, *Politics and Power*, pp 153–55.

24. Martineau, *Politics and Power*, p 138.

25. See Tim Bale, *Sacred Cows and Common Sense: The Symbolic Statecraft and Political Culture of the British Labour Party* (Aldershot, 1999), pp 62–69.

26. Tony Benn, *Diaries*, 3 December 1963.

27. Ibid, 30 August 1963.

28. Castle had taken an interest in Africa throughout the 1950s, partly because of her brother Jimmie's forestry work in the region and partly through Labour MP and pacifist Fenner Brockway's Movement for Colonial Freedom. Hence her pursuit of Lennox Boyd.

29. Currell (*Political Women*, p 30) notes that Wilson appointed six other women to government in 1964: two Ministers outside Cabinet, one Under Secretary, two Parliamentary Secretaries and a government whip. She also points out that while the absolute number of women who have attained such office is low, women MPs have historically had more chance than their far more numerous male counterparts at being appointed to office above the rank of PPS.

30. Martineau, *Politics and Power*, p 162.

31. Ibid, p 163.

32. Castle, *Fighting*, p 136.

33. Castle, *Diaries*, 20 June 1967, and see Martineau, *Politics and Power*, p 169.

34. Castle, *Diaries*, 21 December 1965.

35. Castle, *Diaries*, 30 November 1965.

36. Martineau, *Politics and Power*, p 165.

37. Ben Pimlott, *Harold Wilson*, p 537.

38. Ironically, Castle (*Diaries*, 13 June 1974) records Callaghan reacting to Cabinet criticism of his handling of the EEC renegotiations by threatening to 'chuck in his hand': 'he does', she thought, 'go feminine at times'.

39. See Phillips, *The Divided House*, pp 27–9, also Castle, *Diaries*, 26 March 1976 or *Fighting*, p 267.

40. Martineau, *Politics and Power*, p 165.

41. See Benn, *Diaries*, 9 March 1970 and 7 March 1974.

42. Martineau, *Politics and Power*, p 181.

43. See Geoffrey Dudley, 'The Next Steps Agencies, political salience and the arm's length principle: Barbara Castle at the Ministry of Transport 1965–68', *Public Administration*, 72/2, 1994.

44. See Bale, *Sacred Cows*, pp 129–131, and Castle, *Diaries*, 13 June 1968.

45. 'Why Barbara is King of the Castle', *Daily Express*, 11 March 1968.

46. Castle, *Diaries*, 18 March 1968, see also 28 November 1966.

47. On the disciplinary crisis, see Bale, *Sacred Cows*, pp 158–172. On South Africa, see Bale, 'A Deplorable Episode? South African Arms and the Statecraft of British Social Democracy', *Labour History Review*, 62/1, 1997.

Castle was a past president of the anti-apartheid movement and had helped get the Republic thrown out of the Commonwealth. While it may be true, as some argue, that she (or the threat of her resignation) kept Wilson staunch on southern Africa, it may also be true that her gratitude for his not slipping may have been a significant factor in her dependence on him.

48. See Clive Ponting, *Breach of Promise*, pp 350–2.

49. See Tim Bale, 'Harold Wilson', in Kevin Jefferys (ed.), *Leading Labour: From Keir Hardie to Tony Blair* (London, 1999).

50. Castle, *Diaries*, 5 April 1968.

51. See Minkin, *Contentious Alliance*, and Leo Panitch, *Social Democracy and Industrial Militancy* (Cambridge, 1976).

52. Her concerns are littered throughout her diary long before 1969. See, for example, 22 February 1967 and 25 September 1967.

53. Castle, *Diaries*, 7 May 1969. Her reactions to other rebellions exhibit a similar frustration and failure to appreciate their seriousness; see *Diaries*, 27 July 1967 and 16 January 1968.

54. For instance, the opposition of the TUC's Vic Feather was political; but mixed with it was more than a dash of the personal. He played unpleasantly on her gender and their long mutual acquaintance ('I knew Barbara Castle when she had dirty knickers') to undermine her, and dismissed her frustration at his intransigence and patronising attitude as (surprise, surprise!) 'hysterical' – attitudes and tactics that resonated strongly with his fellow unionists. See Martineau, *Politics and Power*, pp 215 and 218, Robert Taylor, *The TUC: From the General Strike to the New Unionism* (London, 2000).

55. 'Whatever happened to Barbara?', *Spectator*, 9 May 1970.

56. Ponting, *Breach*, p 367; see also Benn, *Diaries*, 3 September 1969.

57. Benn, *Diaries*, 23 June 1970.

58. The profoundly personal collision between the two is an underlying theme of Martineau's recent biography; see *Politics and Power*, p 95.

59. Benn, *Diaries*, 2 May 1972.

60. See Castle, *Fighting*, pp 328–330.

61. Castle, *Diaries*, 4 March 1974.

62. Castle served, alongside her erstwhile enemies and rivals on the so-called Liaison Committee of politicians and trade unionists that prior to 1974 produced the framework document which fed into its manifesto; it was designed to ensure union cooperation in return for a government commitment to economic growth and the welfare state.

63. Castle, *Fighting*, p 480.

64. Castle's other work at Health is best followed in Charles Webster, *The Health Services since the War: Volume II*.

65. Castle, *Diaries*, 4 November 1974.

66. Charles Webster 'The BMA and the NHS', *British Medical Journal*, 1316/7150, 4 July 1998, p 45.

67. See Benn, *Diaries*, 27 October 1975, and Castle, *Diaries*, 20 June 1975 and 18 December 1975.

68. See Castle, *Diaries*, 2–3 December 1975.

69. See Patrick Seyd, *The Rise and Fall of the Labour Left* (London, 1987).
70. See Castle, *Diaries*, 26 March 1976. See also Bale, *Sacred Cows*, p 92.
71. See Benn, *Diaries*, 14 July 1976.
72. See Castle, *Diaries*, 13 June 1968 and 1 July 1968.
73. Castle, *Diaries*, 10 July 1975 and 14 July 1975.
74. See Castle, *Diaries*, 11 February 1975.
75. See Vallence, *Women*, p 179. Out of 206 women candidates only 19 were returned. The Conservatives had eight women MPs, including Thatcher; Labour had 11 – out of a total of 53 who stood.
76. Castle, *Fighting*, pp 584–586.
77. Martineau, *Politics and Power*, p 336.
78. 'Milburn offers big bribe to doctors to stay in the NHS', *Independent*, 22 February 2001.
79. Castle, *Diaries*, 9 June 1975.

Part III
Decline and Renewal Since 1979

11

Tony Benn

Eric Shaw

(Anthony Neil Wedgwood) Tony Benn, b.1925. Labour MP for Bristol South-East 1950–60 (renounced peerage) and 1963–83; MP for Chesterfield 1984–2001. Postmaster General 1964–66; Minister of Technology 1966–70. Secretary of State for Industry 1974–75; Secretary of State for Energy 1975–79. In 1981 he narrowly failed to be elected Labour's Deputy Leader.

> 'Though politicians dream of fame and hope to win a deathless name,
> Time strews upon them when they've gone, the poppy of oblivion.'

> Tony Benn MP, in his final speech in Parliament, quoting from
> his grandfather, former Liberal MP for Glasgow Govan

> All change in history, all advance, comes from the nonconformists.

> A.J.P. Taylor, in *The Troublemakers*

There are, one can say, two sorts of politicians, the *yea-sayers* and the *nay-sayers*: the natural conformists and the instinctive rebels – the troublemakers. There are always many more of the former than the latter, for to elevate oneself in the world of affairs it is always easier to drift with the current than thrust against it. And to be a nay-sayer requires a mix of qualities that few possess: the self-confidence, strength of conviction and steadiness of purpose to survive the public odium that will almost certainly be incurred. Tony Benn was an inveterate nay-sayer

– and for almost three decades was the butt of interminable abuse, ridicule and denigration heaped upon him by the press and political opponents (inside and outside his own party). He was, the noted historian Kenneth Morgan observed in the mid-1980s, feared, despised, 'even hated… canvassers on the doorstep in 1979 and 1983 found that his approach to politics had become Labour's main electoral liability'.[1] Research in 1981 revealed that 73 per cent of a sample believed he held 'dictatorial ambitions', 62 per cent that he was a Communist who sought to make us 'just like Russia', and over a quarter of those intending to vote Labour would reconsider if he became deputy leader.[2]

In 2000 the Political Studies Association, in its 50th anniversary celebration, presented Benn with the award for Britain's 'outstanding parliamentarian', commending him for persistent efforts to reinvigorate British parliamentary democracy and reassert the power of the Commons. This may astonish those many newspaper readers who had been for years instructed that Benn sought (in the words of Anthony Shrimsley, the *Daily Mail*'s political editor) 'to obliterate democracy as we know it'; that 'a cross on the ballot for a party which has Benn waiting in the wings for its top job is a cross for the bleak and cold regimes of Eastern Europe' (the *Sun*); that he was encouraging the 'sort of People's Democracy the Russians set up in Eastern Europe after the war' (Denis Healey); that he was 'a little Stalin' (Frank Chapple, the electricians' union leader); that he had 'the mind of a ranter and the eyes of a fanatic' (the *Express*) and was surrounded by 'sneering, hate-filled creatures' (the *Mirror*). For the *Guardian*'s much-respected political columnist Peter Jenkins, 'popular worries about Anthony Wedgwood Benn appear to be less that he is a leftie than he may be a loonie'. Doubts about his sanity – a useful way of delegitimating political ideas without troubling to explore them – became a common refrain in the press. 'Order of the Bennite Loon. For devotees of crazy political ideas', proclaimed the *Mail* whilst the *Sun*, with its customary subtlety, added: 'Mr Benn – Is He Mad or a Killer?'[3] Not surprising then that the mere mention of the Bristol MP's name in the 1970s and early 1980s could reduce so many ordinary people in the street to splenetic rage. Paul Johnson commented in the *Daily Telegraph* in January 1975:

> anthropologists say that all societies in distress need an object, however innocent, on which to vent their impotent fury… We, it seems, have chosen Mr Benn. Whenever newspaper editors, or economists, or City slickers, or businessmen gather, to ponder the mess and exchange horror-stories of the latest national reverse, Mr Benn's name crops up and he is duly denounced.[4]

TONY BENN   201

That he would become so controversial and (for many) reviled a figure could not have been predicted for a man born with a political silver spoon. He had brains, boundless energy, looks and a winning manner. He was bred in a political family: both his father and grandfather served in the House of Commons and the former's membership of the 1929–31 MacDonald Government gave him early contact with Labour's inner circle. At 18 he joined the RAF, gaining his pilot's wings in March 1945. In 1950, at the age of 25 he was selected and subsequently elected for the (then) safe Labour seat of Bristol South East. Within nine years he had been elected to Labour's National Executive; with gaps, he was to serve on it for a generation. He was appointed Postmaster General in the Wilson administration in 1964 and soon found himself in the Cabinet. In 1966 he was promoted to Minister of Technology and in 1969 his portfolio was expanded into a veritable super-ministry. That year the *Sunday Times* nominated him as 'the only possible contender for the party leadership a decade from now'.[5] In 1974 the politically quite unsympathetic *Times* approved Benn's return to ministerial office as a 'capable administrator'.[6] He was a cabinet member throughout the 1974–79 Labour Government, as Industry Secretary until 1975 and thereafter at Energy.

He was an outstanding communicator, with a remarkable gift for lucid exposition, able to order and marshal facts, ideas and interpretations in exemplary fashion. He could present complex issues with startling clarity, combining forceful advocacy with a calm, measured tone. Barbara Castle reported being 'dazzled by his brilliance in analysing what was wrong with our society and his skill in promoting his ideas'. His capacity 'for putting mundane issues in philosophical context was unmatched, and it was what the rank and file hungered for. He could entrance audiences and lift his speeches to dazzling heights which impressed even non-socialists'.[7] The public image of him as a humourless, wild-eyed fanatic was as far as could be imagined from the truth. Even whilst at loggerheads with Cabinet colleagues between 1974 and 1979 he was 'universally regarded as a personally charming, humorous colleague'. 'Tony,' recalled James Callaghan, could be 'extremely amusing and he sometimes enlivened cabinet with genuine flashes of wit.' He was 'personally courteous at all times', recollected Denis Healey, one of his bitterest foes within the party. 'Besides a silver tongue, he had a pretty wit, and was quite prepared to laugh at himself.'[8]

At the height of his popularity he seemed to be trailing clouds of glory. During the 1980 Party Conference he drew huge crowds as he moved 'from meeting to meeting, as if blessed with ubiquity, to be greeted with revolutionary adulation'.[9] He had – according to Edmund Dell, who stood at the opposite end of Labour's spectrum – 'charm, humour, extraordinary eloquence and a willingness to work which was certainly not emulated among the majority of his opponents in the Party'.[10] Yet, Morgan judged in the mid-1980s, 'this attractive, articulate, energetic man has had a largely unsatisfactory and shapeless career'.[11] For many, his was the cardinal responsibility for Labour's calamitous electoral performance in 1983. 'He came close,' Healey declared, 'to destroying the Labour Party as a force in twentieth century British politics.'[12]

How then can we account for the vicissitudes of his career – his massive appeal to Labour's grassroots and the bitter antagonism he attracted elsewhere? Why does he deserve inclusion amongst the dozen or so key figures outside the ranks of the leadership in the party's recent history? What effect did he have on the party's evolution and for what will he be remembered?

Benn the minister

Benn was an MP for half a century, though his tenure was interrupted twice, once between 1960 and 1963 when, on inheriting his peerage, he was barred from the House and again in 1983, between losing his seat in Bristol South East seat and his return at a by-election the following year as MP for Chesterfield. He finally retired in May 2001 at the age of 76. For the first two decades of his parliamentary life, he was (in Labour party terms) a centrist. He had little enthusiasm for the left-wing Bevanites and the 'obvious relish' with which they reacted to trouble 'brewing' in Labour's ranks disheartened him.[13] But though he voted for Gaitskell against Bevan in 1955, he never really belonged to the revisionist camp either. Within the Parliamentary Labour Party he always remained something of a loner. His main achievement in this period was his campaign to renounce his peerage and retain his seat in the House of Commons. With the passage of the Peerage Act in 1963 he gained a notable triumph. In his first ministerial phase he was 'Mintech Benn', 'the quintessential whizz-kid, developing Concorde with the French, computerising industry, building up Britain's civilian nuclear energy programme as an enthusiast for fast-breeder reactors'.[14]

But all this altered after 1970. Without a doubt the crucial phase of his career was in the years 1970 to 1983 and it is upon these years that we shall concentrate. During this period, fellow frontbencher and one-time ally, Peter Shore later wrote, he was a 'dominant figure in the Labour Party, the principal opponent of majority Cabinet policies, the architect of the so-called "alternative economic strategy" during the successive premierships of Wilson and Callaghan and then, in Opposition again… the creative and destructive genius behind the new model Labour Party'. He assumed the mantle of the left's leader – to the ire of more seasoned campaigners such as Michael Foot and Barbara Castle. His position in the Party grew 'immensely stronger during the period of the Heath Government', as a member of the Shadow Cabinet, a senior figure on the NEC, as Chairman of the Labour Party in 1972 and as one of Labour's most articulate and outspoken figures.[15] In the elections for Deputy Leader of the Party in November 1972, he won 46 votes against the 140 cast for Jenkins and the 96 for Foot – a reasonable score against far more established figures.

His first breach with established thinking, in 1970, was his call for constitutional and institutional reform to break down established concentrations of power – years before commentators claimed this as a defining feature of 'New' Labour. In a major speech he pressed for 'freedom of information legislation on the Swedish model [that] would permit public scrutiny of decision-making'; the holding of referenda on key issues; an opening up of the mass media to those with minority views; the provision of fuller statistical information to encourage informed debate; the integration of the taxation and social security systems to facilitate transparency and eliminate anomalies; the promotion of representative organisations to improve channels of communication between government and the public; and 'devolution of power to regions and localities'.[16] In this and subsequent speeches he anticipated much of the constitutional reform agenda of later years. Immune to the complacency over parliamentary government which traditionally had suffused Labour's upper echelons, he contended – in what became one of the most insistent themes of his numerous public pronouncements – that the advance of democracy had fallen far short 'of any control over the extra-parliamentary centres of financial and economic power'. Nor did it 'even guarantee ministerial or parliamentary power over the apparatus of the state'.[17] He was also responsible for a major constitutional innovation with his suggestion – initially denounced by most of his fellow frontbenchers but later gratefully accepted – for a referendum over the proposed renegotiations over the terms of entry to the European Community negotiated by the Heath Government in 1973.

His critique soon extended to the whole range of policy issues, though they came to be focused on economic and industrial matters. He played a major part in formulating Labour's radical industrial strategy in opposition between 1970 and 1974 and Wilson (probably reluctantly) appointed him Secretary of State for Industry – though he took the precaution of appointing a member of the No. 10 Policy Unit as a 'Benn-watcher' to keep a jaundiced eye on him. Industrial policy was a major bone of contention throughout the 1974–79 Government. The interventionist strategy called, firstly, for the creation of a National Enterprise Board (based on continental models such as the Italian IRI) to operate as a holding company for public enterprises and for the public

stake in private firms; second, for the signing of Planning Agreements
with leading companies in all major industrial sectors, setting targets for
investment, prices, exports and so forth; and third, for the promotion of
industrial democracy. Wilson soon intimated that he intended to scuttle
the strategy and indeed did so. But it remained party policy for years
and had, in Benn, a determined advocate.

This advocacy reflected Benn's belief that capitalism in Britain could
no longer deliver the goods and that only a major extension of planning
and public ownership could revive the economy.[18] Traditionally Labour
governments had sought to balance the wants, aspirations and
expectations of its trade union partners with pressures emanating from
the City, big business and other citadels of economic power. But in the
hazardous economic circumstances of that decade, with stagnant living
standards, massive inflationary pressure, widespread grassroots union
militancy and a business establishment rapidly losing its faith in the
post-war consensus, the balancing act was becoming exceedingly difficult.
Benn's view was that revisionist social democracy – the managed economy
and welfare capitalism – had reached an impasse. In particular, though
acknowledging 'that wage militancy has not got much to do with
socialism' – indeed that it could 'actually damage the prospects of advance'
– he made clear he disagreed with the incomes policy central to the
Government's economic strategy. High wage demands were inevitable,
he contended, 'if we retain an economic system which denies the trade
unions the right to influence profits, investment and dividends'.[19]

The analysis Benn advanced had been proffered by Tawney years before.
Organised labour whilst 'not yet strong enough to impose their will' were
yet 'strong enough to resist when their masters would impose theirs'. The
predicament of trade unionism was that of 'an opposition which never
becomes a government'. This could not for long be sustained – and the
choice would then be between a return 'to the discipline which capitalism
exercised through its instrument of unemployment' or a more positive
role for the unions: the assumption of 'collective responsibility of the
workers for the maintenance of the standards of their profession'.[20] Benn
developed this analysis further. There were, he suggested, three options
for dealing with trade union power: the first was to subdue it through
unemployment and legislative restraints; the second 'to head it off through
participation and involvement at board level' – a window dressing
democracy; the third (his option) was 'to institutionalise it and, through
it, create democracy, which meant real control, shifting the balance of
power and responsibility in favour of labour'.[21] By industrial democracy
he meant the extension of collective bargaining to 'all those decisions that
really determine whether there is wealth creation in society' – including

'investment, products, exports, manpower forecasting and product development'.[22] In effect, the opposition should enter government.

To most senior ministers Benn's combination of industrial democracy and state intervention was both economically and politically a non-starter. 'Vague threats' about workers' control, Healey complained in cabinet committee, had depressed business confidence and 'led to a blight on investment'.[23] If business lacked the confidence to invest, then output, productivity, the balance of payments and employment would all suffer and the Government would pay the electoral penalty.[24] When Benn protested at the proposed emasculation of the NEB, complaining that even the Industrial Reorganisation Corporation of the 1960s had been authorised to purchase shares without consent, Healey riposted:

'Well, we have to maintain the confidence of business.'

'Why just the confidence of business?' I [Benn] asked.

'Because the whole of our future depends on the confidence of business.'[25]

It was, for Benn, an unpalatable point. He had undoubtedly put his finger on a crucial problem but whether he had thought through with sufficient rigour the implications of his strategy, not least for maintaining adequate levels of investment, is another matter. To his exasperated colleagues he exhibited a 'consistent lack of realism, a blank refusal to admit that there were deep-seated problems in the economy, in work practices, in the unions, and in the procedures for pay bargaining, coupled with a denial of the simple facts of inflation or external financial weakness'.[26] Benn was a vigorous protagonist of shop floor power but, in the context of a decentralised and fragmented trade union movement, did this not facilitate sectionalism, wage leapfrogging and insistence upon protecting differentials? In corporatist systems such as Sweden, union organisation was more centralised and shop floor autonomy restricted but was this not more conducive to an all-encompassing approach in which organised labour could give priority to the common interest of all employees, for instance by trading wage restraint for social reforms? But Benn dismissed corporatism – 'the imposition of centralised controls from the top' – as 'unacceptable and unworkable'.[27] Moving towards some variant of Scandinavian corporatism did indeed raise all sorts of difficulties, given the traditions, ethos and institutional arrangements of state, capital and labour in the UK. And the problem of reconciling centralised, elite-level bargaining with participation and accountability – vital issues for Benn – was a very real one. But for the Bristol MP, with his faith in enlarging the prerogatives of shop stewards, the whole approach was in principle objectionable.[28]

This struck a chord with many of the rank and file both within the party and the unions but, even aside from doubts about its viability, politically it was not even on the cards for the 1974–79 Government. For most senior ministers – especially after the collapse of the pay policy and the onset of the disastrous Winter of Discontent in 1978–79 – the question was not how to institutionalise union power but how to tame it. Characteristically, Healey put the matter most forcefully. 'We must redress the balance of power. It is cheaper to strike in Britain than it is in other countries because we give strikers unemployment pay and social benefits.' Callaghan pondered stripping workers in essential services of the right to strike.[29]

In short, Benn and the right-wing majority in the cabinet were approaching the issue of capital-labour relations from radically divergent vantage points. The subservience of the 1970s Labour Government to the 'union barons' has become entrenched in folklore. 'The climate of the time,' according to Roy (Lord) Jenkins, 'was that of ministers finding out what the TUC wanted and giving it to them.'[30] 'The overwhelming power of the trade unions in the Party,' according to one quite typical account, 'meant that the relationship between the unions and the Government was inevitably at times that of patron and dependent.' Benn dissented. 'There are other powers in the land,' he countered, 'beside the trade unions: there's the IMF, which had the power to cut our expenditure by $4 billion and called it "facing harsh reality"; but when the trade unions make their demands we don't look at it that way at all.'[31] Along with the Winter of Discontent, the controversy over the IMF loan was indeed the landmark event of the 1970s Labour administration, for it represented 'a turning point in the philosophical basis of economic policy'. The Ford Administration in the USA was determined to use its control over the IMF to force Britain to eschew the 'profligate' policy of high social spending.[32]

Benn joined other ministers on the left and centre-left – plus the party's leading revisionist thinker, Tony Crosland – in strenuously opposing the loan with its tough conditions. He advocated a complete reversal of policy, including the imposition of import and exchange controls, control of bank borrowing and an interventionist industrial policy, but was very much in a minority. Unlike Crosland he had negligible influence and once the Foreign Secretary had been arms-twisted into switching sides the debate was all but over. Crosland warned that the IMF prescription would have a disastrous effect on investment and on wages policy: 'far from reducing the PSBR [public sector borrowing requirement], the spending cuts would mean higher unemployment, which would in turn mean higher social security payments and lower tax revenue, thus actually increasing the PSBR'. He concluded: 'we have to stop paying danegeld'. When eventually he abandoned his resistance the disconsolate Foreign Secretary (he was to die within a couple of months) told Cabinet that the IMF package – 'wrong economically and socially' – was 'destructive of what he had believed in all his life'.[33] For Benn, the whole episode reaffirmed his belief that it was capital and its political friends, not the unions, who called the tune. Two distinguished economic journalists, writing at the time, agreed. After 1974–5 organised labour 'had very little influence on the broad thrust of policy'. Rather it was the financial markets, whose political clout had expanded by a 'quantum leap', which now emerged as 'the most important influence on policy'.[34]

In fact by the time of the loan the Bristol MP had been politically sidelined. Wilson had used the opportunity of the left's defeat at the referendum over the renegotiation of Britain's terms of entry into the European Community in 1975 to move him from Industry to the less sensitive post of Energy,[35] rendering him 'a frustrated, ineffective figure as a member of government'.[36] As Crosland had predicted, the IMF prescription had fatal effects, paving the way to the grim *finale* of the 5 per cent pay policy and the Winter of Discontent which sealed the fate of the Labour government and ended Benn's ministerial career. But he was by no means distraught. Indeed, the period of his greatest power within the party was about to commence.

Leading the left, 1979–83

By the close of the 1970s Benn had become, as Barbara Castle observed, 'the most charismatic figure on the left'.[37] Politicians rise in the world not simply because of the virtues they may possess but to the degree they embody the hopes, aspirations and expectations of those they seek to lead. 'In normal circumstances a prolonged parliamentary apprenticeship serves to screen out those aspirants whose dynamism, flamboyance, or waywardness has earned suspicion rather than admiration from their colleagues.'[38] But the circumstances were not normal. Benn's critique of Keynesian social democracy was launched at its moment of crisis. His message, that the real options were now a capitalism once more red in tooth and claw (Thatcherism) or real socialism, fell on a receptive audience – the young, mainly university-educated teachers and social workers by then the mainstay of most constituency Labour parties, and the more combative middle-level officials, lay officers and activists within the unions. He articulated their aspirations for a more equal, fairer and participatory society with fervour, clarity and compelling fluency.

Labour's leadership, he wrote in 1977, had always been 'defective', always apt to abandon radicalism when under pressure. Having ascended the political ladder, and savouring the perquisites of office, they ceased to listen to the sound 'heart of the Party'.[39] With the party back in opposition, now was the time to reform Labour's internal arrangements to enforce greater accountability on the party leadership. He was confident that 'the trade unions and the rank and file are stronger than they have ever been... All the growth on the left is going to come up from the outside and underneath'.[40] What was required was to ensure that the right mechanisms were in place. Whilst he did not instigate the drive for constitutional reform, 'he became the figure around whom all the disparate parts of an inherently disunited movement could rally'.[41] The introduction of mandatory reselection of MPs and a wider franchise to elect the leader would, he believed, produce an 'an enormous change, because the PLP, which has been the great centre of power in British politics, has had to yield to the movement that put members there'.[42] He assumed that activists within the constituency parties were representative of the wider membership and shortsightedly ignored the case for one-member, one-vote – which in due course ceded the democratic high ground to Labour's right.

The campaign for constitutional change was furiously fought – and very narrowly and to a degree fortuitously won, and at the cost of exacerbating the Party's internal tensions. Almost immediately, the political climate deteriorated sharply for Labour. A group of senior Labour right-wingers (including Roy Jenkins and David Owen) seized upon the establishment by the special Wembley conference of January 1981 of an electoral college for Labour's leadership to announce the formation of the Social Democratic Party. A pact with the Liberals was soon arranged and a formidable electoral threat to Labour posed. Benn failed to take it seriously, instead activating the new electoral college by challenging Healey for the deputy leadership. He ignored the clamant appeals of those – including the party leader and some within his own camp – who pleaded with him to desist from a course bound to intensify discord.

Benn was defeated by the slimmest of margins.[43] Predictably, far from being 'the healing process' he tagged it, it was an acrid, highly divisive and energy-sapping campaign. It also provoked a right-wing backlash: indeed it was the turning point in the party's history, for from that point on the shift to the right, slow and unsteady at first, but in due course with growing velocity, was relentless. Contesting the deputy leadership was, for the left, a major strategic miscalculation. Benn evinced a faith in the power of will, of resolution – of tenacity in the service of what he considered a just cause – which history, except in the rarest instances, hardly justifies. In reality, the Labour left's power base was exiguous: it rested on the support of party and union activists, some leftist trade union leaders, a handful of radical magazines, a few, generally weak, pressure groups and little else. Against it was arrayed the might of the financial and business establishment, virtually the whole of the media, the main professional associations and the liberal intelligentsia. The labour movement itself was divided, demoralised and steadily shrinking under the double assault of highly unfavourable labour market conditions and manacling legislation being enacted by the Thatcher Government.

The left-wing 1983 manifesto was dubbed by one of Benn's most acerbic critics – Gerald Kaufman – 'the longest suicide note in history'. It ensured that the left would forever be held responsible for the most calamitous defeat in the party's history. Its adoption reflected less the strength of the left than its tactical ineptitude. In contrast to the row over the 1979 manifesto, the 1983 document was accepted almost without debate – despite the fact that the left had by then lost control of the NEC, underlined by the removal the preceding year of Benn from chairmanship of the key Home Policy committee and his replacement by the tough and wily right-wing trade union leader and MP, John Golding. Golding's willingness to virtually nod through a manifesto stuffed with left-wing ideas was a calculated ploy: if the party was going to capsize, it might as well sink to the ocean bed with a red flag flying at its mast.

The 1983 election was a cataclysm for Labour, down to a mere 28 per cent of the popular vote. Benn lost his seat, though he was returned the following year as MP for Chesterfield. But his political career was entering twilight. Already in early 1983 he had confided to his diary that he felt 'the pressure on me now and a sense of isolation, from which Caroline [his wife] thinks I have protected myself by self-deception and optimism. I feel really gloomy and uncertain about the future'.[44] After his deputy leadership bid worries about Benn's inclination to adopt uncompromising stances intensified amongst a growing number of his erstwhile supporters. Although there were divisions on other issues, it was over the disciplining of the Trotskyist Militant Tendency that the definitive break occurred between Benn and former lieutenants such as Michael Meacher, Tom Sawyer and David Blunkett. Benn was reluctant to accept (at least publicly) that the Tendency was more than just another strand of left-wing opinion, but was an entryist organisation boring into the party, to which it felt little allegiance. Equally, he was reluctant to make an issue of their willingness (notably in Liverpool, their stronghold) to use harassment and intimidation against opponents. By the late 1980s the so-called soft left had formed an alliance with the centre and right relegating Benn to the political margin. The extent of his isolation was revealed when in 1988, in a rather quixotic gesture, he challenged Kinnock for the party leadership and was crushingly defeated. He seemed a forgotten man.

Appraisal

How can we make sense of Benn's career? For many, both within and outside the Labour party, the one consistent thread in Benn's career was personal

ambition. In what appeared an act of bewildering celerity, in 1970 he had
metamorphosed from the technocratic, middle-of-the-road cabinet minister,
Anthony Wedgwood Benn, into the radical and plebeian Tony Benn. He
became 'the pied piper of almost every available left-wing cause', unwilling
to spurn any 'fashionable radical cause – that of black activist, feminist,
"gay lib" or Greenpeace environmentalism'.[45] Behind the appearance of almost
beguiling innocence lurked the dedicated schemer, avaricious for power.

This was certainly the tenor of much media comment: the trials of
the Wilson and Callaghan governments created a power vacuum into
which Benn neatly stepped. But several shrewd observers who saw him
at close quarters demurred. 'Although I had more cause then most to
dislike him,' Healey later reflected, 'I did not share the general view of
his opponents that he was an unprincipled careerist.' Edmund Dell –
even further on the right of the Party – agreed. 'It would not be fair to
say of him that he was motivated primarily by thoughts of the leadership
of the Party.'[46] His sharp swerve to the left after 1970 may have won him
friends at the grassroots but it also aroused a deep distrust in the
parliamentary party and the trade union establishment that he was never
to dissipate. His enthusiastic support for the occupation and work-in by
workers at Upper Clyde Shipbuilders (UCS) 'added to his unpopularity
with the great mass of the PLP'.[47] 'Wilson nearly murdered me,' he later
recalled, whilst TUC Secretary Vic Feather 'was furious, absolutely wild
with anger that I was talking to shop stewards when he was trying to get
the whole thing stopped.'[48] In May 1972 he noted that his support for
the UCS work-in and other controversial causes 'have really alienated
everybody. Put quite crudely, I have got to mend my fences'.[49]

But he never did. Prudence could never induce him to eschew a cause
simply because of the unpopularity that might accrue. He was determined
to fight his corner, whatever the odds and whatever the pitfalls. He
certainly did want to become Labour leader. On New Year's Eve 1975 he
wrote that 'if I want to do anything other than frolic around on the
margins of British politics, I must be leader of the Labour Party and
Prime Minister'. But not at any cost. Having established his left
credentials by 1979 many expected that when the contest for the
Callaghan succession began he would tack gently to the centre-left, the
best launching pad, Attlee had said, for a Labourite crown prince. But,
on the contrary, he hardly even bothered (despite the prodding of friends)
to cultivate potential allies on the centre-left. In December 1975 he
ruminated: 'perhaps my approach is too strained'; Frances Morrell, his
political advisor had counselled that he 'must aim to be the man in the
middle' and not simply the spokesman of the radical left.[50] In January
1981 he recorded in his diary that 'I've lost a lot of support in the PLP

by what I've done over the last 18 months and I think I'd better be more patient'. In April, Robin Cook, then a rising star on the left, warned that he was 'becoming isolated on the far left and out of touch with parliamentary opinion'. But his response was to shrug off the advice: 'parliamentary opinion', he opined, 'was out of touch with what is happening in the Party'.[51] In truth, he was not a masterful politician. He came to disparage the political arts: the capacity by patient calculation and realistic appraisal to build coalitions, spin a web of political friendships, accumulate credit in the favour bank, conciliate, flatter, manipulate – in all of this he took little interest.

As Simon Hoggart wrote in the *Observer* in 1980:

> If Mr Benn is so obsessed by power, as so many newspapers seem to think, then he has a funny way of getting it. Had he decided to pursue a quiet, centrist line within the Labour party there is little doubt that his intelligence, diligence, oratorical skills and charm would have made him by now the leading candidate for Jim Callaghan's job.[52]

This brings us to the second interpretation of Benn. He was a zealot, and ideologue or (alternatively) a naive, blundering utopian. Healey mockingly equated him to the avatars of 'feudal socialism' derided by Marx and Engels in the Communist Manifesto: 'Half lamentation and half lampoon... at times, by its bitter, witty, and incisive criticism, striking the bourgeoisie to the very heart's core, but always ludicrous in its effect, through total incapacity to comprehend the march of modern history.' To Morgan he was one of Eric Hoffer's 'True Believers' – the Messiah who can 'harness men's hopes and fears in the service of a holy cause' always tempted to 'the puritanical excesses of the Fifth Monarchy men'.[53] This neatly gels with received wisdom amongst scholars of political parties. Parties – especially those of the left – attract two types of recruits, 'pragmatists' and 'ideologues'. The former tend to be office-seekers who espouse 'marginal social reforms providing collective goods that will attract new voters to the party'; the latter 'value the pure blueprint of a future society and the internal solidarity benefits of party organisation'.[54] Putting the latter in charge is a recipe for defeat for it betrays a blindness to the realities of the modern, highly competitive electoral marketplace. As Downs wrote in a highly influential study, 'parties formulate policies in order to win elections rather than win elections in order to formulate policies'. This, he contended, was rational – by which he did not mean the application of reason to political life, the sense in which the term was traditionally understood on the left. Rational behaviour was the promotion of self-interest, rational political conduct the single-minded pursuit of office to secure for politicians 'income, prestige and power'.[55] From this perspective party politics is driven by the quest for personal advantage. This is inevitable, because man is by nature a self-interested creature and those who plunge into the public domain do so because propelled by 'a perpetual and restless desire of power after power, that ceaseth only in death' (Hobbes). To be effective, party leaders must be 'political entrepreneurs' steering organisations 'that supply public policies demanded by the electorate'.[56] This requires 'a shrewd eye for opportunity, a good hand at bargaining, persuading, reciprocating'.[57] By this yardstick Benn was certainly wanting.

Yet it is a misleading way of posing the issue. Power (as Weber maintained) 'is the unavoidable means, and striving for power is one of the driving forces of all politics'.[58] This a long line of prominent Labour left-wingers, including Aneurin Bevan, Richard Crossman and Barbara Castle fully understood, for without power nothing could be accomplished. The real choice for the politician is not between the pursuit of power or principle but the pursuit of power as means or as an end in itself. At one end of the spectrum is the politician who engages in public life principally because 'he enjoys the naked possession of the power he exerts'. What matters most is the pleasure derived from public recognition and esteem, or the savouring of 'power merely for power's sake without a substantive purpose'. At the other end is the person who embarks on a political career to nourish 'his inner balance and self-feeling by the consciousness that his life has "meaning" in the service of a cause'.[59] For this type power is sought not simply for personal gratification but as a means to 'advance collective purposes'. Sometimes the two can run in tandem: the test is that 'fateful moment when career diverges from cause'.[60]

For Benn there was no ambiguity: politics *was* a calling. The only justification for political engagement was the opportunity thereby afforded 'to think, to act, to argue or to obey or resist in pursuit of some inner call of conscience'. The alternatives were to be servant or opponent of vested power and privilege. He explicitly rooted his political belief in the Judaic-Protestant tradition of social protest. 'My mother brought me up,' he reflected, 'on the Old Testament, in the conflict between the Kings and the Prophets, the Kings who had power, and the Prophets who preach righteousness, and I was taught to believe in the Prophets and not the Kings.'[61] He was remorseless in his denunciation of the modern kings, those who by virtue of their power, status and wealth could chisel for others the shape of their lives.

But he was no ideologue. His mind was of an empirical temper, his views (he often declared) the fruits of pondering on a prolonged immersion in active political life rather than profound and extended study. He was a clarifier and populariser of ideas – and an acute observer of the mechanics of politics as his diaries attest – rather than a creative

or systematic thinker. Though (absurdly) sometimes depicted as a
Marxist, he had little instinctive sympathy for 'scientific socialism'. He
was self-consciously a moralist. Socialism was about the right and duty
of people 'to codify their relationships with each other in terms of moral
responsibility'. 'Without the acceptance of a strong moral code,' he
contended, 'the ends always can be argued to justify the means.'[62] If one
had to place a guiding spirit in the Benn pantheon, it would be not
Marx but Tawney – to Benn, the most effective of all exponents of the
socialist cause. Tawney was fond of quoting William Morris's maxim
that 'fellowship is heaven and lack of fellowship is hell' and this too was
the kernel of Benn's socialism.[63] Like Tawney, he saw 'the moral pressures
released by radical Christian teaching, and its humanistic offshoots as
having played a major role in developing the ideas of solidarity,
democracy, equality and peace'. He summed up his beliefs thus: 'I think
that the moral basis of the teachings of Jesus – Love thy neighbour – is
the basis of it all. Am I my brother's keeper?'[64]

To critics he too often exhibited the earnestness of manner and self-
conscious rectitude of a Calvinist divine – the godly pilgrim amidst the
fallen. In his analysis of Labour leaders, Philip Williams distinguishes
between the 'stabiliser' and the 'pathfinder'. Stabilisers are always 'sound
party men', solid and reliable, the fixers who can balance and reconcile.
The pathfinder, on the contrary, is the politician who feels 'a duty to
lead in a particular direction', driven by his own vision and destination,
able to evoke 'enthusiasm and passion'.[65] Benn was not a 'sound party
man' but a pathfinder, indeed 'by instinct a dissident, an individualist'.[66]
To him the obligations of collective responsibility or party unity counted
much less than acting in accord with one's conscience. He was (in Hazlitt's
use of the term) 'a partisan' – a partisan, that is, of principle who 'can
take up a speculative question, and pursue it with... zeal and unshaken
constancy... he who is as faithful to his principles as he is to himself'.[67]
He possessed a self-assurance born from a secure family background, an
elite public school education, manifold talents and a profound moral
sense of the rightness of his cause. In propounding his ideals he 'brought
his tireless energy, brilliance in argument and a total certainty of the
correctness of his own insights and judgments'.[68] He became increasingly
impatient of the standard techniques of power-building: cajoling,
cultivating, pacifying and mutual back-scratching. Though disposed to
a benign, even romantic, view of the labour movement, any indulgence
he may have felt towards the frailties of humankind did not, as a rule,
encompass senior figures within his own party. 'If we lend ourselves to
the foibles and weaknesses of our friends,' he would have agreed, 'if we
suffer ourselves to be implicated in their intrigues, their scrambles and

bargaining for place and power; if we flatter their mistakes, and not only screen them from the eyes of others, but are blind to them ourselves,' we then become slaves of a political coterie not 'servants of the public'.[69]

He was quick to discern moral weakness, quick to judge. There was hyperbole but also a grain of truth in the comment of Labour MP and broadcaster Austin Mitchell that, in his rousing addresses to Party activists 'he could confirm their worst fears of betrayal and treachery at the top, saying, "You are right. It is so. They will betray. I can show you that they did"'.[70] His pronounced aversion to hypocrisy or self-serving of any sort could spill over into a certain astringency in appraising others – not least longstanding stalwarts of the left. Jack Jones, he confided to his diary as early as September 1973, had 'completely abandoned his serious left wing position'; equally Michael Foot had 'lost the sharp cutting edge of his socialism'. In January 1978 he dismissed Foot as 'lost' to the left and wrote in his diary, after a meeting of the so-called 'husbands and wives' group of left-inclined cabinet members that he felt he had 'nothing in common with any of them'.[71] He became less and less inclined to accept that those (within his own party) who disagreed with him could do so from principle as well as personal ambition. Not surprisingly, his colleagues, left and right, were frequently affronted by what they saw as his 'holier than thou' tone. They came to resent what they deemed (in Barbara Castle's cutting phrase) his 'unctuous pride'.[72] He (candidly) recorded the following exchange with Jim Callaghan, then a beleaguered Prime Minister:

'What are you trying to do?' he [Callaghan] asked.

'Well, Jim, I am trying to be a modest little beacon so that the Party realise that they haven't been deserted.'

'That's so self-righteous.'[73]

'In pursuit of his goals,' Morgan upbraided, '[he] magnified or created structural tensions within his party unique in its history.'[74] There is some truth in this. Labour, Benn at one point deliberated, had to make choices: 'People want to know what the Labour Party will do and I think the process is long overdue; the Labour Party are having a Turkish bath, and the sweat and the heat and the discomfort are very unpleasant.'[75] Like the Old Testament prophets he so much admired, he did not portray in nuanced tones and subtle tints and hues but in bold and audacious strokes. His unyielding pursuit of what he believed to be right distracted him from the strains thereby placed on his party: 'if we look distant, suspicious, lukewarm at one another; if we criticise, carp at, pry into the conduct of our party with watchful, jealous eyes; it is to be feared we shall play the game into the enemy's hands, and not co-operate together for the common good with all the steadiness and cordiality that might be wished.'[76] So it seemed even to some of his supporters who were privately dismayed by his decision to challenge Healey for the deputy leadership (an office of no great practical influence), thereby consigning the party to more months of internal trench warfare. At one point, delivering what Benn called 'a lecture on Party unity', Michael Foot appealed: 'Tony, you are essential... I address your conscience. You are being used by others. You are the most important single member of the Party'. To little avail. 'I won't shut up,' he insisted; he would not be 'cramped by shadow cabinet decisions that are contrary to party policy'.[77] At some point, the line between healthy democratic debate and destructive strife was crossed, and Benn seemed not to notice. A driving conviction of his own rightness, – 'a little beacon', one of the politically elect – fostered an obduracy, almost at times a wilfulness which destabilised the leadership. In due course this served to strengthen the hand of those for whom *any* open debate was a distraction and who insisted upon a tightly centralised and disciplined party as indispensable to electoral success. When taxed for 'control freakery' they would always justify their actions by referring to the debilitating effects of Labour's turbulent years.[78]

Conclusion

With his exceptional ability to communicate his views in a vivid and persuasive fashion and to inspire great loyalty and enthusiasm, Benn was one of those rare politicians upon whom the epithet charismatic could accurately be pinned. His unfailing courtesy, his coolness under fire – his ability to respond, apparently with equanimity, to a torrent of lies, abuse and distortion – was astonishing. In his final years in the House he obtained a degree of respect, reverence even, which had previously eluded him, as a staunch protagonist of the rights of parliament and of its role as scrutineer of executive power. How should he be summed up?

Since his shift to the left around 1970 Benn steadfastly remained a nay-sayer, never faltering in his belief that those who held power must be accountable for the use they made of it. In his final speech to the House, he indicted 'our system' as 'designed to brainwash us into believing that some people are better than us'. Social hierarchies, the obsession with a highly graduated status order, the survival of a peerage training us 'from birth to bow and scrape to someone else' – all this was 'deeply corrupting of the democratic spirit'. He came increasingly to lose faith in his party – or, at least, its leaders and parliamentary representatives. But this only confirmed him in his conviction, like Orwell in *Nineteen Eighty-Four*, that 'if there is any hope it lies with the proles'. 'Governments only listen when there is trouble,' he declared in his last Commons speech. 'My experience of progress is that it begins outside and, through the democratic process, permeates inside. Parliament historically is the last place to get the message.'[79]

With the triumph of New Labour and 'the Third Way', Benn's career seems a study in failure. 'New' Labour has expunged from the party programme much of the radical, challenging spirit he strove so hard to fire. For the effective politician, Weber nominated two pre-eminent qualities: 'passion' – 'passionate devotion to a cause'; and a sense of proportion – a politician's 'ability to let realities work upon him with inner concentration and calmness'.[80] The former Benn had in full measure. If by the latter can be understood a capacity to realistically appraise the balance of forces and draw the correct strategic inferences, Benn lacked it.

In a party system where political initiative is increasingly the prerogative of professional 'political entrepreneurs', and where Labour's egalitarian aspirations have been firmly subordinated to the aspirations of a never-defined and elusive 'Middle England' the type of politics Benn championed seem irrelevant and outdated. But with the passage of years he might come to be judged differently. In an age of slick political marketing, and of political footwork so deft that the most bewildering political turnarounds can be executed with grace, where – as with former Benn allies like Blunkett and Cook – political stands long avowed can be disowned without a blush and with breathless dispatch, in an age 'when politics is a matter of convenience, not conviction [and] only the self-interested prosper'.[81] Benn may come to be viewed less harshly than he was in his political lifetime. His indomitable spirit, his astonishing resilience under the most venomous assaults, reflected his belief – shared with his nonconformist forbears – that precedence should always be given to the promptings of one's conscience. It was this solidity of his convictions that rendered him so indifferent to the rewards that political 'respectability' and 'moderate good sense' could confer. Words penned by Hazlitt about Charles James Fox may stand for him too as a political epitaph:

> He had an innate love of truth, of justice, of probity, of whatever was generous or liberal. Neither his education, nor his connections, nor his situation in life, nor the low intrigues and virulence of party, could ever alter the simplicity of his taste, nor the candid openness of his nature. There was an elastic force about his heart, a freshness of social feeling, a warm glowing humanity, which remained unimpaired to the last.[82]

Further reading

Given a long, full and controversial life in politics there is surprisingly little written on Tony Benn. Jad Adams' study *Tony Benn* (London, 1992) is the only biography covering the main events in his political life. There is an interesting profile in Kenneth O. Morgan's *Labour People – Leaders and Lieutenants: Hardie to Kinnock* (Oxford, 1987). *The End of Parliamentary Socialism* (London, 1997) by Leo Panitch and Colin Leys contains a long and sympathetic discussion of his ideas and career. By far the most important source of information on Benn (and on much else beside) is his own published diaries. In chronological order these are: *Years of Hope: Diaries, Papers and Letters 1940–1962* (London, 1994); *Out of the Wilderness: Diaries 1963–67* (London, 1987); *Office Without Power: Diaries 1968–1972* (London, 1988); *Against the Tide: Diaries 1973–1976* (London, 1989); *Conflict of Interest: Diaries 1977–1980* (London, 1990); *The End of an Era: Diaries 1980–1990* (London, 1992). These published volumes are only a selection from his diaries, which can be inspected by researchers in an archive (together with a compendious collection of other documents) maintained by Mr Benn.

Notes

1. K.O. Morgan, *Labour People – Leaders and Lieutenants: Hardie to Kinnock* (Oxford, 1987), p 312.
2. M. Hollingsworth, *The Press and Political Dissent* (London, 1986), pp 65–6.
3. Cited in ibid, pp 40, 55, 58–1. This is just a taste of the copious detail Hollingsworth supplies.
4. Cited in J. Adams, *Tony Benn* (London, 1992), p 354.
5. Hollingsworth, *The Press and Political Dissent,* p 38.
6. L. Panitch and C. Leys, *The End of Parliamentary Socialism* (London, 1997), p 88.
7. However, she added, 'I had an uneasy feeling from time to time that something was not quite in focus': Barbara Castle, *Fighting all the Way* (London, 1993), pp 446, 504.
8. Morgan, *Labour People*, p 307; James Callaghan, *Time and Chance* (London, 1987), p 444; Denis Healey, *The Time of My Life* (London, 1989), p 471.
9. Peter Jenkins, *Mrs Thatcher's Revolution* (London, 1987), p 117.
10. Edmund Dell, *A Strange and Eventful History* (London, 2000), p 398.
11. Morgan, *Labour People*, p 312.
12. Healey, *The Time of My Life*, p 471.
13. Tony Benn, *Days of Hope: Diaries 1940–1962* (London, 1994), pp 175, 179.
14. Morgan, *Labour People*, p 304.
15. Peter Shore, *Leading the Left* (London, 1993), pp 106, 104.
16. Adams, *Tony Benn*, pp 292–3.
17. Tony Benn, 'Democracy and Marxism', *Marxism Today*, May 1982.
18. Shore, *Leading the Left*, p 106.
19. Benn, *Arguments for Democracy* (London, 1979), pp 43, 155.
20. R.H. Tawney, *The Acquisitive Society* (London, 1961 [1921]), pp 143, 145.
21. Benn, *Conflict of Interest: Diaries 1977–1980* (London, 1990), pp 142: entry for 20 May 1977.
22. Benn, *Arguments for Democracy*, pp 43, 155; Benn, *Conflict of Interest: Diaries 1977–1980*, p 435: entry for 11 January 1979.

23. Benn, *Against the Tide: Diaries 1973–1976* (London, 1989), p 187: entry for 28 June 1975.
24. Ibid, p 212.
25. Ibid, p 327.
26. Morgan, *Labour People*, p 308.
27. Instead he urged the case for democratic socialism, combining 'direct public investment in industry and expanded public expenditure' with 'self-management'. Benn, *Arguments for Democracy*, p 140.
28. During a long train conversation with Keith Joseph – 'great fun' – Benn reported the following exchange: 'He said I was a romantic about shop stewards, and I said he was a romantic about market forces.' Benn, *The End of an Era: Diaries 1980–1990* (London, 1992), p 93: entry for 20 February 1981.
29. Benn, *Conflict of Interest: Diaries 1977–1980*, pp 435: entry for 11 January 1979.
30. Roy Jenkins, *A Life at the Centre* (London, 1991), p 392.
31. D. Barnes and E. Reid, *Governments and Trade Unions: The British Experience, 1964–79* (London, 1980), p 222; Benn, *Conflict of Interest: Diaries 1977–1980*, p 435: entry 11 January 1979.
32. K. Burk and A. Cairncross, *'Goodbye, Great Britain': The 1976 IMF Crisis* (New Haven, 1992), p 129.
33. Benn, *Against the Tide: Diaries 1973–1976*, pp 664–8, 673–4.
34. W. Keegan and R. Pennant-Rea, *Who Runs the Economy?* (London, 1979), pp 122, 131–32.
35. Bernard Donoughue, the Prime Minister's senior policy advisor, commented that he 'thought Tony's contributions on North Sea oil were often excellent and at times prevented the Government from being taken for a ride'. Donoughue, *Prime Minister: The conduct of policy under Harold Wilson and James Callaghan* (London, 1987), pp 150–1.
36. Morgan, *Labour People*, p 307.
37. Castle, *Fighting all the Way*, p 504.
38. P. Williams, 'Changing Styles of Labour Leadership', in D. Kavanagh (ed.), *The Politics of the Labour Party* (London, 1982), p 51.
39. Benn, *Conflict of Interest: Diaries 1977–1980*, p 222: entry for 30 September 1977.
40. Ibid.
41. Austin Mitchell, *Four Years in the Death of the Labour Party* (London, 1983), p 30.
42. Benn, *The End of an Era: Diaries 1980–1990*, p 69: entry for 24 January 1981.
43. Healey was elected on the second ballot by a margin of less than one per cent – his triumph mainly due to the decision made by 37 mainly left-wing MPs who had voted for Silkin in the first round to abstain on the second.
44. Benn, *The End of an Era: Diaries 1980–1990*, p 271: entry for 22 February 1981.
45. Morgan, *Labour People*, pp 301–2.
46. Healey, *The Time of My Life*, p 471; Dell, *A Strange and Eventful History*, p 398.
47. Ibid.
48. Quoted in Panitch and Leys, *The End of Parliamentary Socialism*, p 58.
49. Benn, *Office Without Power: Dairies 1968–1972* (London, 1988), p 428.

50. Benn, *Against the Tide: Diaries 1973–1976*, p 486.
51. Benn, *The End of an Era: Diaries 1980–1990*, pp 75, 116.
52. Quoted in Hollingsworth, *The Press and Political Dissent*, p 74.
53. Healey, *The Time of My Life*, p 471; Morgan, *Labour People*, p 312.
54. H. Kitschelt, *The Transformation of European Social Democracy* (Cambridge, 1994), pp 208–9.
55. Downs, *An Economic Theory of Democracy* (New York, 1955), pp 27–8.
56. K. Strom, 'A Behavioural Theory of Competitive Political Parties', *American Journal of Political Science* 34 (2) 1990, p 574.
57. J.M. Burns, *Leadership* (London, 1979), p 169.
58. Max Weber, 'Politics as a Vocation', in H.H. Gerth and C. Wright Mills (eds), *Max Weber: Essays in Sociology* (New York, 1958).
59. Ibid.
60. Burns, *Leadership*, pp 106, 461.
61. Benn, 'Democracy and Marxism', 1982; Interview With Tony Benn by C.J. Stone, 7 November 2000: www.labournet.net/other/0011/benn.html
62. Benn, 'Democracy and Marxism', 1982.
63. N. Dennis and A.H. Halsey, *English Ethical Socialism: From Thomas More to RH Tawney* (Oxford, 1988), pp 243, 213.
64. Benn, 'Democracy and Marxism', 1982; Interview With Tony Benn by C.J. Stone.
65. Williams, *The Politics of the Labour Party*, p 51.
66. Morgan, *Labour People*, p 311.
67. William Hazlitt, *Sketches and Essays* (London, 1884 [1839]), p 222.
68. Shore, *Leading the Left*, p 106.
69. Hazlitt, *Sketches and Essays*, p 222.
70. Mitchell, *Four Years in the Death of the Labour Party*, p 30.
71. Benn, *Conflict of Interest: Diaries 1977–1980*, p 270; Benn, *Against the Tide: Diaries 1973–1976*, p 62: entry for 26 September 1973.
72. Morgan, *Labour People*, p 312.
73. Benn, *Conflict of Interest: Diaries 1977–1980*, pp 459: entry for 13 February 1979.
74. Morgan, *Labour People*, p 312.
75. Benn, *The End of an Era: Diaries 1980–1990*, p 116: entry for 2 April 1981.
76. Hazlitt, *Sketches and Essays*, p 223.
77. Benn, *The End of an Era: Diaries 1980–1990*, p 168: entry for 11 November 1981; p.156: entry for 1 October 1981.
78. 'The factionalism, navel-gazing or feuding of the Seventies and Eighties' had 'allowed us to be painted as extremist, out of touch and divided.' Hence it was imperative for Labour to be transformed into 'a modern, disciplined party with a strong centre'. See Tony Blair, 'If control freakery means strong leadership, then I plead guilty', *Independent*, 20 November 1998.
79. Benn, *House of Commons Debates*, 9 May 2001.
80. Weber, 'Politics as a Vocation'.
81. George Monbiot, *Guardian*, 12 June 2001.
82. Hazlitt, *Sketches and Essays*, p 437.

12

Roy Hattersley

Lewis Baston

Roy Hattersley, later Baron Hattersley of Sparkbrook, b.1932. Labour MP for Birmingham Sparkbrook 1964–97. Minister of Defence (Administration) 1969–70. Minister of State, Foreign and Commonwealth Office 1974–76; Secretary of State for Prices and Consumer Protection 1976–79. Deputy Leader of the Labour Party 1983–92. Life peer 1997.

Roy Hattersley has inspired frustration and high praise for his complete defiance of political fashion. He was a defiant partisan of Europe and NATO in the 1970s, without for a moment following the fatalism about the Labour Party that led to the formation of the SDP, and a gadfly of the left in more recent times. Hattersley has remained a consistent advocate of equality and social democratic 'Croslandite' ideas for his entire political career, while the Labour Party and the political spectrum have shifted around him. Hattersley has combined a tribal loyalty to the Labour Party with a wry cynicism about its absurdities:

> I knew that I was Labour long before I could begin to explain why it was the only possible party for me. In those early days, my unswerving affection and undying admiration was not for an ideology but for an institution. My allegiance was to dingy rooms over Co-op groceries, rusty duplicating machines which vomited dirty ink and destroyed clean paper, old ladies addressing envelopes with infinite care and obvious difficulty, piles of outdated leaflets that no one delivered

and loudspeaker equipment that dented car roofs but failed to amplify the spoken word. They were all goods and chattels of the Labour Party, a family into which I had been born and for which I felt all the uncritical devotion that sons and siblings instinctively acquire.[1]

Roy Hattersley was born on 28 December 1932 in Sheffield, the son of Frederick Hattersley, a former Catholic priest, and Enid Brackenbury, whom the elder Hattersley married in 1929. As a child he lived close to Sheffield Wednesday's football ground at Hillsborough, acquiring a life-long allegiance to that team, and his support for Labour was acquired in a rather similar way. Sheffield was the first big city to come under sustained Labour control (after 1926) and it was a municipal socialist showcase. Hattersley as a child benefited from its libraries, parks, free concerts and a scholarship to the City Grammar School. His mother was a Labour activist and took him leafleting in the cause of A.V. Alexander, the coalition First Lord of the Admiralty, in the Sheffield Hillsborough constituency in the general election of 1945.[2] He became involved in student politics while at Hull University, and read the socialist and social democratic classics: 'By then I had developed what I believed to be a clear theory of socialism – by R.H. Tawney out of Matthew Arnold'.[3]

Hobhouse, Durbin, Cole and Crosland are all name-checked as influences on Hattersley's political ideas, as is the later work of John Rawls, but much of Hattersley's self-education in the socialist classics was to provide an intellectual framework to support gut loyalty. Hattersley's influences were notably English, secular and Fabian rather than European, religious or sentimental – no Marx, no Methodism and no Tressell either. Hattersley was a natural Gaitskellite, and to this intellectual tendency he added personal loyalty after a chance meeting with Hugh Gaitskell on the day he was elected Leader of the Labour Party in 1955. Hattersley's affiliation to Gaitskell deepened in the early 1960s; he was the Campaign for Democratic Socialism's organiser in the Sheffield Hallam constituency during the anti-unilateralist campaign of 1960–61. Hattersley wrote two years after Gaitskell's death, in words that did not please Wilson, that a Labour Party with both the will and the capacity for victory was 'his greatest and most permanent memorial. Those who fought with him to build the new Labour Party will not, because of minor disagreement or personal dissent, see that work destroyed'.[4]

Hattersley's tribal loyalty was deepened by a spell on Sheffield City Council from 1957 to 1965. The council in those days was governed by strict party discipline even on the most minor matters; patronage extended to seeking a majority of governors in every school. The ruling Labour group was a rather benevolent self-perpetuating oligarchy and although most of the councillors were elderly by the late 1950s they appreciated the value of incorporating younger members into the party elite. Hattersley rose quickly to become Chair of Housing, during which, in 1961, he opened the Park Hill flats complex. Sheffield's hilly terrain made traditional house-building techniques difficult to use and its townscape in the 1950s and 1960s became beribboned by medium-rise concrete blocks. In *Goodbye to Yorkshire* in 1976 Hattersley took pride in the modernity of Sheffield's housing policy during his years, and the high construction standards used, but to later observers it seems a striking example of well-meaning paternalism.

Despite his attachment to all things Yorkshire in general and Sheffield in particular, Hattersley's parliamentary career was based in the West Midlands – a trial run in safe Conservative Sutton Coldfield in 1959, and 35 years as MP for the Sparkbrook constituency in Birmingham. Sparkbrook, south and east of the city centre, was a freak Conservative gain in 1959 which reverted to Labour in 1964 and became steadily safer over the following decades. Hattersley won a 13,573 (39.4 per cent) majority in Sparkbrook's last election as an independent seat in 1992. Hattersley was never even an adopted son of Birmingham, a city many find hard to love, but Sparkbrook did become something of a passion.[5]

During Hattersley's time as its MP, Sparkbrook became an increasingly ethnically mixed seat and Stratford Road a thriving social, cultural and shopping centre for the growing Asian community. By the time of the 1981 census 35.2 per cent of Sparkbrook's population were living in ethnic minority households, the sixth highest proportion in the country.[6] Hattersley and Peter Shore were the first Cabinet-level Labour politicians to represent seats in which ethnic minority voters were more than a small element of the local electorate.[7] As early as 1965 he was dubbed 'Hatterjee' in *Private Eye* and described as the youngest Pakistani immigrant in the government.

Not surprisingly, considering Hattersley's views about equality and the nature of Sparkbrook, racial equality became an important part of Hattersley's political position and he became emotionally committed to the interests of ethnic minorities, particularly British Muslims who were unrepresented in the House of Commons until the election of Mohammed Sarwar in 1997. During the 1980s he was much involved in 'race' issues within the Labour Party, opposing Black Sections (on the grounds that his constituents weren't, for the most part, black, and that the regular party organisation, as in Sparkbrook, should be as open as possible to minorities) and controversially trying to steer a course between his commitments to free speech and Muslim interests during the *Satanic Verses* controversy in 1988–89. Hattersley suggested that as a gesture Salman Rushdie might not publish the paperback edition of the book

that had so offended Muslims; the idea made little sense in principle
and Hattersley's attempt at moderation satisfied nobody. Hattersley wrote
later, with some justice, that:

> Members of Parliament who represent ethnic minorities – unlike their
> colleagues who sit for prosperous suburban seats – are always criticised
> for advancing the claims of their constituents. It is part of the racism
> which afflicts our society.[8]

Labour's long exile from power in 1979–97 meant that several leading
figures never occupied the ministerial jobs that seemed most suitable for
them. Chief among these were Denis Healey never becoming Foreign
Secretary (or Prime Minister), John Smith never serving as Chancellor –
and Roy Hattersley never being Home Secretary. Throughout his
ministerial career (1967–70 and 1974–79) Hattersley never served at
the Home Office, or at Education, despite these areas being his core
concerns as a politician.

Hattersley, straight after the 1964 election, was appointed PPS to
Margaret Herbison, the Minister of Pensions and National Insurance.
Hattersley's ministerial career began in January 1967 with his
appointment as a junior minister under Ray Gunter at the Department
of Labour, which later became a more glamorous sounding position at
the Department of Employment and Productivity under Barbara Castle.
Hattersley has an unenviable record for having been on the scene at
many fateful moments for Labour governments in the 1960s and 1970s.
One of his first jobs was to administer the bizarre Selective Employment
Tax and income restrictions; he followed this by involvement in *In Place
of Strife*, signing the order sending the army into Derry, 'renegotiating'
EEC membership and attempting to hold down wages during the 'Winter
of Discontent'. He did not get the chance to accomplish the things he
really wanted to do, such as make radical change in the education system,
reform the police, or make the tax system more progressive; although
Hattersley's story in this regard merely symbolises the general problem
of trying to change society while managing crisis after crisis.

Hattersley's advance within government was delayed because of the
distrust of Harold Wilson, who was well aware that Hattersley was a
Gaitskell loyalist with links to Roy Jenkins and an ideological affinity
with Tony Crosland. Wilson regarded him as a 'Jenkins man' and warned
Castle when she kept him as a junior minister that everything she said
would be reported back to Jenkins.[9] Castle, however, thought him a
competent minister, and was not too worried about alleged disloyalty:

> Harold won't have Hattersley [as Social Services Minister of State]
> (whose claims I have been pressing) because he is said to have made

three 'disloyal' remarks recently. Dick [Crossman] and I agree this is absurd because, although we don't think Hattersley is a particularly nice man, we know he will make disloyal remarks about anyone, including Roy Jenkins.[10]

Hattersley received his overdue promotion in July 1969 when he was moved to Defence, as the Minister of State for Defence Administration, where he remained until Labour's defeat in the June 1970 general election. His arrival came on the eve of the collapse of law and order in Northern Ireland and the consequent arrival of British troops. Denis Healey was in hospital at the crucial moment and Hattersley signed the order committing the troops.

Hattersley was a loyal member of the pro-European minority of the Labour Party, to the extent of joining the 69 rebels voting with the Heath government in 1971 on the principle of entry to the EC. However, he was not a hard-core Jenkinsite (if one can use a term such as 'hard-core' about such a political position) and tended thereafter the take the Crosland line of placing a higher virtue on party loyalty than demonstrations of European commitment. He was one of the beneficiaries of the departure from the Shadow Cabinet of Jenkins, Lever and Thomson in April 1972, taking a post as Shadow Defence Secretary and at last making it to the front rank of politics. It was a parting of the ways for the Gaitskellites – the term effectively ceased to have meaning after this moment, the group being divided between followers of Jenkins and of Crosland. The Jenkinsites felt bitterness against 'Rattersley' for accepting promotion, but Hattersley won little gratitude from Wilson and his allies as he accepted it so clumsily.[11]

Hattersley was moved to shadow education in 1973. He had always had strong views about education as an important root of inequality in society and took what Tony Benn called 'an absolutely hard line about banning all private education. On health, he's in favour of banning all private provisions because it will destroy the Health Service'. Benn mused that although Hattersley proclaimed an ideology of freedom, the things he seemed most passionate about were actually limitations on freedom.[12] Hattersley announced his determination 'initially to reduce, and eventually to abolish, fee-paying education in this country' to a conference of prep school headmasters in 1973, and promptly became a bogeyman for the private schools and the Conservatives.

Neither did Hattersley's attack on private schools do him much good in the Labour Party; Wilson disowned him and the left, obsessed by procedure, did not support him because he was making policy on the hoof rather than through the intricate formal structure of committees that existed for this purpose. When Labour returned to government in March 1974 Hattersley was not Education Secretary, but one step outside the Cabinet as Minister of State for Foreign and Commonwealth Affairs. Two rather tedious years of European negotiations, meetings with distinguished visitors and jousting with Iceland in the 'Cod War' followed. To counter the effects of endless official dinners, Hattersley took up jogging: 'as I was running I thought I could eat anything I wanted. So I became a rather tubby person who could run four miles a day'.[13]

In April 1976 Callaghan appointed Hattersley to the Cabinet as Secretary of State for Prices and Consumer Protection. This ministry was very much a creature of its times. The last three general elections had seen the parties trading misleading statistics and waving shopping baskets at each other in criticism of each other's record on prices. The ministry was intended to implement the micro-economic aspects of Labour's counter-inflation policy, which had long blamed anti-competitive monopolies and cartels for keeping prices high. The effect of its activities on the general level of retail prices was insubstantial, but it could claim victories here and there on staples such as tea, and its work on takeovers and consumer protection was more effective. As part of the search for something for the ministry to do, Hattersley assumed control of the government's fateful last round of incomes policy in 1978–79, which collapsed in industrial strife. Hattersley worked harder than most in the desperate days leading up to the no-confidence vote of 28 March 1979. He provided two Ulster Unionists, who had been looking for an excuse to vote with Labour, by promising to work on a special price index for Northern Ireland, but it was not enough. In the ensuing election Labour was keen to stress its record on controlling inflation and Hattersley was a prominent campaigner; his finest hour was an unscripted comic double-act with Jim Callaghan on 1 May. But it was to no avail.

On returning to opposition, Hattersley shadowed Environment from 1979 to 1980 during the first skirmishes between the Thatcher government and Labour local authorities, and the introduction of the right to buy at discounted rates for council tenants. Although Hattersley made the fateful pledge to repeal the right to buy, and believed in it, it is unlikely that any other policy would have been acceptable to the Labour Party at the time. In 1980 he moved to shadow the Home Office and performed effectively on issues such as civil liberties and policing, but this was overshadowed by Labour's disunity and the breakaway of the SDP in 1981. Hattersley was a great survivor. His position with regard to the SDP was eloquently described by Ivor Crewe and Anthony King:

Hattersley was like a Catholic curate during the Protestant

Reformation. He did agree with most of the Protestants' aims, and, yes, he did very much want to be a bishop, a cardinal or even pope. But his loyalty to the Labour Party, like the Catholic curate's loyalty to the Church, was of a much more emotional, deep-rooted kind. It was an elemental part of his being. To have deserted the Labour party would have been to desert himself.[14]

Some of the SDP thought that Hattersley had some kind of obligation to join them, and felt a certain bitterness towards him; Hattersley for his part was adamant that the breakaway had retarded Labour's return to electability and kept the Tories in for an extra decade. But this was not his sole analysis of 1983; he realised that Labour's performance in opposition was feeble and its 1983 campaign disastrous: 'we lost because we supported bizarre policies, appeared incompetent and were conspicuously disunited'.[15] Even during the darkest times Hattersley retained an appealing sense of balance:

> I never get stressed out – I am basically a happy person. Even when the Labour Party was going through some pretty rough times I never got overwrought or felt suicidal. I do get physically tired – like when I walk Buster in the hills in Derbyshire – but work never affects me emotionally.[16]

Roy Hattersley was the candidate of the 'right' in the leadership election of 1983, but by current comparison his manifesto reads as a radical document. He returned to his familiar themes of equality and freedom, but also argued that 'we need to re-create the relationship that was built up between the unions and the Labour government during the 1970s' and for 'a massive programme of concentrated spending' on public services. He also favoured the abolition of private medicine and private education. He favoured a minimum wage and an attack on discrimination, two policies which became steadily more mainstream in the 1980s and 1990s, and favoured retaining Britain's membership of the EEC and compliance with NATO obligations. His July 1983 platform was for a more sensible, practical version of the domestic and economic priorities of the 1983 manifesto: 'We can fight the next election on a manifesto which is just as progressive as that on which we lost on June 9 – and win... The British people are not antagonized by socialism. But they are unnerved by unreality.'[17]

Comparing Hattersley's platform with those of his opponents is instructive. Eric Heffer's is a plea for Clause IV socialism expressed in semi-Marxist terms of crisis in capitalism and the dangers of a bureaucratic class. Both Heffer and Kinnock attack the social democratic Crosland tradition to which Hattersley belongs, although Kinnock's is in substance not dissimilar from Hattersley's but with a harder emphasis, calling for maximum as well as minimum earnings and a steeply progressive tax system. The main difference is on nuclear weapons, and Europe which Hattersley favours, Heffer opposes and neither Kinnock nor Shore mentions. Peter Shore's manifesto is the most modernising on offer in 1983, arguing that aspirations to higher education and home ownership should not be denied and drawing attention to the changing class structure.[18]

Had the contest taken place using the old electoral system in which the Parliamentary Labour Party comprised the electorate, the dynamic may have been different. But September 1983 was the first time the party's electoral college system had been used to elect the leader and the trade unions and the constituency parties comprised most of the electorate. Neil Kinnock started with the considerable advantage of the endorsement of the TGWU, and the work he had done to build alliances and prepare the ground in 1982–83. The campaign was a fairly ritual affair and the result was a triumph for Kinnock with 71.3 per cent, to 19.3 per cent for Hattersley and 6.3 per cent and 3.1 per cent respectively for Heffer and Shore. Hattersley was elected Deputy Leader with 67.3 per cent of the vote, to 27.9 per cent for Michael Meacher; Denzil Davies and Gwyneth Dunwoody were also-rans. Hattersley won overwhelmingly in the trade union section (35.2 per cent in the electoral college, out of 40), comfortably among the MPs (16.7 per cent, to 8.8 per cent for Meacher, out of 30) and narrowly among the constituency parties (15.3 per cent, to 14.4 per cent for Meacher, out of 30).[19] The Kinnock-Hattersley combination was described as the 'dream ticket' by the press, the theory being that an axis of left and right at the top could restore party unity.

In 1995 Hattersley said that Labour had elected the right man in 1983. Labour probably could only have been led from the left at that time, and Kinnock was able to dissolve the left alliance that had dominated the party in the early 1980s. A Hattersley leadership would have been unlikely to move as far and as fast to modernise the party because of the 'Nixon in China' factor – a man of the left was needed to make the break with the party's past preoccupations.[20] Kinnock was able to bring fellow left-wingers such as David Blunkett, and eventually Margaret Beckett, along with him because he did not cause tribal hackles to rise from the days of the EEC vote and the 1976–83 civil war. Hattersley would have needed to take more care over maintaining unity and demonstrating that he was not a crypto-SDP politician; he could not have isolated the far left as effectively as Kinnock did after 1985. According to Hattersley, his ambition to be leader ended with the 1983 leadership campaign.

Neil Kinnock appointed Hattersley Shadow Chancellor when he won the leadership in October 1983. It was not one of Kinnock's better ideas and Hattersley was reluctant to move on from Home Office issues and felt that he was 'temperamentally unsuited'.[21] Macro-economics had never been one of his strong points, but Kinnock thought that Hattersley was the man to tear up the Alternative Economic Strategy with which Labour had fought the 1983 election.

Hattersley was facing the Conservatives during the most successful phase of the Thatcher years. Growth was healthy, living standards were rising, inflation stayed relatively low and from summer 1986 onwards unemployment started to fall back from its 3.4m peak. The Conservatives, hubristically, portrayed this record in the 1987 election as an 'economic miracle'. Nigel Lawson as Chancellor personified the arrogant confidence of the Tories in the mid-1980s and his intellectual command over the realm of economic policy easily outclassed Hattersley despite the largely illusory nature of the government's achievements.

Hattersley was arguing a case that ran against the prevailing trends of policy and opinion in the 1980s. Labour's economic policies in 1983–87 had been shorn of the more radical and impractical elements of the Alternative Economic Strategy, but were still a recognisably socialist set of priorities. Hattersley argued the unfashionable case for higher taxes on high earnings and to create disincentives through the tax system on the export of capital, with the aim of rebuilding British industry. Unemployment was naturally key to Labour's economic appeal in 1983–87. Labour's pledge to reduce it to a million was widely believed to be unrealistic in 1983, as were many other of its aspirations. Hattersley told the Shadow Cabinet in July 1986 that:

> In the preparations for previous elections we have almost always committed ourselves to more public spending than the electorate thought credible and the economy could reasonably bear. During the last three years we have largely managed to avoid such self-inflicted wounds.[22]

This did not stop a successful Conservative attack on Labour's plans during the 1987 election, in which taxation played an important part. Lawson's pre-election budget had cut the basic rate of income tax by 2p in the pound, and Hattersley led Labour in opposition to it. Worse was the impression of muddle given during the election campaign about how well-off voters had to be to start losing from Labour's tax and benefit changes. Although Labour did relatively well in Scotland, Wales and northern England, there was little improvement on the 1983 disaster in the south and doubts over Labour's credibility and intentions on the economy played a large part in this defeat. After the election Hattersley moved back to Home Affairs.

Hattersley's political creed was spelled out in greatest detail in *Choose Freedom*, published in 1987. Hattersley's book owed a huge, acknowledged, debt to Tony Crosland, who enunciated the basic principle in conversation with Hattersley in 1977 shortly before he died: 'Socialism is about the pursuit of equality and the protection of freedom – in the knowledge that until we are truly equal we will not be truly free.'[23]

There was nothing non-ideological about Hattersley's approach. Part of his reason for writing *Choose Freedom* was that the pragmatism and flexibility of democratic socialists was not a strong enough basis to fight against the new right and also repel extreme left boarders from Labour's decks. 'For too long the mainstream of the Labour Party believed that it was possible to combat bad ideas by opposing ideas in general.'[24] The definition of 'socialism' and socialist ideology was an important matter to Hattersley in the 1980s in a way that it was not to Blair in the 1990s.

By installing freedom as the core of socialist belief, Hattersley was attempting to change the perceptions of freedom in politics. The word had become associated with Thatcherism and neo-liberal economics, and Labour was seen by many voters as a patronising party that told people what to do. Hattersley put the case for freedom as more than the absence of coercion and restraint, but as extending choice and opportunity as widely as possible.

While free-market reformers emphasise the idea of 'equality of opportunity' and New Labour claims to stand for 'more than equality of opportunity', Rawls, on whose *Theory of Justice* Hattersley bases much of his egalitarian case, is concerned with equality of outcome. Equality of outcome is often set up as a straw man – 'it's ridiculous to favour a situation where everyone gets the same money – we're all different, aren't we?' – but to Hattersley inequality is a socially produced phenomenon – differences between humans are natural; equality of outcome means that society does not organise itself to produce inequality.

Throughout his political career Hattersley stressed his linkage of equality and freedom as the central tenet of socialist belief. He was not attracted by the traditional left belief in public ownership as the core of socialism, saying in 1978 that:

> The great ideal of democratic socialism can neither be expressed nor achieved by a doctrine solely concerned with economic organisation. Forms of economic organisation can contribute to its attainment, but they cannot in themselves constitute a socialist society. If socialism is about freedom as well as equality, the Federal Republic is 'more socialist' than East Germany. We ought not to be afraid to say so.[25]

Most books expounding the views of active politicians are doomed to a short life; who now recalls the details of David Owen's *Face The Future* (1980) or Peter Walker's *The Ascent of Britain* (1977)? The main exception to the pattern has been *The Future of Socialism* by Anthony Crosland (whose later works like *The Conservative Enemy* or *Socialism Now* proved more ephemeral).[26] Hattersley's update of Crosland occupies a middle position, neither totally forgotten nor a regular entrant in the canon of the literature of the British socialist tradition. It is still on some reading lists for university courses on political thought.

Despite superficial similarities, *Choose Freedom* was not a forerunner of New Labour. Hattersley broadly believes in markets, but takes a traditional social democratic approach to their practical limitations. 'In education and health, scarce resources must be distributed according to need, not purchasing power. The public utilities – transport, energy and telephones – cannot be judged according to their own short term market related performance because of their effects on other industries and the community at large.' Monopolies, by their nature, are also not subject to the competitive disciplines of the market; in the rest of the economy the market is the best mechanism 'but in most sectors it cannot be left to itself'.[27] Government would directly run the public utilities and, where appropriate, monopolies, and reserve the right to intervene in the market sector to meet social objectives and conduct macro-economic policy by affecting investment, profits and exports. 'Public ownership, in the form of state corporations centrally owned, planned and administered, is essential for the public utilities.'[28]

Hattersley's thought on markets was mostly about demolishing the instincts that governed 'sentimental socialist circles' which regarded competition as antithetical not to monopoly but to co-operation: 'Socialists certainly believe in co-operation, but the repetition of its virtues does not solve any of the problems concerning the way in which we allocate resources.'[29] 'Socialism's concern for freedom, as well as its dependence upon the success of an efficient economy, requires support for the market system in large parts of the economy.'[30]

> To the devotees of private enterprise, the free-market mechanism is a system to be spoken about with reverence but only to be supported when it operates in their sectional interests. Socialists should apply the same rule. When the market serves our ends, it should be encouraged. When it does not, it should be discarded in favour of whatever process directly encourages the more equal – and therefore more free – society which we aim to create.[31]

However, on power and ownership Hattersley owed as much to Stuart Holland as to Anthony Crosland. Worker co-operatives, industrial democracy and a spread of worker and state ownership throughout industry was commended: 'when we consider the make-up of the mixed economy, we should begin to penetrate the entire system instead of selecting a whole sector of private enterprise for head-on assault and capture.'[32] Ownership is peripheral to Hattersley's socialism and his thoughts on the matter lack the detail of his theoretical discussion of equality and freedom. While more appreciative of the market mechanism than most of his colleagues, he was also able to countenance arguments for intervention that other social democrats found uncongenial.

Redistribution is a more important practical concept to Hattersley than nationalisation: 'there are an infinite number of ways in which the tax and benefit system can be used to promote equality.'[33] Specific suggestions he offered in 1987 were a lower-rate tax band at the bottom of taxable income, restriction of mortgage and pension relief to the basic rate and abolition of the National Insurance upper earnings threshold. An increased tax take would come not so much raising higher rates as eliminating loopholes and allowances. Hattersley was an early advocate within the Labour Party of a statutory minimum wage, previously resisted as an intervention in an area more properly left to trade unions. Some of these specific ideas were continued under New Labour, including the lower-rate tax band and the minimum wage, but the anomalies of the National Insurance system remain sacrosanct.

To recall that Hattersley was regarded as a hard-line right-winger is to expose the idiocy of the definitions of left and right prevailing in the 1970s and 1980s within the Labour Party. The litmus test issues, of support for the EC and NATO, as Hattersley pointed out, had little to do with the nature of society, the fundamental business of socialism. In terms of the state's role in the economy, redistribution, racism and other social issues there is much more that unites Hattersley with the self-described radical left than with New Labour, but this was obscured by the tribalism of the times. Kinnock and Hattersley managed to soften the edges and dissolve the left bloc, but the left itself made the decisive move.

The decision of Tony Benn to launch a quixotic challenge to Neil Kinnock for the leadership of the Labour Party in 1988 posed a considerable risk for Roy Hattersley. The threat came not so much from Benn's running mate Eric Heffer as from John Prescott, who had earlier backed out of contesting the deputy leadership to avoid a divisive contest but entered the fray once Benn and Heffer had mounted their challenge. Prescott was part of the mainstream left, and had the merit of actually being interested in the job of Deputy Leader, believing that it should be used as a base to rebuild and inspire the Labour Party. Once Prescott became Deputy in 1994 he put this into practice with considerable success, but in 1988 the leadership closed ranks around Hattersley.

The vote for Hattersley in the deputy leadership contest of 1988 was something of a turning point in the history of the Labour Party. Hattersley won with 66.8 per cent overall, a fraction down on his showing in 1983 mainly because Prescott polled better among the trade unions and MPs than Meacher had in 1983. Hattersley's support in the constituency parties was significantly up, with 18.1 per cent to 7.8 per cent for Prescott and four per cent for Heffer. Hattersley's support was particularly strong in constituencies which had balloted their members. It was a signal that the left, so powerful in the constituencies that they had given Benn a four to one majority over Healey in 1981, no longer held sway at the party grass roots and there was real support for the leadership and the policy review.

Also in 1988, Hattersley drafted the Labour Party's statement of *Aims and Values*, which was intended to supplement and update Clause IV without actually rewriting the clause itself. It was based around the ideological principles of *Choose Freedom*, as amended by the Shadow Cabinet who found Hattersley's original draft too enamoured of competitive markets.

Hattersley's resignation as Deputy Leader after the 1992 election was followed by a plunge into writing. One argument jokingly advanced for voting Labour in 1992 was that if Labour won Hattersley would have no time to write another sprawling novel like *The Maker's Mark* (published by Macmillan in 1990). He had been more prolific than most top-level politicians throughout the 1980s, but after 1992 he was omnipresent in the media. The sheer quantity of Hattersley's literary output over the years is daunting, as is its variety. He has written books about subjects as diverse as the future of democratic socialism and the life of Buster the dog, and his journalism also runs the gamut between impassioned political writing and quirky *Endpiece* observations about anything that takes his fancy. When outside earnings were first tallied properly after the 1995 Nolan Report, Hattersley topped the charts as the highest earner – £105,400 – thanks to his writing, and his honesty in listing payments received in full. Hattersley was a frequent feature on television, but became most famous for a 1993 non-appearance on the quiz show *Have I Got News For You*, when he was replaced as Paul Merton's colleague by a tub of lard.[34] He published his political memoirs, *Who Goes Home?* – in which he deprived future biographers and essayists of most of their best lines by telling all his best anecdotes – in 1994.

In 1997 he retired from the Commons and took a peerage. Since then he has enjoyed his biggest literary success with *Buster's Diaries* and has continued to write for the press. Hattersley has frequently criticised the Blair government, particularly on its deviations from the comprehensive principle and for keeping Chris Woodhead at Ofsted in 1997–2000. The Labour Party he knew and loved, he feels, has effectively ceased to exist. He is given to recalling Harold Wilson's statement that the Labour Party is a crusade or it is nothing: 'the logical implications of which are too appalling to contemplate.'

Hattersley was not without his faults. On a bad day he could be pompous, vain and disorganised, but the criticism most commonly made of him was that of unprincipled ambition. This was unfair. Ambition in politics is neither rare nor discreditable, and his writings display stronger and more consistent principles than most of his contemporaries. As a man of good will who enjoyed a good lunch, he sometimes gave the image of vagueness and flabbiness, but his faith in Labour, forged in South Yorkshire childhood, was tough and durable. Hattersley's pleasant life, like that of many of his generation, was lived out thanks to Labour's values. Unlike others, Hattersley always kept the faith.

Further reading

There is no full-length biographical study of Hattersley, but his own memoirs *Who Goes Home?* (Little, Brown, 1995) are entertaining and surprisingly revealing, and he earlier wrote a fuller memoir of childhood, *A Yorkshire Boyhood* (Chatto and Windus, 1983). His *Choose Freedom* (Michael Joseph, 1987) is a considered statement of his political values, while the companion volume *Economic Priorities for a Labour Government* (Macmillan, 1987, with Doug Jones) is more ephemeral. His relationship with his dog is well covered in *Buster's Diaries* (Little, Brown, 1998).

Notes

1. Roy Hattersley, *Goodbye To Yorkshire* (London, 1976) p 32.
2. Roy Hattersley, *A Yorkshire Boyhood* (London, 1983) is a memoir of childhood; see also Roy Hattersley, *Who Goes Home?* (London, 1995).
3. *Who Goes Home?*, p 14.
4. *Sheffield Telegraph,* 18 January 1965, as collected in Roy Hattersley, *Between Ourselves* (London, 1994) pp 317–21.
5. See for instance the essays collected in Roy Hattersley, *Between Ourselves*, particularly 'Up for Adoption', pp 51–4.
6. Strictly, the proportion is of those living in households whose head was born in the New Commonwealth or Pakistan.
7. Though senior NEC figures in the 1970s such as Ian Mikardo and Norman Atkinson represented ethnically diverse London seats.
8. *Who Goes Home?*, pp 300–02.
9. Barbara Castle, *Diaries 1964–70* (London, 1984) p 422: entry for 4 April 1968.
10. Ibid, p 605: entry for 23 February 1969.

11. The episode is well told in *Who Goes Home?*, pp 110–114.
12. Tony Benn, *Against the Tide: Diaries 1973–76* (London, 1989) pp 571–2: entry for 27 May 1976.
13. *Daily Express*, 24 August 1999.
14. Ivor Crewe and Anthony King, *SDP: The Birth, Life and Death of the Social Democratic Party* (Oxford, 1995) p 531, Chapter 4, note 10.
15. *Guardian*, 22 January 2001.
16. *Daily Express*, 24 August 1999.
17. *Labour's Choices*: Roy Hattersley, Fabian Tract 489, Fabian Society, July 1983.
18. *Labour's Choices*: Roy Hattersley, Eric Heffer, Neil Kinnock, Peter Shore, Fabian Tract 489, Fabian Society, July 1983.
19. David Butler and Gareth Butler, *Twentieth Century British Political Facts* (Basingstoke, 2000) p 147.
20. The analogy is with President Nixon's recognition of and visit to the People's Republic of China; his prior record as a vehement anti-communist enabled him to break with the previous US policy while a president with a less right-wing reputation would have justifiably feared arousing opposition.
21. *Who Goes Home?*, pp 260–1.
22. As quoted in Roy Hattersley and Doug Jones, *Economic Priorities for a Labour Government* (Basingstoke, 1987) p 13.
23. Roy Hattersley, *Choose Freedom* (London, 1987) p xix.
24. Ibid, p 19.
25. Roy Hattersley, *Managing the Mixed Economy*, Lecture to Yorkshire and Humberside Regional Management Centre, 20 January 1978.
26. Even this tends to confirm the pattern, as *The Future of Socialism* was written when Crosland was out of parliament and the two later works were the products of an active MP.
27. *Choose Freedom*, pp 170–1.
28. Ibid, p 185.
29. Ibid, p 150.
30. Ibid, p 209.
31. Ibid, p 210.
32. Ibid, p 191.
33. Ibid, p 234.
34. *Between Ourselves*, 'Upstaged by a tub of lard – allegedly', pp 310–12. This was actually the latest in a series of last-minute non-appearances by Hattersley, which is why HIGNFY resorted to the tub of lard joke. Merton won.

13
Gordon Brown

Brian Brivati[*]

(James) Gordon Brown, b.1951. Labour MP for Dunfermline East since 1983. Shadow Chief Secretary to the Treasury 1987–89; Shadow Trade and Industry spokesperson 1989–92; Shadow Chancellor 1992–97. Chancellor of the Exchequer since 1997.

The place of Gordon Brown in a volume on Labour lieutenants is, by definition, problematic because he might still attain the top spot; indeed much commentary by journalists centres on the way he in fact runs the country already. His life and career is a work in progress and not the final canvas ready for the contemporary historian to judge. However, Brown's career to date is already as substantial in achievement as that of anyone else in this volume, and more so than most. His contribution to the modernisation of the Labour Party, his tenure as Chancellor of the Exchequer and his increasing stature on the world stage would make him a key figure in the post-1945 Labour Party. But the combination of all these things with the intellectual drive behind his approach, the coherence of the content and the message of his style of democratic 'socialism' and the unapologetic nature of his politics make him the outstanding Labour figure of his generation. It is to underestimate Tony Blair to see Brown as the only real force in the government but it is nevertheless the case that Brown is the most powerful and influential Chancellor since David Lloyd George and there is no reason yet to write off his chances of occupying the top job.

James Gordon Brown was born on 20 February 1951 at Giffnock, southwest Glasgow. He was the son of John Brown, a minister of the church, who married Elizabeth Souter in 1947. They did not live long in Glasgow; his father was transferred back to his native Fife in 1954 and Gordon grew up in Kirkcaldy. There were two key influences – both formative and symbolic – on the early life of Gordon Brown. The first was the socially conservative, if not to say authoritarian, world of provincial Scotland in the 1950s. This was a provincial Scotland that centred, for Brown, on the Church – a church that was deeply imbued with a sense of the communitarian social responsibility of the affluent for the deserving poor. The second influence was a progressive social experiment in education that took the young Brown through accelerated schooling to University. Progressive yet conservative, this was a schooling premised on learning by rote, examination and punishment. Gordon Brown's childhood was cross-cut by the conflicts inherent in the evolving spirit of the age. On the one hand, there were the politically progressive aspects of his father's ministry and the social experimentation of his schooling, and on the other an oppressive and hierarchical Scotland emerging later than the rest of the United Kingdom from the long dark night of Victorian moralism.

The context into which Brown was born is a significant clue to an aspect of his character that occasionally seems to puzzle English journalists: his self-confidence. Gordon Brown is a born member of a ruling elite. In the community into which he was born his father was a member of the social elite and the Labour movement represented the political class. This was the 'aristocracy of Labour' in which there was little sense of inferiority or deference based on social class. Brown's father's politics connected him to a Labour movement that was the dominant political force in the local state and his faith connected him to another source of self-assurance. Faith in both a spiritual and a temporal sense bred confidence and, if not a feeling of a personal manifest destiny, then certainly not an ounce of intellectual or social humility.

This sense of worth was married to an innate intelligence and capacity for work that made Gordon Brown a prodigy. He started at Kirkcaldy West School at the age of only four, for reasons that remain unclear, and despite being much younger than the other pupils was always racing through his reading and arithmetic ahead of the rest of the class. His closest friend and one who remains close to him, was his brother John. Together John and Gordon applied their intelligence and energy to some highly precocious occupations. They invested the immense reserves of childhood concentration into producing a newspaper that they sold for charity. At the age of eight, Gordon Brown was the sports editor of the

Gazette – which had a circulation of 500. The sports reporting showed that for all their serious application and moral purpose, the Brown boys also exhibited perfectly normal passions for football and other sports. The content of the *Gazette* was earnest and the game was constructed in a serious and purposeful manner. The only difference between the Brown brothers and other children is the application they brought to the task and the work they devoted to it.

Brown's schooling, and idyllic yet serious sounding childhood, was overtaken by a progressive experiment in educational selection being run by Fife county council at the time. He was sent up, at the age of only ten, to the academic, selective Kirkcaldy High School and taught intensively. He took his O Levels at the age of 14 and Highers at 15, scoring five straight A grades and entering Edinburgh University at 16 to read history. Brown viewed the hothouse experience harshly: 'I was a guinea pig, the victim of a totally unsighted and ludicrous experiment... at sixteen I had more problems than years.'[1] To compound the psychological problems induced by this hothousing, at the very end of his Kirkcaldy High School years Brown was injured while playing rugby. He had been an active and successful competitor in tennis, athletics and rugby at school and town level until the 1967 injury when his eyes were severely damaged – he lost sight in his left eye. Treatment for the eye injuries meant that he missed his studies in the autumn term of 1967 and began in spring 1968.

Even this short delay left him extremely young to be attending university. He was transplanted from a world in which he was the leader in academic terms and had the secure base of his brothers and the social position of his family to lean back on, into a new and wider world. His capacity to survive the Kirkcaldy experiment suggests an immense reserve of personal strength but also that core of solid ambition that sets top-flight politicians out from other people. He was now faced with a new environment to conquer: a freakishly young undergraduate, with physical disability to come to terms with and with all the standard apparatus of late teenage angst to master.

All students arriving at university try to find themselves, some by moving as far and as fast as they can away from the identity with which they arrived, others by trying to recreate as much of it as possible. Brown set out into student journalism and politics: the arenas that most closely resembled the universe of his home life in which he had been a master.

After a quiet period Brown came to prominence with a scoop. In 1970 the student newspaper revealed that the university, contrary to official denials, had considerable investments in oppressive firms in South Africa. The affair was most embarrassing to the right-wing principal of the university, Michael Swann, who was a nationally prominent opponent of student power. He told Ted Short, the Education Secretary in January 1969 that Senate representation for students was 'wrong in principle and was exceedingly dangerous in practice'.[2] However, thanks to the tradition in Scottish universities of a Rector, elected by students, who chaired the university Court, there was a channel for student action in Edinburgh. Rectors were usually political or entertainment figures, whose involvement in university governance was minimal, but the opportunity had always been there for a student Rector. First, Brown organised the campaign of a friend, Jonathan Wills, who was elected in 1971, and then he was himself elected to a three-year term in 1972. Swann and Brown vehemently disagreed about how the university should be run and the balance between secrecy and openness in government. Swann left for the BBC in 1973 and his successor came to better terms with Gordon Brown.

The role as Rector established Brown's national reputation in Scotland. Within the Labour Party he was seen as a figure of the left though not the outside left in the sense of flirting with extra-parliamentary methods. His left credentials were accumulated in specifically Scottish terms through the politics of devolution.

In contrast to much of the English left at this time, Brown was arguing for decentralisation of power as the mechanism for social and economic transformation. In 1975 he made a major intellectual contribution to Labour thinking on devolution and nationalism as editor and contributor to *The Red Paper on Scotland*.[3] The British left since the 1930s had generally seen a strong central government as the most effective mechanism for the pursuit of social justice, and worked for nationally uniform levels of provision. In *The Red Paper* Brown argued that:

> Scottish socialists cannot support a strategy for independence which postpones the meeting of urgent social and economic needs until the day after independence. But neither can they give unconditional support to maintaining the integrity of the United Kingdom – and all that entails – without any guarantee of radical social change.

Brown's *Red Paper* was very much a product of its times, when the left was in optimistic and expansive mood and the prospect of building socialism in Britain – or an independent Scotland – seemed immediate. Brown argued for left-wing measures such as a shopping list of industries as candidates for nationalisation and the erosion of the power of the market. Its analysis of power was influenced by Antonio Gramsci's work.[4]

Throughout his university career Brown had been an increasingly prominent Labour Party activist and won a place on the Scottish executive and the selection for the Tory-held Edinburgh South constituency in 1976. Although Labour had never won the seat before, the Conservative vote in the area was eroding; had the election come in autumn 1978 Brown might well have won, but in May 1979 he had to be content with a further reduction of the Conservative majority. Devolution was a divisive issue within the Labour Party in Scotland in the 1970s. Brown was an active partisan of the pro-devolution cause and spoke at dozens of meetings to argue the case in the 1979 referendum campaign.

As Brown's political activities had increased, his academic career waned. He finished his doctoral thesis on Labour in Scotland in the 1920s in 1982, ten years after he had begun. He followed this with a 1986 biography of James Maxton, the leader of the ILP. In the meantime he switched, like Peter Mandelson – another student politician with Labour Party ambitions in the period after the 1979 election – from academic life to television journalism, though this career was always subservient to his political career. As well as keeping his place on the Scottish party executive he cultivated links with the trade union movement, principally the Transport and General Workers' Union, and joined that union's approved parliamentary panel.

The Scottish Labour Party was slightly semi-detached from the internecine war that engulfed the Labour Party in the earlier 1980s. Only two Scottish MPs joined the breakaway SDP and the left in Scotland was more independent of the Bennite organisation than its English equivalent. In turn, many on the hard left viewed the Scottish party as the tool of the trade union movement and essentially an extension of the Scottish establishment. Brown himself was perhaps best characterised as an unreliable member of the left; his voting record on the executive was independent and he was regarded with suspicion by the leaders of the left, though in policy terms he approved many of their ideas. He would call himself a *Tribune* left-winger at this time, a designation that described an emotional and symbolic attachment to a particular reading of the party's past more accurately than it explained positions on contemporary political questions. Brown was, as most Labour people were at the time, a supporter of the party's Alternative Economic Strategy and believed in the extension of government intervention and ownership in the economy, Keynesian techniques of reflation and a rapid redistribution of income and wealth.

Both Brown and Tony Blair were the beneficiaries of Labour's doomed legal action against the recommendations of the Boundary Commission in 1983. The party had selected candidates for the seats under the old boundaries, and once the legal action failed there was a scramble for nominations to seats under the new boundaries that was not finished when

Margaret Thatcher called the election on 9 May. Like Sedgefield, Dunfermline East was a newly created safe Labour seat with no identifiable predecessor and therefore an open nomination, although a canny T&G official had arranged that the union would sponsor the constituency.

Dunfermline East does not contain the town of Dunfermline. It is instead a collection of gritty ex-mining and industrial towns between Dunfermline and Kirkcaldy – Cowdenbeath, Cardenden, Bowhill and the naval dockyard town of Rosyth. It also includes a few more middle-class coastal towns, including North Queensferry, just across the Forth bridges from Edinburgh, where Brown bought a house. On 16 May, the day Labour's disastrous national campaign officially began, Gordon Brown became Labour candidate and was duly elected on 9 June. Even in that dire year, Brown polled more than half the vote and his majority was 11,301. Brown joined the small Labour intake of 1983.

Though new to the House of Commons, Brown was promoted quickly. This was in part a reflection of the lack of talent in the parliamentary Labour Party after the 1983 election and in part because of his already deep political experience. In November 1985 Brown joined the front bench as a member of John Smith's trade and industry team, with a particular brief over regional policy. After the 1987 election, Brown was elevated to the Shadow Cabinet as Shadow Chief Secretary to the Treasury and deputised for Shadow Chancellor John Smith during Smith's recovery from his October 1988 heart attack. It was an opportune time to speak for Labour on economic affairs; the short-term boom that the Tories called an economic miracle was coming to an ignominious end amid rising inflation and higher interest rates and Nigel Lawson's star was fading. Brown used the opportunity to project himself into Labour's front rank and Kinnock duly rewarded him a year later with promotion at the expense of Bryan Gould to shadow Trade and Industry. Brown was the leading figure of the loose group the media described in the mid and late 1980s as YAKs – young, able Kinnockites. Another member was Tony Blair, who joined the front bench before Brown did but was his junior in political experience and learned a lot of political skills from Brown, with whom he shared a parliamentary office early in the 1983 parliament.

While recognised as an up-and-coming figure, Brown was not at this stage a prime mover in terms of changing Labour's policy. He was deputy to Smith during the 1987–89 Policy Review and took over trade and industry after the review had reported and set the course of policy in the run-up to the 1992 election. This was a long period of political success for Brown. From 1988 to 1992 he increased his status within the party and in the country at large and built a close working relationship with John Smith. He was perceived at the time of the 1992 election as Labour's leading moderniser, but his position slipped in the two years after the election. Labour's defeat was widely associated, not completely accurately, with the shadow budget of John Smith and some of the problems associated with that rubbed off on Brown. If Labour seemed too puritanical, too Calvinist, too traditional, above all too *Scottish*, Brown was not the answer. In addition, Brown seemed depressed by Labour's fourth failure and was slow to respond. This was very uncharacteristic for him. An aide during the late 1980s remembers being frequently woken by Brown at 7am and told to issue a press release on an obscure subject. Up to this point the pace and intensity of Brown's working life had been unrelenting. However, in the aftermath of the defeat, it was Tony Blair who went on a media offensive on the day after the election and thereby established an initial momentum, which carried him through to the top.

It was a crucial media moment in which people needed a Labour story to balance the Conservative story, Blair provided it and the balance began to shift away from Brown towards Blair. Brown's position was made worse by his personal style, which is still crumpled to say the least, and by personal circumstances. A closeness to gay activists in the party, staying in the same hotels as these groups at party conferences, when coupled with bachelorhood had inspired the inevitable speculation about his sexuality. In fact it was not these unfounded rumours that mattered so much as the image contrast with Blair's photogenic family.

These image problems were compounded by the difficulty Brown and Smith had in exploiting the collapse of the Conservatives' economic policy in September 1992. Both men had been even more enthusiastic about membership of the ERM than the Conservatives.

As Shadow Chancellor, however, Brown was at the centre of policy for the first time. He scrapped the 1992 proposal to raise national insurance at the higher end and up-rate pensions and child benefit. Brown also built up a network of loyalists and admirers. He recruited Ed Balls, a professional economist, as his economic adviser and Charlie Whelan as his press spokesman at the end of 1993. He depended heavily on Balls in developing his thinking on economic management and the welfare to work programme, and would occasionally get carried away by academic excitement, most notoriously when he referred to 'post-neoclassical endogenous growth theory' in a speech in 1994. Whelan's role was as a street-fighting operator to promote Brown's interests and do down his opponents. Brown's parliamentary allies included Nick Brown, Nigel Griffiths (who had won Edinburgh South in 1987) and Douglas Henderson; Brown support was particularly strong in Scotland and the North East. He has continued to build support, for instance by diligently entertaining members of the 1997 intake.

Brown had never been reticent about his ambitions to lead Labour or his view that he was the right man to lead the party, but after the death of John Smith in 1994 he faced the excruciating experience of having to give ground to a politician with much less intellectual and political authority but a much sharper image. A media groundswell took place for Blair during May 1994, confirmed by public opinion polls suggesting Blair was the most likely to win a general election. After much agonising, Brown eventually came into line and confirmed his intentions to Blair at the famous dinner at Granita's in Islington on 31 May.

Until 1994, Brown had never been a subordinate political figure to anyone in his generation, and it was a difficult moment. According to a biography by Paul Routledge, with which he and aides had co-operated, Brown felt cheated. He and Blair had resolved not to stand in a leadership election. At the time they discussed the issue Brown was the more senior and had assumed that he had a pact to stand for the leadership with Blair's support. Thereafter the relationship with Blair was a complicated one, often compared to a marriage. Though such a relationship at the heart of a political party is not unusual, rivalry and friendship can rarely survive at the very top of politics.

Despite the tensions, Brown and Blair formed an effective partnership during the most successful period ever enjoyed by an opposition party (1994–97). Brown was an early supporter of rewriting Clause IV and devised the welfare to work strategy that was central to Labour's political approach. In January 1997 he pursued the policy of reassurance even further by announcing that Labour would be sticking to the Conservative spending plans for the first two years, and would not raise income tax rates during the first parliament. Brown made a cost-free gesture to his party by letting it be known that he had argued for a 50p higher rate band but been overruled by Blair.

Brown was duly appointed Chancellor of the Exchequer on 2 May 1997, and provided the most startling break with the past during Labour's first week. He announced that interest rates would in future be set by the Bank of England's Monetary Policy Committee, in effect making the Bank of England independent. This was an early signal of Brown's approach to economic management, which centred on the idea of 'prudence'. Adherence to the spending plans, paying off vast amounts of the national debt and relinquishing control of interest rates were all 'prudent' measures: 'no return to boom and bust' was repeated endlessly and the contrast between Labour's economic record and the Tory years was the key theme of Labour's election campaign in 2001. In autumn 1997 the government's line on the Euro emerged after a messy spin operation – Brown was not an enthusiast for early entry and going in before the next election was effectively ruled out. The political battle over the timing of the decision remains, at the time of writing, a core second-term issue.

1998 was not a good year for Brown. It began with a furore over the Routledge biography, which was compounded by a briefing from someone very close to Blair that the Chancellor suffered from 'psychological flaws'. In July, the first comprehensive spending review reported, with claims made that an extra £40bn was going to be spent, a figure that turned out on closer inspection to rely on double counting. Later that month the reshuffle was a purge of Brown supporters within the government. The Paymaster-General, Geoffrey Robinson, was gradually sinking because of disclosures about his business affairs and was only spared in the reshuffle because of Brown's intercession. Robinson went in December, and his house loan also took down Peter Mandelson, the controversial Secretary of State for Trade.

The details of Gordon Brown's budgets provide a blueprint for the technocratic and managerial basis of his governmental political ideology. His first budget was presented on 2 July 1997. Its main feature was the introduction of the New Deal welfare to work programme funded by the imposition of an approximately £3bn windfall tax on the profits of the privatised utilities; there were adjustments to the excise duties and relatively modest increases in health and education spending.[5] The heart of the budget was the combination of the imposition of a commitment to restrict levels of spending to those planned by the Conservatives and the introduction of the workfare programme. At a stroke much of the political economy of the Labour Party since 1945 was abandoned because it was perceived to have failed those it was intended to benefit. It is not the case that only the market economy was offered in its place – the minimum wage and the workfare programme go beyond merely a market economy. It was the case, however, that even the diluted form of social market economy that John Smith favoured had been abandoned, as had been the commitment to universalism.

The 1998 budget was much more a holding operation. The main feature was the Working Families Tax Credit paid directly or via pay packets from October 1999. A child care tax credit was introduced for the low paid, child benefit was increased, the National Insurance floor raised, £500m provided for public transport, and a 1p cut made in corporation tax. This was followed in 1999 by a budget which gave, in Brown's words:

> a better deal for work, a better deal for the family, a better deal for business – for a Britain now united around values of fairness and

enterprise, and I commend this Budget not just to the House but to
the country.

The main features of this budget were a cut in basic rate of income tax
(effective in 2000) and a 10p starting rate (1999), along with the removal
of MIRAS and married allowance. This was followed, in March 2000,
by a package that would 'unite the whole country' in 'a Budget for all
the people'. There was to be 'radical reform' to business taxation; the
Chancellor said that his reforms would allow the UK to 'meet and master
a tide of technological change'. The emphasis was on increased spending
at the time, although comment later focused on the 'stealth taxes'. What
followed in March 2001 was 'a budget for families', which contained
the same mix of tax and welfare reforms that had characterised previous
budgets. In each budget, and between budgets, the levels of public
expenditure and the distribution of that expenditure has been regularly
announced. Increases have featured as reflections of a core commitment
to public services, but the structure of the public sector has been
stubbornly slow to change.

By 2001 Gordon Brown had served nine years as Shadow or real
Chancellor, the longest continuous stretch anyone has ever had speaking
for a party on economics. At the time of writing, the conflict between
the government's rhetoric on public services and the resources that have
been devoted to them has reached a crisis point. There is a struggle in
the very heart of the government between Brown's vision of a more social
market economy, in which the public elements of the partnership are
given a more substantial role, and Blair's vision of the public-private
partnership. The choice in many ways remains the same as it did in
1997 between a Rhine economic model and an Atlantic one. The political
choice has been made and we are all new democrats now. The economic
and social choice will now follow: will we be new social democrats? It is
often said that a Prime Minister can choose to be either his own Foreign
Secretary or his own Chancellor. The way in which this conflict over
public and private is resolved in the second term, along with the separate
but related debate on Euro membership, will determine the extent to
which it is the Chancellor who has managed to be his own Prime Minister.

In the history of the Labour Party many Labour leaders have been
outshone by more powerful key colleagues: Bevin and Attlee and Healey
and Callaghan being the obvious examples. Moreover, stories of
Chancellors plotting to replace Labour Prime Ministers are also common:
Dalton and Attlee, Jenkins and Wilson. Anthony Crosland was arguably
more important to revisionism than Gaitskell lived long enough to be.
Being Prime Minister is not in and of itself a guarantee of dominance,
either in terms of policy or personality. However, no other Labour

lieutenants, whether or not they went on to the top prize, have played such a key role in the history of the party and the country.

For the natural party of opposition, which Labour was in the twentieth century, it is not particularly surprising that prime ministers are not necessarily the most important political figures. What matters most, in the party that is playing catch-up to the party of government, is to have people who think about power: how to get it, how to use it and how to keep it. Bevan thought more creatively than anyone else in the Labour movement about how to use power and applied that thinking to the construction of the National Heath Service, but he lacked the self-discipline necessary to be a dominant force in the winning of parliamentary elections. Crosland thought, in different ways but with equal force of passion and superior force of applied logic, about how to use the power of the state to further the aims of democratic socialism. Wilson won power by utilising a clever mix of the rhetoric of Bevan and the logic of Crosland. Healey was a key Minister in two administrations and saved the Party from disintegration by remaining loyal but he was incapable of building the alliances necessary to capture the leadership.

Brown is the only post-war Labour politician to function in each department of the pursuit of power. He has a clear strategy for how to get power and a concept of government designed to hold on to power once acquired. Much more than the clever trickery of a Peter Mandelson, Gordon Brown's electoral strategy – securing the core vote while tying in the floating voters with economic predictability – is capable of replication over time. In the long run, Peter Mandelson's strategy – the maximisation of contingent and short-term circumstances – would have been only as effective as John Major's. Mandelson delivered the mobilisation of short-run preferences of a sufficient majority for a single victory. Brown, like Margaret Thatcher or the Scandinavian social democratic parties, is building a majority intended to last. His political strategy has set out to combine heavily divergent forms of political economy: effective welfare in a market economy, rising expenditure on public services without increased taxation and so on. Therefore it links the pursuit of power with the use of power from day one. This linkage is the key to longevity because it builds wide-ranging but potentially stable electoral coalitions.

In getting to this position of political leadership and potential dominance, Gordon Brown has clearly continued to sacrifice, almost as he has done since childhood, private spheres for public actions that bring recognition. The price is to make him appear much more of a Wilsonian character than a Crosland or a Bevan. While there is a private hinterland, enhanced by his marriage to Sarah Macaulay, it was overwhelmed by politics in the period up to 1997. In singled-minded careers such as this is huge personal danger. When one returns from the great game the danger is that the self has disappeared. There is, as the hollow figure of Margaret Thatcher at the 2001 election testified, nothing actually there when the light goes out. It is not that Brown is psychologically flawed. Rather he is as much psychologically flawed as any driven alpha male. If he were in business or sport, his single-mindedness would barely elicit a comment from the sorts of people who criticise his conduct; he would be a typical male in the city, a large competitive law firm or a management consultancy. That this is clearly an insane way to live should be obvious; that Gordon Brown is one amongst many men who chose to live like this should be equally obvious. The contrast with Crosland or Bevan is that they seemed to retain more of a life beyond the call of politics, while Harold Wilson had almost nothing else except the great game.

We would not question Brown's state of mental health if he were in another line of work. Nor would we be so fascinated by his political self-confidence if he were a Tory. Brown is part of the Scottish Labour Party aristocracy: a natural party of social and political dominance in a deferential and socially conservative country. Brown and the other Scottish members of the New Labour elite have a self-confidence and faith that was nurtured by being the dominant force in the society and culture in which they grew up. This has informed their conduct of politics and explains much of their style: secretive, manipulative and highly effective. It also explains a large part of their ideological flexibility. Being born to govern allows much greater scope for flexibility in the policies you set out to implement when you achieve power and the changes that you are free to make in order to achieve that power.

In earlier sections of this essay I have placed the word 'socialist' in inverted commas when relating it to Gordon Brown's political philosophy. This sort of hedging is necessary when dealing with a politician who so clearly understands the power and importance of symbols. It is well known that Brown has consistently entertained the party faithful and trade unionists at No. 11, in contrast to the pop stars and millionaires invited to No. 10. In all these gatherings, and at party meetings, Brown talks a language of social and political change that embraces the terms and phrases of socialism, is organised around the aspirations of Labour activists and expresses his ambitions as poverty alleviation and unemployment reduction. In the details of the measures introduced by Brown's budgets there is much attention to cutting unemployment, reducing poverty and in his international statements on third world debt relief, there is clearly more than just lip service to the traditional Labour objectives.

But none of this, and very little that the Blair administrations have done, can be described as socialism. Brown is not a socialist in the mould of Maxton; he is barely a democratic socialist in the mould of Tony Crosland. His approach, the approach of the government and the new British political consensus, is based on a combination of European social democracy and North American New Democratic ideology. One of Brown's predecessors as Labour Chancellor, Hugh Gaitskell, predicted in 1951 that British politics would increasingly come to resemble American politics: a bickering over inessentials. The evidence of New Labour in power since 1997 is that, on macro-economic questions, this is exactly what has happened. The central tenets of what Brown calls socialism and which he endorsed in his earlier writings, have all been abandoned not merely because of a changed political and economic context but because of a sense that they do not work to alleviate poverty and end powerlessness. It is not the case that Brown has moved politically as far as the circumstances in which he finds himself have changed. That would be to underestimate his interest in political ideas: economic intervention, the question of ownership, the use of direct taxation, the universal definition of welfare based on citizenship and entitlement have been jettisoned because they do not work, as well as because they do not win elections. Brown personifies that failure of the left not so much in the mechanics of electoral politics but in the efficacy of socialist ideas in action. In the place of socialism and social democracy there is now an enlightened managerialism delivered by the foremost member of the new British elite. Perhaps rather than new democrats, or even new social democrats, we are all human resource managers now.

Further reading

The range of sources on the political career of Gordon Brown, especially after 1990, is immense. If you put his name into the search engine at the *Guardian*'s online archive you get 5,376 responses; the other broadsheets and magazines will be comparable. Amid these are some profiles, especially around budgets. There is a wealth of information and a plethora of often rather slanted analysis about Brown. The authorised life is *Gordon Brown: The Biography* by Paul Routledge, published in 1998 with an updated paperback later in the year and more updates to follow. This is very high quality journalism, immensely resourceful research, though having full access to the papers no doubt helped. The problem is that it sacrifices any attempt at analysis for potential headlines. The also authorised, *Gordon Brown: The First Year in Power* by Hugh Pym and Nick Kochan, published in 1998, has all the same qualities of research and well-paced journalistic style but lacks the headline grabbing 'insights'. Beyond these, Brown crops up in the various collections on Chancellors of the Exchequer and portraits of New Labour personalities, amongst which Andrew Rawnsley's *Servants of the People* is the best, but otherwise, as the story has not yet finished, there is, of course, no authoritative study.

Notes

* I would like to thank Dr Paul Auerbach for commenting on an earlier draft of this essay and, for background research, Lewis Baston, Senior Research Fellow at www.kingston.ac.uk/cusp.

1. Written by Gordon Brown in May 1967, found by Paul Routledge in research for *Gordon Brown* (London, 1998), pp 37–9.
2. Meeting with Swann, 31 January 1969: Public Record Office file ED188/340 (1969).
3. Edinburgh University Student Publications Board, 1975.
4. Neal Ascherson, 'Life on the Anti-Eurodiluvian Left', *Guardian*, 5 November 2000.
5. Hugh Pym and Nick Kochan, *Gordon Brown: The First Year in Power* (London, 1998) is a crucial work on this and the rest of Brown's agenda as Chancellor.

Index